The
Glorious Body
of Christ

The
Glorious Body
of Christ

A Scriptural Appreciation
of the One Holy Scripture

R. B. KUIPER

THE BANNER OF TRUTH TRUST

THE BANNER OF TRUTH TRUST
3 Murrayfield Road, Edinburgh EH12 6EL
PO Box 621, Carlisle, Pennsylvania 17013, USA

✱

© 1966 Wm. B. Eerdmans Publishing Co.

✱

First Banner of Truth Trust edition 1967
Reprinted 1983
Reprinted 1987
Reprinted 1998
Reprinted 2001

ISBN 0 85151 368 9

✱

✱

Printed by Bell & Bain Ltd, Glasgow

To

My Wife

Faithful Helpmeet
Wise Counselor
Diligent Student of the Word

CONTENTS

The Glorious Body of Christ

PREFACE

That a crying need exists for a popular presentation of Christian doctrine, in particular of the Reformed faith, is to my mind beyond question. This volume represents an attempt in that direction with reference to the teaching of Holy Scripture concerning the church of Christ.

In different periods of the history of Christian doctrine the major emphasis has been on different truths. Today the theological limelight is turned largely on the doctrine of the church. This constitutes one reason for my writing on that subject. Another reason is more personal. In my teaching of Practical Theology over a period of some twenty-five years I have of necessity given much attention to ecclesiology. And because the church, particularly its Protestant manifestation, in spite of the current interest in ecclesiology, is not being held, either by the world or by its own membership, in the high esteem to which it is entitled, I have chosen to write specifically on its *glory*.

From October, 1947, to February, 1952, I contributed monthly articles to *The Presbyterian Guardian* on "The Glory of the Christian Church." In response to numerous requests those articles are here reproduced. Of the many alterations and additions that were made only Chapter 26 on the church's Supreme Task needs to be specified. It is an adaptation of a contribution by me to the December, 1952, and January, 1953, issue of *Torch and Trumpet*. I wish to thank the Presbyterian Guardian Publishing Corporation and the Reformed Fellowship, Inc., for permission to revise and re-publish that material.

When I wrote the aforementioned articles I was a minister in the Orthodox Presbyterian Church. I had previously been, and am now again, a minister in the Christian Reformed Church. I had also held a pastorate in the

Reformed Church in America. However, in my description of the glory of the church I did not have in mind any particular denomination but rather the church described in the Apostles' Creed as "catholic." And it may not be forgotten that any body of believers, in order to deserve to be denominated a Christian church, must be a manifestation of the church universal, which is Christ's body.

This study is intended to be pre-eminently Scriptural. Occasionally the creeds of Christendom are quoted and outstanding theologians are recognized, but my chief concern is to give the reader some glimpses of the marvelous glory of the body of Christ as that glory shines forth resplendently from God's infallible Word.

—R. B. KUIPER

Grand Rapids, Michigan

INTRODUCTION

HAS THE GLORY DEPARTED?

The Word of God tells us that Christ's church is glorious. Not only does history ascribe to it a past that is in many respects glorious and does prophecy predict for it a glorious future, it is *essentially* glorious. The Christian church is glorious *in its very nature*.

Today the glory of the church is thickly veiled. It is no exaggeration to assert that in the main it presents a picture of advanced decadence and extreme feebleness.

To be sure, not everyone will subscribe to that evaluation. There is much talk in our day of a religious revival the world over, especially in these United States of America; and the fact that a larger percentage than ever before — six out of ten — of our population holds membership in one church or another is cited as conclusive evidence of that revival. The church is said to be advancing from glory unto glory. However, that judgment excels in superficiality.

To measure the glory of the church in terms of numbers is, to say the least, precarious. When the Roman emperor Constantine, in the year 323, gave official recognition to the Christian church, he, in the words of one historian, "clothed the church in royal purple." In consequence its membership increased by leaps and bounds. Church membership became the fashion. Perhaps history is repeating itself. In fact, there can be little doubt that it is. Once more church membership is becoming fashionable. It enhances one's respectability. Likely many who join the church are Christians only in name.

Due to the influence of Rabbi Liebman, Bishop Sheen and Dr. Norman Vincent Peale many are flocking into the churches in quest of peace of mind; yet few seem to realize that the one and only way to achieve peace is through the atoning blood of Jesus Christ. Nor is it generally understood that the Christian life is one of constant warfare. He who is at peace with God is by that very token at war with Satan, the world and the flesh.

True, the impact of evangelist William Franklin Graham's preaching is nothing short of phenomenal. Through it many thousands from every walk of life are being led into the churches. This may be a harbinger of better days ahead for Protestantism. However, it is a disturbing fact that many of Graham's converts unite with churches that adulterate the gospel. And history teaches that the results of mass evangelism are difficult to appraise. Unless it is accompanied by intensive study of the Word of God, its fruits usually have not proved abiding.

Let it be said emphatically, the church is where the truth is. Sound doctrine always has been, is today, and ever will be the foremost mark of the true church. But who dares to assert that there is today in the churches a rising tide of interest in doctrine? By and large people do not go to church to learn about God from His infallible Word, but rather to be tranquilized. And that the glory of God is both the beginning and the end of common worship does not seem to occur to them.

The fact remains that the Christian church of our day finds itself in a sorry plight. It seems despicable rather than glorious. However, that fact renders insistence on its essential glory all the more necessary.

The following chapters constitute a series that sets forth from various viewpoints the inherent glory of the church of Christ, which is His body. By way of background, it may be well first to enumerate a few of the factors that have contributed to its apparently sad state at the present time.

The world has ever opposed the church and always will. The struggle between the seed of the woman and the seed of the serpent is not only perennial but perpetual.

Yet it can hardly be said that today the world hates the church with a violent hatred. Particularly in these United States the world rather slights the church. It regards the church with a benevolent tolerance as a harmless, perhaps even somewhat helpful, but not overly useful institution. That attitude itself casts a serious reflection upon the church. If it were strong and active, as it ought to be, the world would oppose it much more vigorously. Persecution by the world is a badge of honor for the church. Did not Jesus pronounce blessed those who are persecuted for the sake of righteousness, and does not that beatitude apply to all faithful followers of the Lamb (Matthew 5:10-12)? But by and large the church of our day and our land has lost that badge and forfeited that blessedness. And that is another way of saying that the church's most imminent peril issues from its own household. A few threats from within may be named.

WORLDLINESS

The term *worldliness* is often used loosely. Many who denounce worldliness eloquently are abruptly silenced when asked to define it. To some the word suggests certain specific amusements, to others it connotes little more than a mode of feminine dress. That some of such things may properly be classified under worldliness cannot be denied. But the term has a much broader application.

There is a type of worldliness which is extremely prevalent in the church and is doing it untold damage, yet is hardly recognized as worldliness. In fact, the very watchmen on the walls of Zion are particularly guilty of it. It is to count greatness as the world is wont to do, to stress externals at the expense of spiritual values. Savonarola, the Florentine forerunner of the Reformation, decried it thus: "In the primitive church the chalices were of wood, the prelates of gold; in these days the church hath chalices of gold and prelates of wood." That church is said to flourish which grows rapidly in numbers, even though it does not grow in grace and the knowledge of the Lord. That church is deemed prosperous which has a costly stone structure and keeps enlarging it, even though it fails to build up its members as lively stones into a spiritual house. Instead of faithfully proclaiming the Word of God and fervently praying that the Lord may so bless its proclamation that such as are being saved will daily be added to the church and that the saints will be built up in the most holy faith, the pastor puts on special attractions and membership drives in a concerted effort to swell the rolls of his church and to realize the ambition that it may possess the most imposing edifice in the community. All the time the requirements for church membership are progressively — more precisely, retrogressively — lowered and the demands of church discipline are progressively — rather, retrogressively — ignored. And never once does it occur to the pastor that this is the worst possible way for the church to command the respect of the world, nor does he realize that thus his church is forfeiting the favor of God.

The aforenamed is a somewhat subtle form of worldliness found within the church. That more brazen forms abound may be asserted without fear of contradiction. How true is the oft-repeated indictment of church members that they can hardly be distinguished from the men and women of the world. The most outstanding sin of ancient Israel was that, instead of upholding its distinctiveness as Jehovah's chosen people, it was ever and anon imitating its heathen neighbors. That sin is rampant in the church today.

MODERN DISPENSATIONALISM

Strange though it may seem, there are within the church true believers who do injury to the church by belittling it. Prominent among them are dispensationalists.

The notes in the Scofield Bible have for several decades now exerted a strong and widespread influence on American fundamentalism. Sad to say, that influence has not been unqualifiedly wholesome. On the contrary, the Scofield Bible has been instrumental in gaining many adherents for the errors of dispensationalism. In his *Prophecy and the Church* Oswald T. Allis has masterfully exposed those errors, and there are signs that his warnings have not gone altogether unheeded. Yet the leaven of dispensationalism has not been purged from the church and it continues to do serious detriment.

Modern dispensationalism openly belittles the church. It says that Christ purposed at His first coming to establish a kingdom with Jerusalem as its capital and Himself, seated on the throne of His father David, as its king. However, when the Jewish nation rejected Him as king, He decided, we are told, to postpone the kingdom until His second coming and in the interim to found His church. But the church is not nearly as important as the kingdom. In the dispensational scheme it is merely a parenthesis, an interlude, time-out, so to speak, in the divine chronology.

The low view of the church which dispensationalists hold has led many a minister of that persuasion to cease striving for the doctrinal soundness of his denomination. More than a few pastors who vowed at their ordination to strive for the purity of the denomination are today, to say the least, slighting that vow. Perhaps they faithfully proclaim the heart of the gospel from their own pulpits, but when another minister in the self-same denomination denies the precious truth that Christ's death on the cross was a sacrifice by which He expiated sin and satisfied the divine justice, it does not occur to them to charge him with heresy in the courts of the church. An outstanding minister of the dispensational school once said: "The denomination means nothing to me." At that, his denomination did not subscribe to the independent or congregational type of church government.

Dispensationalism must bear some, although by no means all, of the blame for the general neglect by American

Protestantism of important aspects of the covenant of
grace. It has come to pass that the majority of Protestant
churches hardly count the children of believers as church
members. What is even worse, they fail miserably to
provide anything like adequate religious instruction for
these children. The sad fact is that hardly any Protestant
church in America today insists on a consistent program
of Christian education for children of the covenant. Small
wonder that hosts of such children are lost to the church.
That surely bodes ill for its future.

Not by any manner of means is modern dispensationalism to be equated with modernism. Modernism denies
many cardinal teachings of Christianity and thus rejects
the Christian religion. Dispensationalism, contrariwise,
adheres to those truths that have come to be known as
"the fundamentals." But the regrettable fact remains
that it does violence to the Scriptural teaching of the church
and detracts more than a little from the church's glory.

Doctrinal Indifference

The Bible describes the church as "the pillar and ground
of the truth" (I Timothy 3:15). That is a clear and emphatic way of saying that it is the church's task to *uphold*
the truth. Just as clearly and just as emphatically Scripture teaches that it is the church's business to *proclaim*
the Word of truth (e.g., Matthew 28:18-20, Acts 1:8).
That being the case, the church has no more destructive
enemy in its midst than indifference to the truth.

There are those within the church who deny the most
cardinal doctrines of the Christian religion. Deniers of
the Bible as the infallible Word of God and, consequently,
of the Scriptural teachings of the Holy Trinity, the deity
of Christ and the vicarious atonement are found in the
church's pulpits and in seminary chairs. That, of course,
is deplorable beyond words. But an even sadder fact must
be recorded. It is that in most instances the church is
not concerned to cast those false teachers out. If the

church had a zeal for the truth, it would rid itself of them;
but of that most churches have no thought. Church members by and large do not know what truth is, nor do they
care to know. The churches are filled with Pilates who
ask sneeringly, "What is truth?" What they mean to say
is: "I don't know, you don't know, nobody knows, nobody
can know; let's quit quibbling about truth." The Presbyterian Church in the U.S.A. has perhaps the best doctrinal
standards of all Christendom. The Westminster Confession of Faith and Catechisms are the ripest, and likely
the noblest, creedal products of the Protestant Reformation. Yet in the early twenties of the present century
some twelve hundred ministers of that denomination put
their signatures to the *Auburn Affirmation* and by so doing
expressed the view, not only that the doctrine of the
inerrancy of Holy Scripture is harmful, but also that it
does not matter whether or not a minister in that communion believes in Christ's virgin birth, His bodily resurrection, the miracles of the Bible generally, or the satisfaction view of the atonement. The silly notion is still
held widely that Christianity is only a life, not a doctrine.
Church union at the expense of truth is demanded on every
hand. Any number of church members applaud the alco-
holic who requested a minister to tell him the difference
between modernism and fundamentalism, and, on being
advised to repeat the question when he would be sober,
retorted that then he would no longer care to know.

Thus it has come about that many of the Protestant
churches in America are tainted with modernism, which
is not a brand of Christianity but a denial of it, and that
several of them are so definitely under the control of theological liberalism as no longer to deserve to be called
Christian churches. The so-called middle-of-the-roaders
must bear much of the blame.

One often hears it said that modernism, characterized
by rationalistic denial of the supernatural and the substitution, under the influence of Friedrich Schleiermacher and

Albrecht Ritschl, of subjective religious experience for objective divine revelation, has now been supplanted by the "new orthodoxy," popularly known as Barthianism. If that were true, it would constitute no great, if indeed any, gain; for Barthianism, too, is essentially modernist. It accepts many of the conclusions of the higher critics and denies the plenary inspiration of Scripture. Cornelius Van Til was not wide of the mark when he denominated it *The New Modernism*. However, it simply is not true that the older modernism has all but vanished; and to suppose that it has, is evidence of almost unbelievable naiveté and a well-nigh complete lack of doctrinal awareness. The legend that the liberalism of Harry Emerson Fosdick has had its day may well be a ruse by which the father of lies would lull the faithful to sleep. And it is by no means inconceivable that the present prevalence of Barthianism will prove to be of short duration. Its blatant irrationalism would seem to point in that direction. If and when that comes to pass, classical liberalism in one form or another will ride as high as ever. It is as old as the church and, no doubt, will plague the church to the end of time. Now, as always, the church's attitude to it must be that of uncompromising intolerance.

*   *   *   *

When the ark of the covenant had been taken by the uncircumcised Philistines, the widowed wife of the priest Phinehas gave birth to a son, and she named him *Ichabod*, saying: "The glory is departed from Israel" (I Samuel 4:21). The question may well be asked whether today the glory has not departed from the church. It would seem that *Ichabod* had better be chiseled over its gates.

And yet, unbelievable though it may seem, applicable to the church of all ages, also of this age, is the exultation of the Psalmist: "The Lord loveth the gates of Zion more than all the dwellings of Jacob. Glorious things are spoken of thee, O city of God" (Psalm 87:2, 3).

Chapter 1

THE ANTIQUITY AND PERPETUITY
OF THE CHURCH

ITS BIRTHDAY

How old is the Christian church?

In the counsel of God the church existed from eternity. At a subsequent point in this study of the church's glory that truth will be considered. At this juncture we are concerned with the church in history. The question is how long ago in human history the church originated.

Two answers have been given to that question. Christian theology generally says that the church originated in the garden of Eden immediately after the fall of man, when God promised a Saviour and man accepted that promise in faith. On the other hand, many take it for granted that the outpouring of the Holy Spirit at Pentecost, a little more than nineteen hundred years ago, marks the birthday of the Christian church.

Which of those answers is correct? That can best be decided in the light of a definition of the church. If we know precisely what the church is, it should not be difficult to determine whether or not it existed before Pentecost. Now the Apostles' Creed defines the church as "the communion of saints." It is just as correct to say that it is the communion of believers. Was there a communion of believers in Old Testament times? There certainly was. Ever since the fall of man there has been but one Saviour, the Lord Jesus Christ, and but one way of being saved; namely, through faith in Him. As New Testament saints are saved through faith in the Christ of history, so Old Testament saints were saved through faith in the

Christ of prophecy. The Christ of prophecy and the Christ
of history are, of course, identical. And so Isaiah, David,
Abraham, Abel and a host of others were members of the
one body of Christ, His church. And if we assume, as
undoubtedly we may, that Adam and Eve believed the
promise of God that the seed of the serpent would indeed
bruise the heel of the seed of the woman, but that the
woman's seed would bruise the serpent's head (Genesis
3:15), then it may be asserted that they constituted the
first Christian church.

Its Maturity

It must not be thought that the church was mature
from the day of its birth. It did not come to maturity
until the Holy Spirit was poured out upon it. And that
makes Pentecost incomparably the most important turning point in its history. It also accounts for the fact that
the glory of the church under the new dispensation is far
greater than was its glory under the old.

The church of the new dispensation has a fuller revelation. Whereas the Old Testament saints had to be content
with the shadow of things to come, we may walk in the
full light provided by Him who is at once the Son of
God, the effulgence of the Father's glory, the express
image of the Father's being (Hebrews 1:3), and the Lamb
of God who takes away the sin of the world (John 1:29).
And it was He who on the day of Pentecost made good
His promise to grant unto His church the Spirit of truth
to lead it into all the truth (John 16:13).

The church of the new dispensation has a greater freedom. It is no longer in the position of a little child which
needs to be told in minute detail what to do and what not
to do, but it has attained majority (Galatians 4:1-7).
Not only has the ceremonial law, which prescribed the
worship of ancient Israel, been abolished; the liberty of the
New Testament church concerns also the moral law of
God. It is indeed in sacred duty bound to keep this law,

but it delights in doing so, and that is the very essence of liberty. To be sure, that liberty was not unknown to the Old Testament saints, for the Psalmist found God's commandments sweeter than honey and the honeycomb (Psalm 19:10). Yet it is enjoyed in larger measure by the New Testament church because upon it the Holy Spirit was poured out as never before, and "where the Spirit of the Lord is, there is liberty" (II Corinthians 3:17).

The church of the new dispensation has a visible form all its own. Time was when the church was bound up with the patriarchal family. Subsequently it was bound up, though not identified, with the Israelitish nation. But at Pentecost it came into its own as a distinct organization.

The church of the new dispensation is universal. In Old Testament times the church was confined almost entirely to the nation of Israel. Only occasionally and by way of exception was a gentile received into the church. Ruth, the Moabitess, affords an outstanding example. But at Pentecost cloven tongues as of fire sat on the heads of the disciples and they proclaimed the great works of God in many languages. Men were present from all over the Mediterranean world, both Jews and proselytes. Many of them were converted and received by baptism into the Christian church. They were the firstfruits of the great harvest that would be gathered in from the field of the world.

ITS CONTINUITY

Much more could be said about the greater glory of the New Testament church. But after all had been said that could be said, the fact would still remain that the church of the new dispensation is the continuation of the church of the old dispensation, and also the further fact that the church of Jesus Christ in both those periods is glorious indeed. What deserves to be stressed is that the very continuity of the church contributes greatly to its glory.

Of that the apostle Paul wrote in glowing terms to the

gentile Christians at Ephesus. After reminding them that
once they were aliens from the commonwealth of Israel
and strangers from the covenants of promise, he went
on: "But now in Christ Jesus ye who sometimes were far
off are made nigh by the blood of Christ. For he is our
peace, who hath made both one and hath broken down the
middle wall of partition between us, having abolished in
his flesh the enmity, even the law of commandments contained in ordinances, for to make in himself of twain one
new man, so making peace; and that he might reconcile
both unto God in one body by the cross, having slain the
enmity thereby; and came and preached peace to you
which were afar off and to them that were nigh. For
through him we both have access by one Spirit unto the
Father. Now therefore ye are no more strangers and
foreigners, but fellow-citizens with the saints and the
household of God, and are built upon the foundation of
the apostles and prophets, Jesus Christ himself being the
chief cornerstone, in whom all the building fitly framed
together groweth unto a holy temple in the Lord" (Ephesians 2:12-21).

As was remarked in the introduction to this study, according to dispensationalism the church was non-existent
before Pentecost, and even when the Son of God came to
earth it was not His purpose to build a church. He came
to establish a kingdom, but when the Jewish people rejected Him as king He decided to postpone the kingdom
until His second coming and in the interim to found a
church. Thus the "church-age" becomes relatively insignificant, a mere parenthesis. But the truth is that the
church was founded already in Eden and will continue to
the end of time, yes for ever and ever.

Christ's church is continuous to the point of the most
glorious perpetuity. It embraces all the ages of human
history and will extend through the boundless ages of eternity. Instead of being a temporary substitute for something better, it constitutes the very heart of the eternal

plan of God. And instead of comprising the believers of but a few centuries, it is the communion of God's elect of all ages, the countless throng of all who are written in the Lamb's book of life from the foundation of the world and will dwell eternally in the city which has no need of the light of the sun, neither of the moon, because the glory of God lightens it and the Lamb is the light thereof (Revelation 21:23).

Chapter 2

THE CHURCH VISIBLE AND INVISIBLE

A distinction is often made between the visible church and the invisible church. That distinction is both valid and valuable, but it must not be supposed that there are two Christian churches, the one visible, the other invisible. There is only one church of Jesus Christ, for He has but one body. However, this one church has different aspects, and two of them are wont to be distinguished as visible and invisible.

THE MEMBERSHIP OF THE VISIBLE CHURCH

The visible church consists of all who are enrolled as church members. It is not difficult to determine who they are, for their names appear on the registers of churches. With little effort an accurate count of them can be made. To be sure, this is not always done. Some churches have a way of juggling figures so as to make their membership appear larger than it actually is. But such camouflage is not hard to see through.

Very strictly speaking, the membership of the visible church coincides with that of the invisible church. And since the invisible church consists of the regenerate, only they rate as members of the visible church. To use a biblical expression, only the regenerate are *of* the visible church (I John 2:19). However, it cannot be denied that there may be, and actually are, unregenerate persons *in* the visible church. Hence it may be said to comprise both believers and unbelievers, such as are truly Christians and such as are merely professed or nominal Christians. The little circle of the twelve apostles, which was the nucleus of the New Testament church, contained the traitor Judas Iscariot. The church at Jerusalem, upon which the Holy Spirit had recently been poured out, harbored such pious frauds as Ananias and Sapphira. Membership in the visible church does not guarantee eternal life. There is every reason to fear that in these days of exceedingly lax requirements for church membership and the almost total neglect of ecclesiastical discipline the unsaved within the visible church constitute much more than a sprinkling.

THE MEMBERSHIP AND GLORY OF THE INVISIBLE CHURCH

On the other hand, the invisible church consists exclusively of those who by the grace of the Holy Spirit have been born again. It is not difficult to understand why this aspect of the church should be characterized as *invisible*. We cannot tell with certainty who have been regenerated and who are in an unregenerate state. Only God omniscient is able to do that. Occasionally a pastor will talk as if he can without fail name the "born again ones" in his flock, but that is arrogant presumption. It is altogether likely that Luther was right when he predicted that on his arrival in heaven he would meet with two surprises: he would miss many whom he had confidently expected to see there, and he would meet many concerning whose Christianity he had had serious doubts. It is well to remember, too, that he added that the greatest wonder of all would be that unworthy Martin Luther would be there.

From the fact that the invisible church consists solely of regenerate persons it follows that this aspect of the church is glorious indeed. Every single member of it has been delivered from the power of darkness and translated into the kingdom of God's dear Son (Colossians 1:13). Of all its members it may be said: "Ye were sometimes darkness, but now are ye light in the Lord" (Ephesians 5:8). "As lively stones" they are "built up a spiritual house, a holy priesthood" (I Peter 2:5). They are washed,

they are sanctified, they are justified in the name of the
Lord Jesus Christ and by the Spirit of God (I Corinthians
6:11). Together they constitute the body of Christ (Colossians 1:18). To be sure, they have not attained perfection; yet even now they have the victory over sin and the
devil through their Lord Jesus Christ. In Him they are
perfect.

THE GLORY OF THE VISIBLE CHURCH

But what of the glory of the visible church?

Consisting as it does of believers and non-believers, it
must of necessity be far less glorious than is the invisible
church. That is a sad fact. In the course of history it
has also proved to be an exceedingly troublesome fact.
Churchmen have struggled long and hard with the problem whether measures should not be taken to remedy the
impurity of the visible church and, if so, what should be
done about it. To the present day there is nothing like
unanimity on that question. Three divergent views may
be named.

Throughout its history there have been groups within
the Christian church which insisted on what has come to
be known as the "pure church" idea. They restricted
membership to such as were conscious of having been born
again and could give a more or less glowing account of
their conversion. They deemed it both necessary and possible to keep all unregenerate persons outside the church.
Here the Novatians of the third and following centuries
and the followers of John Nelson Darby in recent times
may be named. This view had considerable currency
among the early Congregationalists of New England. It
is an extreme view and savors of fanaticism. It places
undue emphasis on subjective religious experience. It
overlooks the inability of men to determine who are regenerate and who are not. Instead of solving the problem
presented by the impurity of the visible church it would
destroy that problem.

Others have gone to the opposite extreme. They have adopted a "laissez-faire" policy and ignore the problem. Consequently they would exercise no judicial ecclesiastical discipline. Frequently they appeal to the well-known parable of the tares (Matthew 13:24-30, 36-43) in support of their position. They interpret — rather misinterpret — that parable to teach that the church may not attempt to separate tares from wheat in its midst. The adherents of this view are exceedingly numerous in our day. In effect they would let the purity, and hence the glory, of the visible church go by default. At a subsequent point in this series the parable concerned will be considered more fully. Suffice it at this juncture to say that time and again the Word of God unequivocally commands the church to cast out wicked members, and it is a sound hermeneutical principle that any given passage of Scripture must be interpreted in the light of Scripture as a whole.

There is a third view. It excels in balance and is based squarely on the infallible Word of God. On the one hand it admits that the visible church cannot be kept perfectly pure. Its most godly, most faithful and wisest officers are far from infallible in seeking to distinguish between wheat and tares. But on the other hand it insists firmly that the church is in sacred duty bound to keep itself as pure as is humanly possible and to that end must exercise discipline, if need be to the point of excommunication. Did not the Lord ordain that, if an offending brother refuses to heed the admonition of the church, he is to be regarded "as a heathen man and a publican" (Matthew 18:17)?

The conclusion of the matter is that the visible church is glorious insofar as it resembles the invisible church. Visibility and invisibility are two aspects of the one church of Jesus Christ. For that simple and conclusive reason the visible church must manifest the invisible. Admittedly, the resemblance of the one to the other is never perfect. But in some instances the visible church is no

more than a caricature of the invisible. Then it is inglorious. In a great many instances the visible church seeks
feebly to reflect the invisible. Then its glory is dim. By
the grace of God there are also instances in which the
visible church concertedly emulates the invisible. Such a
church is truly glorious.

It follows that the glory of the visible church does not
consist in such externals as costly edifices, artistic stained
glass windows, richly appointed furnishings, dignified
vestments and talented preachers. A church may have all
these and yet be so inglorious as not to deserve being called
a church of Christ. Not even long membership rolls
necessarily betoken glory. They may evince vainglory.

The glory of the visible church is reflected in its members
and consists in their loyalty to Jesus Christ. That church
is glorious which acknowledges Christ as its Saviour and
Head, and itself manifests His body.

Chapter 3

THE CHURCH MILITANT AND TRIUMPHANT

The distinction between the militant church and the church triumphant is a common one. By the former is meant the church on earth, by the latter the church in heaven. Therefore, when some one has fallen asleep in Jesus it is not unusual to say that he has been translated from the militant church to the church triumphant.

That both those aspects of the church of Christ are glorious is evident, and that the church in heaven is far more glorious than the church on earth goes without saying. But what seems not to be generally understood is that the church triumphant has not yet attained the glory for which it is destined. Nor is it unusual for the glory of the militant church to be underrated. The truth of the matter is that the church triumphant is for the present in some respects not altogether as glorious as is ordinarily supposed and that the militant church is considerably more glorious than is commonly thought. It may even be said that the militant church is already triumphant, and the triumphant church still militant.

THE INCOMPLETE GLORY OF THE CHURCH TRIUMPHANT

Far be it from us to detract from the glory of the church in heaven. That it is free from all sin and perfect in holiness means that it is exceedingly glorious. So does the fact that, sharing in the glory of Christ, seated at the right hand of God, it reigns with Him over His earthly subjects. Its glory exceeds the power of human imagination. Its splendor is such as eye has not seen, ear has not heard,

31

and as never arose in the heart of man (I Corinthians 2:9).

And yet it cannot be denied that after the consummation of all things the church in heaven will be even more resplendent than it is today. Its present state, however glorious, is preliminary. A few respects in which it remains to be perfected may be named.

Obviously, the membership of the church triumphant is not yet complete. Nor will it be complete until the last believer has gone to glory. And that will not occur until the second coming of our Lord. The saints who then remain alive will, without the experience of dying, join the church triumphant. Then the sum total of God's elect will be gathered into one as never before. Then the perfect body of Christ, comprising all its constituent members, will appear. Then the roll will be called up yonder and not one whom Christ purchased with His blood will be absent. That will be glory for the church and also for its Head. "In the multitude of people is the king's honor" (Proverbs 14:28).

A church can be no more glorious than are the members that constitute it. That holds also of the church triumphant. But the saints in heaven have not yet attained the acme of glory. It may even be said that their salvation is still in process. Their bodies are resting in the dust. And not until those bodies, sown in corruption, dishonor and weakness, have been raised in incorruption, glory and power, and as spiritual bodies have been united with their sinless souls, will death be swallowed up in perfect victory.

The Bible tells us that the church in heaven has longings which will not be satisfied until the Lord's return to judgment. In one of his visions John saw under the altar in heaven the souls of them that were slain for the Word of God and for His testimony, and he heard them crying with a loud voice: "How long, O Lord, holy and true, dost thou not judge and avenge our blood on them that dwell on the earth?" (Revelation 6:10) This is not a demand for personal revenge but a militant prayer for the vindication of divine justice and the manifestation of the glory of God in the annihilation of His foes. Therefore we read that when Babylon is destroyed the inhabitants of heaven shout: "Alleluia; salvation and glory and honor and power unto the Lord our God: for true and righteous are his judgments; for he hath judged the great whore which did corrupt the earth with her fornication, and hath avenged the blood of his servants at her hand" (Revelation 19:1, 2).

THE GREAT GLORY OF THE MILITANT CHURCH

Our age is one of ecclesiastical pacifism. Instead of opposing error most churches tolerate it and many even enthrone it. That doctrinal error is sin, occurs to very few churches indeed. Flagrant immorality and social injustice are frowned upon, but other forms of worldliness are rampant among church members. Judicial discipline is seldom exercised and heresy trials are relegated to the middle ages. Historic differences among denominations are played down and church union is all the vogue. And when men of integrity and courage put forth concerted efforts to purify the church, they are soon ousted as disturbers of the peace of Zion.

It is more than time that the church be reminded that militancy is of its essence. When a church ceases to be militant it also ceases to be a church of Jesus Christ. The church on earth is glorious, not in spite of its militancy, but precisely because of it.

A truly militant church stands opposed to the world both without its walls and within. Thus its militancy proves that, while it is in the world, it is not of the world. The church's militancy evinces the antithesis between the children of God and the children of the devil. That antithesis is absolute. It is active, too. It is not the antithesis of black and white which exist quite passively and peacefully alongside each other, let us say on a garment, but it more closely resembles the antithesis of fire and water in violent conflict with one another. To be sure, the church would have the men and women of the world saved, and it never loses sight of the fact that omnipotent grace can in the twinkling of an eye transform an enemy into a friend. Yet, paradoxical though it may be, the fact remains that not only is the world at enmity with the church, but the church is also at enmity with the world.

Positively put, the church's militancy is proof of its holiness. As the light of the world it cannot but strive to expel the darkness of sin. As custodian of the truth it zealously upholds the truth of God against error. Thus militancy becomes synonymous with glory.

A truth frequently overlooked is that the militant church is victorious. Not only is it certain of triumph in the end, it is victorious here and now. This is not to say that its members have attained moral perfection. It does not even mean that some of its members are free from all known sin, as the Victorious Life Movement would have us believe. On the contrary, every one of its members must confess: "In many things we offend all" (James 3:2). And yet in a very real sense the militant church is victorious. Christ, its Head, has vanquished Satan and the world, sin and death; and His body, the church, shares in His victory. Therefore the apostle Paul, after crying out in self-abhorrence: "O wretched man that I am, who shall deliver me from the body of this death?" in the very next breath exults: "I thank God through Jesus Christ, our Lord" (Romans 7:24, 25). In his labors in the gospel the same apostle encountered the strongest sort of opposition; yet he gloried: "Thanks be unto God, which always causeth us to triumph in Christ" (II Corinthians 2:14). And the author of Hebrews comes close to identifying the militant church with the triumphant when he says: "But ye are come to mount

Zion and unto the city of the living God, the heavenly Jerusalem, and to an innumerable company of angels, to the general assembly and church of the firstborn, which are written in heaven, and to God, the Judge of all, and to the spirits of just men made perfect" (Hebrews 12:22, 23). Therefore we sing:

> Yet she on earth hath union
> With God the Three in One,
> And mystic sweet communion
> With those whose rest is won.

One day the victory of the militant church will be consummated. It will be merged with the church triumphant. An angel said to John on the isle of Patmos: "Come hither, I will show thee the bride, the Lamb's wife." And he beheld "that great city, the holy Jerusalem, descending out of heaven from God, having the glory of God . . ." (Revelation 21:9-11).

Chapter 4

THE CHURCH TRANSCENDENT

There are, of course, a great many organizations in the world. It is hardly an exaggeration to say that they are countless. One of them is the Christian church. But it must not be thought that the church is merely one of many organizations. In important respects it differs so radically from all others that it may be said to be, not just at the head of the class, but in a class by itself. It far transcends all other organizations.

ITS DIVINE ORIGIN

The great majority of organizations in the world were originated by man. They were conceived in the mind of man and brought into being by human effort. That is true, for example, of such relatively unimportant organizations as book clubs and automobile clubs, of such influential organizations as the National Association of Manufacturers, the American Federation of Labor and the Congress of Industrial Organizations, of so colossal and potentially powerful an organization as the United Nations, and also of such religious organizations as the National Council of the Churches of Christ in America, the National Association of Evangelicals, the American Council of Christian Churches and the World Council of Churches. All of these organizations and a host of others were brought into existence by the will of man.

The church, on the other hand, was brought into being by God Himself.

The very word which the Greek New Testament employs to designate the church stresses that truth. It tells us that the church consists of those who have been *called out* from the world. It was God who did the calling. And He called not only by His Word but also by His Spirit. He called irresistibly, effectually.

In the counsel of God the church existed even before the creation of man. This means that only God can have originated it. Paul told the Christians at Ephesus that God had chosen them in Christ before the foundation of the world and had predestinated them unto the adoption of children (Ephesians 1:4, 5). Nor were they chosen merely as so many individuals. God regarded them as a group, "the household of God" (Ephesians 2:19). No doubt, John Calvin had that in mind when he spoke of the doctrine of election as the heart of the church.

Very early in human history man rebelled against his Maker. At once God stepped in and divided our race in two. To His right He placed the seed of the woman, to His left the seed of the serpent. Instead of commanding them to be at enmity with each other and leaving it to their discretion whether or not to obey, He declared: "I will put enmity between you" (Genesis 3:15). Thus by a divine fiat were the church and the world separated from each other and set in opposition one to the other.

After some centuries Abraham appeared on the scene. It was not Abraham who sought God, it was God who called Abraham from his pagan surroundings. Nor did God merely offer Abraham His friendship and invite him into a covenant; without waiting for Abraham's consent God established the covenant of grace with him and his seed after him (Genesis 17:7). God's declaration made the covenant an accomplished fact. Henceforth the patriarchal family was the church.

In the fullness of time God sent forth His Son to redeem the elect, to save those whom the Father had given Him. That, too, was a sovereign act of God, in no way dependent on the will of man. And because the redeemed constitute the church of God, Scripture tells us that He purchased the church with His own blood (Acts 20:28).

When Peter, as spokesman of the twelve, had confessed Jesus to be the Christ, the Son of the living God, the Lord replied: "I say unto thee that thou art Peter, and upon this rock I will build my church" (Matthew 16:18). He was referring specifically to the church in its New Testament aspect. The Son of God declared Himself to be its founder.

At Pentecost He built this church. He did it by supernatural, miraculous intervention. To the accompaniment of the sound as of a mighty rushing wind and cloven tongues as of fire, He poured forth the Holy Spirit upon the disciples, and they proclaimed the great works of God "with other tongues, as the Spirit gave them utterance" (Acts 2:4). Through the renewing influence of the same Spirit three thousand were saved and received into the church.

Christ keeps building His church throughout the ages. Every time a living member is added to the church this is done through His activity. The ablest minister of the gospel that ever lived was no more than a means by which it pleased the Lord Christ to build His church. It was the Lord, not Peter, nor his fellow apostles, who added daily to the church at Jerusalem such as were being saved (Acts 2:47).

How unmistakable that the church is a creation of the Triune God!

Its Supernatural Essence

It must not be supposed that the church is the only institution of divine origin in the world. At least two other institutions can lay claim to the same distinction. They are the family and the state.

The second chapter of Genesis contains the story of the first wedding. It was not man's idea but God's. God said: "It is not good that the man should be alone." So God caused a deep sleep to fall upon Adam, took one of his ribs, made a woman of it, and brought her to Adam that she might be his wife. Thus God established the human family (Genesis 2:18-24).

The thirteenth chapter of Romans teaches that the state is divinely instituted. We are enjoined to be subject to the civil magistrate because "there is no power but of God: the powers that be are ordained of God" (vs. 1). And when Pilate said to Jesus: "Knowest thou not that I have power to crucify thee and have power to release thee?" He replied: "Thou couldest have no power at all against me except it were given thee from above" (John 19:10, 11).

Does it follow that the family, the state and the church are equal in glory? Not by any manner of means. Although all three are of divine origin, yet the family and the state are in one category, the church is in quite another. And the latter category far transcends the former.

Of the three only the church is said by Holy Scripture to have been founded by Christ. This certainly does not mean that He had nothing to do with the origination of the family and the state. The three persons of the Holy Trinity always work together. Yet it is highly significant that Christ said only: "I will build my *church*" (Matthew 16:18). The reason lies at hand. Christ is the Saviour, and the church consists of the saved. And that can be said, neither of the family as such, nor of the state.

The family and the state belong to the realm of the natural. Unregenerate persons can, and often do, constitute a family. While the Bible unmistakably condemns the marriage of a believer to an unbeliever, it may not be said that wedlock is for Christians only. And while Christians should by all odds be the best citizens, citizenship is not restricted to them.

The church, on the other hand, belongs to the sphere of the supernatural. Only those who have been born from above and, in consequence, have by a true faith received Christ as Saviour and Lord are its living members. The unregenerate in the church, however many they may be, are not *of* the church. The church is holy and its members are saints. They are indeed "elect according to the foreknowledge of God the Father, through sanctification of the Spirit, unto obedience and sprinkling of the blood of Jesus Christ" (I Peter 1:2). They constitute "a chosen generation, a royal priesthood, a holy nation, a peculiar people" (I Peter 2:9).

*   *   *   *

How clear that no other institution in all the world is comparable to the Christian church in point of glory! The glory of the greatest, wealthiest, most powerful and most resplendent empire of all history was as nothing, yes less than nothing, in comparison with the glory of the church of Christ.

Small wonder that of all the countless organizations in the world the Redeemer fondly claims only the church as His very own. "Upon this rock," said He, "I will build *my church*." The church alone is "his body, the fullness of him that filleth all in all" (Ephesians 1:23).

Chapter 5

UNITY AND DIVERSITY

Some years ago Wendell Willkie wrote a best seller entitled *One World*. It was a plea for the harmonious co-operation of all nations. Mr. Willkie's aim was most laudable, but his book suffered from oversimplification and superficial optimism. He did not reckon sufficiently with the depravity of human nature in general nor with the ungodliness of Marxian Communism in particular. Today the world is exceedingly far from being one. Scripture tells us that it will not be one until God has established the new earth.

The plight of the Christian church seems almost as sad as that of the world. To all appearances it, too, is a house divided against itself. It resembles a beautiful vase that, fallen from its perch, lies shattered in a thousand pieces. It is like a grand structure transformed by an exploding bomb into a tangled heap of wreckage.

One Church

Unbelievable though it may seem, the church of Jesus Christ is really one.

This truth is presupposed in the Apostles' Creed, which makes mention of "a holy catholic church" in the singular and defines this church as "the" — the one and only — "communion of saints." To be sure, according to the same creed the church's unity is a matter of faith rather than sight, but that does not detract a whit from its reality.

The Word of God teaches the unity of the church unmistakably, repeatedly and emphatically. It is no exag-

41

geration to assert that this is one of the most outstanding teachings of the New Testament. It tells us, for instance, that the church has one Head (Ephesians 1:22), one Spirit (I Corinthians 12:13), one foundation (I Corinthians 3:11), one faith and one baptism (Ephesians 4:5), and that it is one body (I Corinthians 12:12).

That being the case, the question arises why Jesus, in the seventeenth chapter of John's gospel, prayed for the unity of believers. Referring to the apostles, He said in the eleventh verse: "Holy Father, keep through thine own name those whom thou hast given me, that they may be one as we are." And in the twenty-first verse, with the believers of succeeding ages in mind, He continued: "That they all may be one; as thou, Father, art in me and I in thee, that they also may be one in us." Surely, if the unity of believers is a reality, it would seem superfluous to pray that it may come to pass.

Many present-day advocates of church union take it for granted that Jesus prayed in John seventeen for the organizational unity of His followers. Glibly they quote the Saviour's prayer for the unity of believers in support of the wholesale wiping out of denominational boundaries. But even he who runs may see that Jesus was thinking primarily of the *spiritual* unity of believers. He prayed that they might be one *as He and the Father are one*. No doubt, He also desired that this unity might become manifest, for He added: "That the world may believe that thou hast sent me"; but that in no way alters the fact that the unity for which He prayed was specifically spiritual.

Indisputably, the Lord prayed for the spiritual unity of His church. And so the question remains how this prayer may be reconciled with the fact that spiritually the church *is* one. A comparison may help discover the answer. The Christian is holy. Every Christian is a saint. It may even be said that in principle he is perfect. And yet, how obvious that the very best Christian needs to grow in holiness and has a long way to go before he shall have attained the goal of perfection! In much the same way the spiritual unity of all who believe in Christ is indeed a present reality, but its fullest realization and the attainment of its highest degree lie in the future. The spiritual unity of the church is both real and to be realized.

The fact remains that the church of God, far from being a tangled heap of wreckage, is even now God's own perfectly proportioned temple, built upon the foundation of the apostles and prophets, with Jesus Christ Himself as the chief cornerstone, in whom all the building is fitly framed together and all believers are built together for a habitation of God through the Spirit (Ephesians 2:20-22). God omniscient sees it thus. So does God's child with the eye of faith.

MANY FORMS

That there is considerable variety among individual Christians and also among groups of Christians cannot be disputed. There is no good reason why anyone should care to dispute it. Uniformity among Christians is not necessarily a good. When carried to extremes, it becomes an evil. It can be shown that complete uniformity within the church would not enhance its beauty but rather detract from it.

Theologians often speak of the multiformity of the church. By and large they regard it as a good. However, few have stopped to define the term, and that has led to confusion. Sad to say, the term *multiformity* has even been used to cover a multitude of sins.

It has been made to include heresies. One instance may be cited. There are, no doubt, greater heresies than Arminianism. Pelagianism is far worse. But Arminianism, too, is error. Let no one say that the difference between the Reformed faith and Arminianism is merely one of emphasis, the former stressing the sovereignty of God, the latter the responsibility of man, and that therefore it is desirable that there be both Reformed churches and Arminian churches. Obviously, human responsibility is a corollary of divine sovereignty. Because God is sovereign, man is responsible to Him. Therefore, precisely because of its strong emphasis on divine sovereignty the Reformed faith stresses human responsibility strongly also. But Arminianism does violence to both. Not only does it encroach upon the absolute character of God's sovereignty, it also adjusts the demands of God's law to the enfeebled powers of man. Now all doctrinal error, Arminianism too, is sin. And to make sin look respectable by casting about it the cloak of multiformity is itself sin.

Again, the term *multiformity* has often been employed to excuse schism within the church. Schism is sinful division. To leave one denomination in order to found another is an extremely serious matter, and it may be done only for compelling reasons. When division occurs in the body of Christ on some insignificant issue as, for instance, whether leavened or unleavened bread should be used in the Lord's Supper, there is joy among the fallen angels. Multiformity and schism are by no means synonymous.

If churchmen could make up their minds to use the term multiformity only for permissible differences and not for sin, that would remove much misunderstanding and might well promote the unity of the church.

It is not difficult to think of permissible differences. In the interest of uniformity Rome has adopted one language, Latin, for its services of worship throughout the world; but surely there is room within the church of Christ for any number of languages. Three legitimate modes of baptism are found within the church — immersion in water, pouring on of water and sprinkling with water. What does it matter whether a minister wears a Geneva gown, a Prince Albert, a cutaway coat with striped trousers, or just an ordinary suit of clothes in the pulpit? The Scotchman has the reputation of being stolid and usually there is something stolid about his worship, while the African is more emotional and this, too, is reflected in his mode of worship; but instead of finding fault with each other for this difference, they should hold one another in high esteem.

Such multiformity does not obscure the unity of Christ's church, but rather causes it to stand out the more boldly. Unity that comes to expression in uniformity may well be, and usually is, superficial. On the other hand, unity that constitutes the background of multiformity is necessarily deep. For us to be at one with those who are like us is easy; to be at one with those who are unlike us is possible only if a profound unity underlies surface differences. Cicero, pagan though he was, made the wise observation that love surpasses friendship in that, while friendship is esteem of one for another who agrees with him, love is esteem of one for another who differs from him.

By the same token, diversity short of sin, instead of detracting from the glory of the church, enhances it. How much more beautiful is a building constructed of stones of different shapes and sizes than is a structure of blocks all of which look alike! As the human body derives its beauty from the variety of its members, so does the body of Christ. When love rises above uniformity and embraces multiformity, the greatest of Christian virtues comes to glorious expression.

Chapter 6

UNITY AND DIVISION

The spiritual unity of Christ's church is an undeniable reality. It is one body, even the mystical body of Christ.

Nothing can destroy this spiritual unity. Not even the apparently hopeless division of the church into almost countless sects and denominations destroys it. On the other hand, it must be admitted that the present division of the church does greatly *obscure* its unity. And that is a sad fact. It gives rise to the question whether the church is not in sacred duty bound to put forth a concerted effort to remedy this evil.

In the main there are three attitudes to that question. They may be called *extreme denominationalism, extreme unionism* and *realistic idealism.*

EXTREME DENOMINATIONALISM

A great many Christians are of the opinion that the spiritual unity of believers is the only thing that matters and that their organizational unity is of little or no account. Some go so far as to regard organizational *disunity* as a virtue rather than a vice.

As might be expected, those of this persuasion do not hesitate to found new denominations for insufficient reasons. The Reverend Smith, let us say, cannot see that Scripture teaches the secret rapture of believers. Elder Jones is not only convinced that this tenet is Scriptural, but he makes it a hobby. His conscience will give him no rest unless he stirs up a rumpus. If the outcome is a split in the church, what of it? Briefly put, extreme denominationalism makes the blunder of identifying multi-formity with denominationalism.

Perhaps the most striking manifestation of extreme de-nominationalism is the "undenominational" church. Its members will vow that they have no use for denomination-alism, but the fact is that they would carry it to the n-th degree, for they want every particular church, every single congregation, to be a denomination by and unto itself.

That such denominationalism is far removed from the pattern of the apostolic church is evident. In the days of the apostles there were significant differences among believers in various localities, yet all particular churches were united in one Christian church, and denominations were entirely out of the question. The fifteenth chapter of Acts tells us that certain problems which plagued the gentile churches were considered by the apostles, together with the elders of the mother-church at Jerusalem, and that their decisions were deemed binding on all the churches. It is a very far cry from the teaching of Acts fifteen to the undenominational church.

It is just as evident that extreme denominationalism puts the spiritual unity of the Christian church under an opaque bushel and thus detracts in no small measure from its glory. And that is really sinful.

The conclusion is warranted that this attitude toward division within the church of Christ deserves unqualified condemnation.

EXTREME UNIONISM

The opposite pole from extreme denominationalism is extreme unionism. It is advocated by the Roman Catholic Church and by most modernist churches of our day.

Rome takes the position, not merely that there ought to be but one church, but that there actually is but one church. That one church is the Roman church itself. All other churches so called are said to be utterly unworthy of that name. They should repent of their departure from the true church and return to it.

The modernist plea for union, while hardly less urgent than the Roman plea, is differently motivated. Back of the latter plea lies the preposterous assumption that Rome has a monopoly on the truth; behind the modernist plea lurks the flippant notion that doctrinal differences among denominations are negligible, that doctrines, in fact, do not greatly matter. Indifference to truth is one of the most outstanding characteristics of the modernist ecumenical movement of our day. Forgetting theological dissension that is behind, the churches should merge, we are told, for a united campaign to do away with social injustice and to evangelize the world.

The folly of that sort of reasoning is both great and obvious. According to the Word of God the church of Christ is "the pillar and ground of the truth" (I Timothy 3:15). The church is custodian and defender of the truth. It follows that the truth is far too great a price for the church to pay for organizational unity. If it should attain to perfect organizational unity at that price, it would only have succeeded in destroying itself. For the church is where the truth is, and the church which sells such truths as the deity of Christ and the satisfaction of divine justice by His sacrificial and substitutionary death on the cross has been transformed into a "synagogue of Satan" (Revelation 2:9).

More than one leader of the liberal ecumenical movement would unite the church of Christ by annihilating it.

Revelation 13 informs us that all that dwell upon the earth whose names are not written in the Lamb's book of life will worship the beast that has risen out of the sea (Revelation 13:8). The fulfillment of that prophecy probably has several stages, but beyond all doubt the final stage will be the religious unification of practically the entire human race under Antichrist. That the vaunting, but compromising, ecumenism of our day is contributing to the hastening of that event, must be set down as a distinct possibility.

* * * *

Neither extreme denominationalism nor extreme unionism has a remedy for division within the church of Christ. The former has no interest in a remedy and would let the disease run wild. The latter offers a remedy that is more fatal by far than the disease. Must we conclude that there is no remedy? The answer of *realistic idealism* to that question remains to be presented.

In the meantime it must be remembered that the spiritual unity of Christ's church continues a reality. Existing division obscures the church's unity but does not destroy it. Extreme denominationalism accelerates division and thus obscures the church's unity more than ever, but cannot destroy it. Extreme unionism spells the destruction of the church, but will never be permitted actually to destroy either the church or its unity.

Christ Jesus, the glorious and omnipotent Head of the church, at the right hand of God, guarantees its continuity. With the continuity of the church itself is bound up the continuity of its unity. For unity is of the essence of the body of Christ.

Chapter 7

THE IDEAL OF VISIBLE UNITY

REALISTIC IDEALISM

It can hardly be denied that ideally the church of Christ should be *one* in outward appearance as well as inner reality. In that respect it ought to resemble the apostolic church, which certainly was intended in the main as a pattern for the church of succeeding ages. When, in His high-priestly prayer, Christ pleaded for the spiritual unity of believers, He must have had in mind also the outward manifestation of that unity, for He said: "That the world may believe that thou hast sent me" (John 17:21). What needs to be emphasized is that visibility and invisibility are two aspects of the one church and that, therefore, the visible church should manifest the attributes of the invisible — with the obvious exception of the attribute of invisibility. Indisputably one of the most glorious attributes of the invisible church is its unity. In the measure in which the visible church fails to manifest that attribute, outward appearance belies inner reality.

For that reason the notion, which has long been prevalent in orthodox circles, that denominationalism is perfectly proper insofar as it is occasioned by God-appointed natural factors, must be rejected. The fact that Christians speak different languages is a poor excuse for their dwelling apart in different denominations. As it is, there are denominations in which several languages are employed. It is difficult to see why a dozen or more could not be used in one communion. Again, if geographical distance ever was a valid reason for denominationalism, it can hardly be so regarded in this age of fast travel and

almost instantaneous communication. It is not nearly
as far from New York to Shanghai today as it was from
Jerusalem to Rome in the days of the apostle Paul. And
as for differences in racial traits, Christians do well to
remember that in Christ there is neither Greek nor Jew,
Barbarian nor Scythian, white man nor colored.

The ideal is clear. However, no less clear is the fact
that the basic cause of division within the church of Christ,
namely sin, is operating as powerfully today as it was in
the past and that beyond all reasonable doubt it will continue to operate as powerfully in time to come. That is an
exceedingly hard fact which must be faced with utmost
realism. He who does that will, to put it mildly, deem extremely unlikely a united church at any time before the
Lord's return. It is hardly an exaggeration to assert that the
expectation of a united church in this dispensation is an
unwarranted anticipation of the new heaven and the new
earth.

Idealistic Realism

Shall we then discard the ideal? God forbid. It is of
the essence of Christianity to strive for the unattainable.
Fully aware that he will not reach the goal of moral perfection in this life, the Christian must yet press on with
might and main toward that very mark. Likewise, though
convinced that it will continue divided until its Head
comes back, the church must labor incessantly at healing
its breaches. In a word, in the matter of ecumenism we
surely should not permit idealism to run wild, but neither
may we make realism an excuse for a do-nothing policy.
On the one hand, we must see to it that our idealism remains realistic; on the other hand, it is no less important
that our realism remain idealistic.

A few suggestions are in order as to how we may, with
both our feet on solid ground, strive toward the ideal of
visible unity for the church of Christ.

First, we must have the courage to refuse to recognize
as Christian certain self-styled Christian churches. The

truly Christian denominations should declare apostate
such churches so called as have officially denied cardinal
Christian truths. Most assuredly, this should not be done
lightly and least of all pharisaically. But if Unitarianism
by its denial of the Holy Trinity has patently forfeited
every claim to the Christian name, it is difficult to see
how a church which has wittingly and willfully accepted
the control of modernism, with its denial of the essential
deity of Christ and such supernatural events as His virgin
birth and bodily resurrection, has any right to be called
Christian. Such a church should be denominated a false
church and declared outside the Christian fold. If that
were done, one of the greatest obstacles to the unification
of the visible church would be eliminated. For theological
liberalism, in spite of all its clamor for ecumenism and
church union, is working more effectively toward the disruption of the church of Christ than is any other force.
The first need of the church of this day is not union, but
division; however, division unto union.

Second, those denominations on which liberalism has
made inroads but which have not yet surrendered to this
enemy of Christianity should forthwith bring the doctrinal issue to a head. If that were done, almost every
denomination in our land would presently be in the throes
of controversy. Before long many of them would perhaps
be split wide open. But precisely that may have to occur
if the visible church is ever to present a united front.
When the Prince of peace declared that He had come not
to send peace on earth but a sword (Matthew 10:34), He
had in mind the fact that the one and only way in which
true peace can come is by the destruction of false peace.
Almost without exception the denominations of our land
and day are enjoying — or pretending to enjoy — a false
peace. Truth and falsehood are walking hand in hand.
Surely, erring members ought to be given every reasonable opportunity to repent; yet so vigorously must falsehood be condemned and truth upheld that their respective

adherents will part company. That will mean division, but division which is prerequisite to genuine unity.

Third, conservatives must humbly confess that they, too, have sinned and done violence to the visible unity of the body of Christ. Their sin has taken many forms but has usually been rooted in a failure to bow unreservedly before the Word of God. While avowedly accepting the Bible as the Word of God, conservatives have often set up human reason instead of Scripture itself as the ultimate interpreter of Scripture. For instance, instead of permitting both the sovereignty of God and the responsibility of man to stand without any soft-pedaling of either, for the simple and conclusive reason that both are taught unmistakably and emphatically in the Word of God, many who would be known as Bible-believers have done violence to divine sovereignty in a determined effort to square it with human responsibility before the bar of human reason, and at least a few have become guilty of the reverse procedure. By this type of rationalism the visible church has been disrupted. Again, it is by no means unusual for conservatives to place human tradition on a par with divine revelation. The Pharisees of Jesus' day had nothing like a monopoly on the sin of thus denying the sufficiency of Holy Scripture. Nor does the Roman Catholic Church. Protestant churches have been split by the demand of serious-minded Christians that church members live by eleven or twelve commandments instead of ten. It is at this point that the virtue of piety degenerates into the vice of piosity. At the same point the sin of sectarianism has frequently raised its ugly head. To divide the church on what according to the Word of God is an "indifferent" matter; that is to say, a practice which God has neither condemned nor commanded, is the essence of sectarianism. Once more, failure to keep the various teachings of Scripture in balance with each other and the consequent stressing of one or some of them out of all proportion to others, have frequently destroyed the visible unity of

Christ's church. Riding a theological hobby is by no means an innocent pastime. Of such sins it behooves churches everywhere to repent, and from them they must desist.

Fourth, churches which unqualifiedly accept the Bible as the infallible Word of God and are agreed on such basic teachings of the Bible as the Holy Trinity, the eternal Sonship of Christ, the deity and personality of the Holy Spirit, the vicarious atonement, salvation by grace, the visible personal return of the Lord Jesus Christ, the resurrection of the body and the everlasting separation of believers and unbelievers, but differ honestly as to the interpretation of certain other — perhaps even important though less basic — teachings of Scripture should be willing to learn from each other. So far as possible they ought also to co-operate with one another. To mention but a few examples, there is no good reason why they should not co-operate in the distribution of Bibles and insistence on the church's God-given, hence inalienable, right to proclaim the gospel both at home and abroad by any of the usual means of communication, radio and television included. United efforts along such lines will not only facilitate the work of the several churches engaged in them, but will also tend to manifest their essential oneness.

Finally, there are Christian denominations which are so similar in their interpretation of the Word of God that they can without compromising their convictions merge with each other. It may be said without hesitation that organizational unification is their solemn duty. For them to continue divided is sin. It is difficult, for instance, to justify the separate denominational existence of the conservative Baptist churches in the northern part of these United States and the equally conservative Baptist churches of the south. And beyond all doubt those Reformed and Presbyterian churches which are truly Reformed in doctrine and truly Presbyterian in church government should proceed toward organic union and thus make a worthwhile contribution to the realization of the ideal of the visible unity of the Christian church. The establishment, in 1946, of the Reformed Ecumenical Synod was a noteworthy step in that direction. May the future prove it to have been only the first step.

To strive without sacrifice of truth for the visible unity of the body of Christ is to enhance its glory.

Chapter 8

HOLINESS

In the Apostles' Creed Christians the world over say that they believe a "holy catholic church" and they go on to describe the church as "the communion of saints" or holy persons. Surely, that creed of all Christendom puts much emphasis on the church's attribute of holiness.

HOLINESS AS A FACT

Just what does it mean that the church is holy? In what sense is it holy?

Obviously the church is not perfect. Its individual members are imperfect, and collectively they cannot be otherwise. The very best church member is a poor Christian; therefore the very best church has many spots and wrinkles.

Yet the church is truly holy. It is "a holy nation" (I Peter 2:9). It is holy in a twofold sense: objectively or ceremonially, and subjectively or ethically.

According to Scripture any person, and for that matter any thing, that is taken out of the world and set aside for the service of the holy God is holy. For instance, the tabernacle and the temple of the old dispensation, together with their furniture and all that pertained to them, were holy. And so were the priests who ministered in those places. But holiness in this sense is not ethical. Material things are never ethically good or bad, virtuous or sinful. Things simply have no moral quality. However wholesome a glass of milk may be, it is not pious, and however whiskey may be abused, it is not itself wicked. It is just as obvious that not all the priests who served in the Old

Testament sanctuaries were saints at heart. Of some of them it is recorded that they were exceedingly wicked. A striking example is afforded by Hophni and Phinehas, the sons of Eli, with whose behavior God was so thoroughly displeased that He destroyed them. And was it not the high priest Caiaphas who pronounced Jesus worthy of death because He claimed to be the Son of God?

Objective or ceremonial holiness, then, does not guarantee ethical or subjective holiness. However, to despise it for that reason would be a serious mistake. God Himself sets great store by it. When God separates someone from the world and assigns him to His service, He is giving no small honor to that person. Precisely that honor God has bestowed upon His church.

But the holiness of the church is not thus exhausted. The church of Christ is holy also in the ethical sense. Its members have been regenerated by the Holy Spirit. However many unregenerate individuals may be enrolled as members of the visible church, all true and living members of the church have been born again. They have received hearts of flesh for hearts of stone. Consequently they love God and walk in His ways. It cannot be denied that they frequently do the things they would not and fail to do the things they would; nevertheless they "delight in the law of God after the inward man" (Romans 7:22). In principle they are perfect, and their lives manifest the beginning of perfect obedience. They are no longer "the servants of sin" (Romans 6:17). For them to live in sin is out of the question. Therefore Scripture boldly asserts of them: "Whosoever is born of God doth not commit sin; for his seed remaineth in him: and he cannot sin, because he is born of God" (I John 3:9). Not merely a few outstanding members of the church are saints, as Rome would have us think; all true church members are. In spite of the many blemishes that marred the church at Corinth the apostle Paul addressed its members as "saints" (I Corinthians 1:2, II Corinthians 1:1). The church is indeed "the communion of saints."

What glory! The church of Christ is the one and only organization in the world which is holy in this sense. That makes it incomparably the most glorious of all earthly societies.

Nor must it be thought that the church's holiness is a mere ornament that adds to its glory as a sparkling necklace may enhance the beauty of a fair woman. No, its holiness is its very essence. Holiness constitutes it the church. The church is synonymous with holiness.

HOLINESS AS A DUTY

From the fact of its holiness it does not follow that the church may rest on its laurels. On the contrary, it must constantly be at war with the enemy that would destroy its holiness. Again, the church may not rest satisfied with the degree of holiness which it has attained. It must ever strive toward greater heights. In a word, the church's holiness is not only a glorious fact but also a most solemn duty.

The foes that would prevent the church from progressing in holiness, and would even rob it of its holiness, are often described as the world, the devil and the flesh. For practical purposes the three may be subsumed under the one term *worldliness.*

Just what is worldliness? In general it is the exact opposite of holiness. But a more specific answer may prove helpful.

There are those who have externalized the difference between the church and the world. The Amish, for example, a strict branch of the Mennonites, hold that a Christian should be recognizable from his apparel and should refuse to ride in an automobile. While it must be admitted that the antithesis between the church and the world has certain external implications, the view just described suffers from unwholesome extremism.

In the minds of a great many Christians worldliness is synonymous with "worldly amusements." It must be noted here that an amusement is properly described as worldly only when it is sinful. The mere fact that worldly people in large numbers indulge in a certain pastime does not make it worldly. For instance, many worldly folk play golf, but that is no reason why it should be condemned. On the other hand, there are amusements which are so obviously sinful that church members should not think of participating in them. Gambling and most forms of modern dancing are examples. Many "movies," too, are abominably filthy and sacrilegious.

There are in every age certain sins that may be described as regnant. One of the regnant sins of the world in our day is sexual immorality and resulting divorce. Against such sins especially must the church be on guard if it would maintain its holiness. Once it lets down the bars set up by Holy Scripture against such evils, it will inevitably be overwhelmed by a tidal wave of worldliness.

What few Christians seem to realize is that a church may take a strong stand against certain flagrant sins of the world and yet be decidedly worldly. That is a fact worth dwelling upon.

In every church which is truly alive there are bound to be differences. These differences may concern significant doctrines. Then church members must try to convince each other from the Word of God. Thus they may make a valuable contribution to the holiness of the church, for God is wont to sanctify His own through the truth. The thing for them not to do is to organize opposing factions and to attempt by political maneuvering to get the church to adopt a certain view. For that is the worldly way of doing things. It is worldliness.

Not all the officers of a church are equally talented. Some have as many as five talents, others have fewer. In consequence, positions of honor and trust are more or less unequally distributed. That is unavoidable and perfectly proper. Not every minister or elder will make a good moderator of a general assembly or an efficient president of a synod. But as a result it is not unusual for jealousy and envy to spring up. The leaders of a church not infrequently follow the bad example of Jesus' twelve disciples and vie with one another for honor. That, too, is worldliness.

Again, there are churches which pride themselves on their firm stand against worldliness and yet want to be great as the world counts greatness. They think in terms of costly stone edifices rather than lively stones that are built up a spiritual house (I Peter 2:5). They strive after statistical rather than spiritual prosperity. That also is worldliness.

The conclusion is inescapable that the Christian church, in order to maintain its holiness, must indeed discipline those of its members who indulge in the flagrant sins of the world, but that is not enough. It is no less necessary that the church cast out such forms of worldliness as are less obvious but more insidious and not a whit less malignant.

And in order that it may *progress* in holiness the church must delve ever more deeply into the truth of God's Holy Word. Did not Jesus pray: "Sanctify them through thy truth" and declare: "Thy word is truth" (John 17:17)?

Chapter 9

CATHOLICITY

A good dictionary defines catholicity as "universal prevalence or acceptance; universality." The Christian church is truly universal, and its universality is an outstanding aspect of its glory.

PREVALENT MISINTERPRETATIONS

It is regrettable that the catholicity of the church is sometimes misunderstood. Two misinterpretations are particularly prevalent. On the one hand, there are those who take too narrow a view of it; on the other, there are those who view it too broadly.

The Church of Rome calls itself The Catholic Church. By claiming catholicity for itself it bars every other communion from the church universal. According to this view the universality of the church does not extend beyond the Church of Rome. That is indeed a restricted universality.

On the contrary, many Protestants take far too loose a view of the catholicity of the Christian church. They recognize as constituent parts of the universal church any and all groups that call themselves churches. That is the opposite extreme of the Roman view and is not a whit less erroneous. Communions which deny the Holy Trinity or tolerate deniers of the deity of Christ in their membership, and perhaps even in their ministry, have beyond all doubt forfeited the honor of being counted as Christian churches. They are "false" churches. That fact is overlooked, and even denied, by many leaders of the liberal ecumenical movement. Then too, there are self-styled

churches which in reality are mere sects. Difficult though
it often may be to distinguish between a church and a
sect, when a new denomination is founded for reasons
which in the light of Scripture must be deemed picayune
the sin of schism is committed, and that which comes into
being is not a church but a sect. The warning of the
Belgic Confession remains pertinent: "We ought diligently
and circumspectly to discern from the Word of God which
is the true Church, since all sects which are in the world
assume to themselves the name of the Church" (Article
XXIX).

OLD TESTAMENT ANTICIPATIONS

In order to get the proper slant on the catholicity of the
Christian church, one must compare the church of the old
dispensation with that of the new.

It has often been said that the church of the old dispensation was confined to the people of Israel and therefore was national, not universal, in its scope. It cannot
be denied that by and large that was true. God established
the covenant of grace with Abraham and his seed. "He
sheweth his word unto Jacob, his statutes and his judgments unto Israel. He hath not dealt so with any nation:
and as for his judgments, they have not known them"
(Psalm 147:19, 20).

However, that is by no means the whole story. The
Old Testament may be said to teem, not only with prophecies and promises of coming universalism, but also with
actual anticipations thereof. At the very time when God
called Abraham out of his heathen surroundings in order
that he might become the father of a peculiar people, He
told him: "In thee shall all families of the earth be blessed"
(Genesis 12:3). Nationalism was never an end in itself,
but from the outset was a means to the end of universalism. The seventy-second Psalm is one of many that speak
of Messiah's universal reign. "He shall have dominion,"
we are told, "from sea to sea and from the river unto the

ends of the earth" (Psalm 72:8). Through the evangelical prophet God issued the universal invitation: "Look unto me and be ye saved, all the ends of the earth" (Isaiah 45:22). At God's command the prophet Jonah preached the gospel of repentance to the heathen city of Nineveh. Rahab of Jericho and Naaman, the Syrian, as well as Ruth, the Moabitess, turned from paganism to the true and living God.

NEW TESTAMENT REALIZATION

It is not until the new dispensation, however, that the universality of the Christian church comes to its full realization.

When, toward the close of Jesus' public ministry, certain Greeks wanted to see Him, He was deeply moved and said: "I, if I be lifted up from the earth, will draw all men unto me" (John 12:32). This He said referring to His crucifixion. When He was about to return to heaven from Mount Olivet, He commanded His disciples: "Ye shall be witnesses unto me both in Jerusalem, and in all Judea, and in Samaria, and unto the uttermost part of the earth" (Acts 1:8). On the day of Pentecost there were present at Jerusalem men "out of every nation under heaven." Many were converted and received by baptism into the Christian church. The Ethiopian eunuch was converted through the teaching of Philip, the Roman centurion Cornelius with his household through the preaching of Peter. Most significant of all, Paul became God's chosen vessel to carry the gospel far out into the gentile world. The book of Acts tells the story of the triumphant march of the gospel from Jerusalem, the capital of Jewry, to Rome, the capital of the world.

In a word, in the new dispensation the church of Christ breaks completely through the dikes of nationalism and flows out over the whole earth. Before Christ's return the gospel will have been preached to all nations. In heaven the redeemed sing to the glory of the Lamb: "Thou

wast slain, and hast redeemed us to God by thy blood out
of every kindred and tongue and people and nation"
(Revelation 5:9).

PRACTICAL APPLICATIONS

The fact of the catholicity of the Christian church has
a great many practical applications. A few of them will
be specified.

In the past there have been several national churches,
and some persist to the present day. The Church of England is an outstanding example. But if catholicity is an
attribute of the Christian church, it follows that a national
church is a contradiction in terms. It is not even correct
to describe the church of Christ as international. It is
supra-national. That is to say, it far transcends all
nationalism.

For that reason, among others, the principle of the
separation of church and state must be upheld. Just because Pentecost marks the end of a national church it
spells the separation of church and state. Often the precise
application of that principle is admittedly difficult to make,
but beyond all doubt the church may never brook inter-
ference by the state with its spiritual affairs. The
church's right, for a significant example, to preach the
gospel both at home and abroad is not dependent on the
consent of the state, but was bestowed upon it by its divine Head and is therefore inalienable.

The church must ever be on its guard against anything
that may detract from its catholicity. Therefore it must
avoid sectarianism. The term "sectarianism," though
often abused, is not difficult to define. The church cannot
possibly take Scripture too seriously. It follows that insistence within the bounds of Scripture on the exact formulation of Christian doctrine or the exact delineation of
Christian ethics may never be deprecated as sectarianism.
Yet precisely that is often done. But when one teaching
of Scripture is stressed out of all proportion to others,

and again when men presume to add to the teaching of
the Word of God — then it is that sectarianism puts in its
appearance. Concretely, when a church stresses human
responsibility at the expense of divine sovereignty, as does
Arminianism, or when, after the manner of hyper-Calvin-
ism so called, it does the reverse, that is sectarianism.
Again it is patently sectarian to take the position that
even the most moderate use of wine as a beverage is under
any and all circumstances sin, for that view finds no
support in Holy Scripture. Whatever form sectarianism
may assume, it is always a great evil because it makes
for narrowness, prejudice and bigotry and is bound to
obscure that glorious attribute of the church which is
known as catholicity.

A violation of the church's catholicity which is not unusual even among Protestants is to equate to all intents
and purposes one's own denomination with the church of
Christ. There are, no doubt, denominations that have
degenerated into false churches. There are also denominations that are sects rather than churches. But after
those subtractions have been made, it still remains true
that no one denomination anywhere is the whole Christian
church.

The most important positive implication of the church's
catholicity is its solemn duty to proclaim the gospel of
Jesus Christ to all nations and tribes on the face of the
globe, and to receive all who believe, of whatever race or
color, into the church by holy baptism. In the Christian
church "there is neither Greek nor Jew, circumcision nor
uncircumcision, Barbarian, Scythian, bond nor free; but
Christ is all and in all" (Colossians 3:11).

In the winter of 1909 Arthur Balfour lectured in Edinburgh on *The Moral Values Which Unite the Nations*. He
named such matters as common knowledge, common com-
mercial interests, diplomatic intercourse and the bonds of
human friendship. When he had finished and the resounding
applause by the audience had subsided, a small voice from

the balcony queried: "But, Mr. Balfour, what of Jesus Christ?"   One could have heard a pin drop.   The leading statesman of what was then the greatest Christian empire in the world had been rebuked by a Japanese student.

Only a few years ago there was much enthusiastic talk about "one world."   Many were so gullible as to believe that the conclusion of the second world war and the organization of the United Nations would usher it in. Today there is general disillusionment.   No wonder.   The indispensable prerequisite of one world is a universal church. Only then will there be one world when every knee shall bow at the name of Jesus and every tongue shall confess that Jesus Christ is Lord (Philippians 2:10, 11).

Chapter 10

APOSTOLICITY

Is apostolicity an attribute of the Christian church? Some have answered that question in the affirmative, others in the negative. The correct answer is both Yes and No. In a very real sense the church of the new dispensation has the distinction of being apostolic; in another sense it is not apostolic.

THE APOSTOLIC FOUNDATION

When Peter had confessed Jesus to be the Christ, the Son of the living God, the Lord pronounced him blessed and then went on to say: "I say unto thee that thou art Peter, and upon this rock I will build my church" (Matthew 16:18). Just what is "this rock"?

Rome says that the rock is the apostle Peter, and it makes this statement of Jesus the cornerstone of its doctrine of the papacy. Peter, it insists, was the first pope. In view of the fact that the name Peter means *rock*, it must be admitted that at first blush it seems logical to identify Peter with the rock on which the church is built. However, there are weighty objections to that interpretation. To name but one, the New Testament says elsewhere that the church is built upon the foundation of the apostles and prophets, Jesus Christ Himself being the chief cornerstone (Ephesians 2:20). Significantly the church is here said to be built upon all the apostles, not just one of them. No pre-eminence is ascribed to Peter over the others.

Many are certain that the rock of Matthew 16:18 is none other than Christ Himself. But that interpretation is farfetched and fanciful. Jesus was, of course, speaking

67

to Peter — as well as of him — when He said, "I say unto thee that thou art Peter," that is, "a rock." Now the disciples could not possibly have understood Him to refer no longer to Peter but to Himself when He added, "And upon this rock I will build my church," unless He accompanied the latter statement with the gesture of pointing to Himself. But the text contains not the slightest inkling of such a gesture.

Is "this rock" the confession that Peter had made? That Peter's confession elicited from the Lord the words under consideration is self-evident. Beyond doubt, the confession and the rock are closely related to each other. It does not follow, however, that they may be identified. When Jesus said, "I say unto thee that thou art Peter," that is, "a rock," and then added: "Upon this rock I will build my church," He was obviously thinking not only of Peter's confession, but also of his person.

Very likely "this rock" is none other than the confessing Peter as representative of the apostles. That interpretation puts the emphasis demanded by the verse on both Peter's confession and his person. It fits admirably into the context. Peter made his confession in reply to Jesus' question: "Who say ye that I am?" "Ye" is plural. Peter answered, not for himself alone, but for the twelve. That makes it likely that in His response the Lord regarded Peter as representing his fellow apostles. Then, too, this interpretation harmonizes perfectly with Ephesians 2:20, which, in describing the foundation of the church, speaks not of one apostle, but of "the apostles."

The conclusion is warranted that Matthew 16:18, as well as Ephesians 2:20, teaches that the foundation of the church is apostolic.

Doctrinal Apostolicity

In what sense is the foundation of the New Testament church apostolic? A perfectly safe answer is that the church is founded upon the *teaching* of the apostles.

That is unmistakably implied in the Matthew passage which was just considered. It was not merely on the occasion of Peter's stating the doctrine that Jesus is the Christ, the Son of God, but precisely *because* of Peter's confessing this doctrine, that Jesus said: "I say unto thee that thou art Peter, and upon this rock I will build my church." Specifically as confessors of that truth the apostles are the foundation of the church.

That the teaching of the apostles is the foundation of the Christian church is no less patently implicit in the Saviour's high-priestly prayer. Said He: "Neither pray I for these alone, but for them also which shall believe on me through their word" (John 17:20). He had in mind, in addition to the apostles, the church of succeeding ages. It consists of all who believe on Christ through the teaching of the apostles. And that is only another way of saying that acceptance of apostolic doctrine is of the very essence of the church.

The question might be asked whether the statement that the foundation of the church is apostolic does not contradict Paul's emphatic declaration, "Other foundation can no man lay than that is laid, which is Jesus Christ" (I Corinthians 3:11). But that difficulty vanishes quickly and completely when one recalls that the church is founded upon the *teaching* of the apostles. What did they teach but Christ? Christ was the sum and substance of their teaching. Did not Paul say that he determined to know nothing save Jesus Christ and Him crucified (I Corinthians 2:2)? To say that the teaching of the apostles is the foundation of the church is the exact equivalent of saying that Christ is its foundation.

It is highly significant that one of the ecumenical creeds, the confessions of faith to which the entire historic church has subscribed, came to be known as "the Apostles' Creed." To be sure, the apostles did not compose this creed. The idea that it consists of twelve articles because each of the twelve apostles contributed one article must

be dismissed as ridiculous. The truth is that it is the
product of growth and did not acquire its present form
until long after the death of the last of the apostles.
Nevertheless its name says precisely what it is: a summary of the beliefs and teachings of the apostles.

Obviously, this brief creed is nothing like a complete
summary of apostolic teaching. For instance, it does
not name that interpretation of Christ's death which the
apostles taught so unmistakably — that it was a substitutionary sacrifice for the expiation of sin by the satisfaction of divine justice. Nor does this creed dwell on
the teaching of the apostles on such important matters as
Christian conduct and the government of the church. The
foundation of the Christian church includes many apostolic
teachings besides those which are enumerated in the
Apostles' Creed.

It may not be concluded that, in order to merit the
distinction of apostolicity, the church of succeeding times
must be patterned in every detail after the church of the
apostolic age. There are those who teach this, but it is a
position which the apostles themselves never took. For
instance, in the apostolic church there were "charisms,"
special gifts of the Holy Spirit, such as speaking with
tongues and miraculous healing. In I Corinthians 14 the
apostle Paul discouraged the use of at least one of such
gifts, and there is abundant evidence that they ceased
when special revelation was completed. For another example, there is not a shred of evidence that the apostles
intended that the apostolic office should be continued in
the church after their death. They never appointed men
to succeed them in their office. The apostolic office was
confined to the church of the apostolic age. There are
no successors of the apostles.

ORGANIZATIONAL SUCCESSION

Certain churches lay claim to apostolicity in the sense
of their being exclusively, or nearly so, the uninterrupted

continuation of the organized church as it existed in the days of the apostles. Particularly do they boast of their clergy as the unbroken succession of the bishops ordained by the apostles. This view is known as "apostolic succession" and is held by the Greek Catholic, the Roman Catholic and the Anglican churches. It is interesting that the last named body asserts that all three possess apostolic succession, the second concedes it to the first but not to the last, while the first regards its possession by either of the others as exceedingly doubtful.

One serious fallacy in these claims to apostolic succession is that they completely overlook the fact that organizational succession does not guarantee doctrinal succession. To say nothing of the other two communions just named, the Roman Catholic Church has departed very far from the teaching of the apostles. Does it not deny that doctrine which lies at the very heart of apostolic teaching — justification by faith only? For that reason, among others, the Reformers of the sixteenth century did not hesitate to pronounce Rome a false church. Organizational succession without doctrinal succession is worthless. A church that possesses the former but has lost the latter is no longer a church of Jesus Christ. Our Reformed fathers were right when they said that "succession of doctrine" rather than "succession of persons and places" is a mark of the true church. (See Bavinck, *Gereformeerde Dogmatiek*, Vol. IV, p. 353.)

Nevertheless it must be maintained that a true church of any time and any place has the distinction of possessing organizational as well as doctrinal apostolicity. The apostles themselves constituted the nucleus of the organized church of the new dispensation and during their lifetime they built that church. The church which they organized has never passed out of existence and never will. The divine Head of the church has promised that. To be sure, it has experienced many upheavals, but no upheaval has ever destroyed it. That holds even of that great upheaval known as the Protestant Reformation. The simple fact is that the Protestant churches which emerged from that upheaval were the continuation of the apostolic church. Admittedly, today the organized church does not manifest that unity which marked it in the days of the apostles but is marred by division. And yet it remains true that every church which is truly a Christian church, and not a synagogue of Satan nor a mere sect, is the organizational succession of the apostolic church.

Perhaps an illustration will help clarify this point. Think of a tree. It has one trunk. The trunk divides into, let us say, two branches. These again divide into smaller branches. As the tree keeps growing, more and more branches appear. However, every once in a while dead wood has to be pruned away. It may even be that a considerable part of one or both of the two large branches issuing directly from the trunk must be sawed off. To go a step farther, one or the other of those branches may have to be done away with entirely. But whatever may happen to the tree, is it not true that at all times all its living branches, whether great or small, are a continuation of the one trunk? In much the same way every true church since the apostolic age is a succession of the church of the apostles.

The true church is founded upon the apostles. It has the twofold distinction of possessing doctrinal and organizational apostolicity.

Chapter 11

ILLUMINATION

There are two views of the illumination of the Christian church, which represent opposite extremes. On the one hand, Rome holds that the church is illuminated to the point of infallibility. It lays claim to two infallibles — an infallible Bible and an infallible church; hence an infallible interpretation of the Bible by the church. On the other hand, certain Anabaptists, individualists of the Protestant Reformation, stressed the right of private interpretation of the Word of God to the point of practically ruling out the illumination of the church by the Spirit of truth. Today a great many Protestants, including numerous fundamentalists, take the Anabaptist position.

Both of those views suffer from extremism. The truth lies between them.

THE MYTH OF AN INFALLIBLE CHURCH

The infallibility of ecclesiastical councils is an ancient teaching of the Roman church. While it never retreated from that position, experience taught it that the infallibility of many is difficult to maintain. Therefore it arrived eventually at the doctrine of the infallibility of one, the head of the church, the pope. The Vatican Council of 1870 declared him to be infallible in his official pronouncements on matters of faith and morals.

It is clear that this position goes far beyond anything taught in the Bible. It is no less clear that it does violence to the Word of God. It denies the sufficiency of Holy Scripture by placing another infallible alongside it. Some Roman Catholic theologians even go so far as to place the church above the Bible. They argue that the Bible, having been produced by the church, owes its existence to the church and derives its authority from the church.

Every good Protestant stands aghast at such presumption. However, it is easily explained in the light of the basic Roman Catholic teaching concerning the church. Not only does Rome teach that the church is of divine origin. Every Protestant will agree to that. Nor is Rome satisfied to teach that the church is supernatural in its essence. To that again every true Protestant will subscribe. Rome goes much farther. It actually holds the church to be divine; it deifies the church. And since infallibility is a divine attribute, that attribute is ascribed to the church.

Thus Rome becomes guilty of the most heinous of all theological heresies, the fruitful mother of a legion of others — that of wiping out the difference between the Creator and the creature, the Infinite and the finite, the Divine and the human.

THE RIGHT OF PRIVATE INTERPRETATION

It stands to the everlasting credit of the Reformers of the sixteenth century that they rebelled against the doctrine of ecclesiastical infallibility. They upheld the infallibility of the Bible alone. In consequence they insisted that every individual Christian has the right of private interpretation of the Word of God.

It is often said that the Reformers taught the universal priesthood of believers. That is a perfectly correct statement. In defiance of the Roman Catholic hierarchy, they rejected a special class of men in the church known as priests and maintained that every single believer is a priest. However, it is no less correct to say that the Reformers taught the universal prophethood of believers. Every believer, according to them, has the right to interpret the Word of God and to teach it to others. In so doing he is not bound by the church's interpretation. The

Reformers themselves made diligent and vigorous use of that right.

Occasionally one hears it said that private interpretation of Scripture is condemned by II Peter 1:20, 21 — "No prophecy of the Scripture is of any private interpretation, for the prophecy came not in old time by the will of man; but holy men of God spake as they were moved by the Holy Ghost." Even a hasty look at this passage will reveal that it has no bearing on the subject in hand. The reference is not to the *interpretation* of Scripture, but to *its origin.* Peter is here speaking of the interpretation, not of *Scripture,* but of the *future.* He says that prophecy in Scripture came into being, not through human interpretation of the future, but through the divine inspiration of holy men.

The universal prophethood of believers is based squarely on Holy Scripture. Moses' prophetic wish: "Would God that all the Lord's people were prophets" (Numbers 11:29) and Joel's beautiful prophecy: "And it shall come to pass afterward that I will pour out my Spirit upon all flesh; and your sons and your daughters shall prophesy, and your old men shall dream dreams, your young men shall see visions; also upon the servants and upon the handmaids in those days I will pour out my Spirit" (Joel 2:28, 29), were fulfilled when, on the day of Pentecost, the Holy Spirit was poured out, not only on the apostles, but on *all the disciples,* cloven tongues as of fire sat upon *each of them* and *they all* began to speak with other tongues the wonderful works of God (Acts 2:1-11).

THE FACT OF AN ILLUMINATED CHURCH

Does it follow that the individual believer may flippantly brush aside the historic Christian church's interpretation of the Word of God? Some extremists of the sixteenth-century Reformation did that, and their numerous spiritual descendants today do likewise. But that is a serious error.

An elderly church member once said to his youthful pastor: "In my study of the Word of God I have a great advantage over you in your study of the Word. You are biased by your knowledge of the church's creeds; I have no such bias but am led directly by the Holy Spirit." That was a highly presumptuous saying. It ignored the significant fact that throughout the centuries the Spirit of God has been leading the church into the truth and that the truly great creeds of Christendom are the products of that guidance. To disparage the historic confessions of faith is a heinous sin against the Holy Spirit. The slogan "No creed but Christ," however well intended, is an insult to the Spirit whom Christ has poured out upon His church.

Jesus' promise: "When he, the Spirit of truth, is come, he will guide you into all truth" (John 16:13) was addressed to the twelve, not as so many individuals, but as the nucleus of His church. At Pentecost the Holy Spirit was poured out, not merely on the individual disciples who were present, but definitely on the *church* of the new dispensation. In fact, this event marked the birthday, not of the Christian church as such, to be sure, but of the church in its New Testament aspect. The apostle Paul states that to the church of the old dispensation "were committed the oracles of God" (Romans 3:2). Likewise the church of the new dispensation is custodian of the Word of God. The same apostle describes "the church of the living God," the generic church, as "the pillar and ground of the truth" (I Timothy 3:15).

In consequence there runs through the history of the Christian church from the beginning to the present, and there will continue to run through its history from the present to the end of time, a line of truth or orthodoxy. In spite of all the errors that have at different times crept into the church, and in spite of the frequent prevalence of error, the Spirit of truth has never departed from the church, nor will He depart at any time in the future.

Often only a small minority of the membership of the church has adhered to the truth, but a remnant according to the election of grace has never failed, and that remnant has ever constituted the true church. In the future, too, there will always be a true church.

A bit of history of doctrine will afford an example. Inspired Paul taught salvation by the sovereign grace of God, and he taught it without the slightest compromise. God the Father chose His own from eternity. He did it sovereignly, without regard to any foreseen good in them. God the Son by His passive and active obedience merited salvation for the elect so fully that precisely nothing is left for them to merit. And saving faith, by which they lay hold on the Saviour and all His benefits, is the sovereign gift of the Holy Spirit. That is the Pauline doctrine of salvation, and it constitutes the very heart, not only of the teaching of that apostle, but of the whole of Scripture. By the fifth century it was lost almost entirely out of sight. Then the Spirit of truth girded St. Augustine to reassert it. Before long it was again eclipsed, and almost complete darkness settled down upon the church. But in the sixteenth century Luther, Calvin, Knox and others, aroused by the Spirit of truth, once more boldly proclaimed salvation by grace. Soon this precious truth was again compromised, this time by the synergists in Lutheran circles and the Remonstrants in Holland. But vanquished it never was. In the nineteenth century it was upheld unswervingly by a whole constellation of brilliant Reformed theologians — among them the Hodges and Warfield in America, Kuyper and Bavinck in the Netherlands. Today the churches that hold unqualifiedly to the Scriptural teaching of salvation by grace are few and far between and withal so small as to be almost negligible. Yet the Reformed faith, of which this truth is the very essence, is still found in the church of Christ. It always will be. The Spirit of truth will see to that.

In one sense the church of Christ is not infallible. Most

assuredly it can err. It has erred grievously in the past. It errs exceedingly grievously today.   But in another sense it is infallible.   It will never lose the truth.   The truth will never perish from the church.   As there always has been a body of believers upholding the truth of God, so there always will be. The church of the past was, the church of the present is, the church of the future will be — the pillar and ground of the truth.

In that respect, too, the Christian church is indeed glorious.

Chapter 12

PROGRESSIVENESS

The Christian church is generally regarded as a conservative institution. The notion is prevalent that it not only *is* conservative, but *must* be. Conservatism is widely thought to be one of its most essential attributes.

That view of the church is quite correct, but it is correct only so far as it goes. In a very real sense the true church has always been progressive as well as conservative, and it is no less important that the church be progressive than that it be conservative. Its progressiveness is an important aspect of its glory.

In Bible Times the Church Was Progressive

The church of God as depicted in both the Old Testament and the New was progressive. Significantly, its progressiveness was not so much a matter of its own choice as of God's making. God caused the church to progress by giving it a progressive revelation.

The Bible did not on a certain day fall down as a finished product from heaven to earth. On the contrary, it was written by divinely inspired human authors over the extended period of some sixteen centuries. From a small beginning it grew to completion. In consequence God's people on earth were all the time gaining more knowledge concerning God and His relations to men. The church progressed because and as God revealed Himself progressively.

Modernists tell us that the progress found in the Bible involves contradiction. They say that the later books of the Old Testament contradict the earlier on several points and that the New Testament frequently contradicts the Old. For instance, the God of the Old Testament is said to be a cruel despot, while the God of the New Testament is a loving father. That, of course, is a false statement. Liberalism holds a basically wrong view of Scripture. The Bible never contradicts itself.

Another erroneous view of progress in special revelation is that the Old Testament is completely silent on important truths which come to light for the first time in the New Testament. The fact is, as St. Augustine has said, that the New Testament is latent in the Old and that the Old becomes patent in the New. The relation of the two is like that of the bud and the flower. The entire flower is present in the bud, but the content of the bud does not come fully to view until the full-blown flower appears.

Misrepresentation of progress in Scripture aside, progress is a fact. In consequence the church of Bible times could hardly help progressing. Of the many examples that might be given only one will be cited. It concerns an important aspect of the Biblical doctrine of the church itself.

The calling apart of Abraham from his heathen surroundings was a significant event in the history of the establishment of the church. It is extremely meaningful that the account of that event contains a distinct note of universalism. Said God to Abraham: "In thee shall all families of the earth be blessed" (Genesis 12:3). However, it is clear that the same event marks the beginning of a national church. Nor can it be denied that, in spite of frequent prophecies and even anticipations of universalism, the church of the old dispensation was confined almost entirely to Israel as a nation. God showed His word unto Jacob, His statutes and judgments unto Israel. He did not deal so with any other nation, and as for His judgments, they did not know them (Psalm 147:19, 20). In line with this nationalism was the instruction which Jesus gave to the twelve when He sent them out to preach:

"Go not into the way of the gentiles, and into any city of the Samaritans enter ye not" (Matthew 10:5).

It was not until the Saviour's death on the cross that the bud of universalism burst into full bloom. Shortly before His death He said: "I, if I be lifted up from the earth, will draw all men unto me" (John 12:32). After His resurrection He commanded His apostles and His church to make disciples of all nations (Matthew 28:19) and to be His witnesses in Jerusalem, in all Judea, in Samaria, and unto the uttermost part of the earth (Acts 1:8). At Pentecost Jews and proselytes from "every nation under heaven" (Acts 2:5) were converted through the preaching of Peter and received into the church. It is a noteworthy fact that the church required some time to grow accustomed to its universality. Peter himself needed a supernatural vision to prepare him for preaching the gospel to a Roman centurion (Acts 10). And the apostles had to argue the matter out in a conclave at Jerusalem before they were ready to receive gentiles into the church without their first having passed through the door of Jewry (Acts 15). But universalism won the day. God saw to that.

How clear a case of progress in divine revelation and of consequent progress by the church!

In Subsequent Times the Church Has Been Progressive

It might seem that, when the Bible was completed, the church would cease to progress. However, that was by no means the case. Special revelation is indeed complete in Holy Scripture, but the progress of the church has not thus come to an end. In a most important respect the church of every age needs to progress; namely, in its *understanding* of the Scriptures. As a matter of history the Spirit of truth has throughout the centuries led the church into an ever better and deeper understanding of the Word of God.

It must not be thought that this progress has been uninterrupted. To suppose that, would betray extreme ignorance of church history. In certain periods the church seemed almost to have lost the truth. It must also be borne in mind that not all that calls itself a church is actually a church of Christ. At different times considerable portions of the church have apostatized. Yet, beyond doubt, the illumination of the historic Christian church by the Holy Spirit has been progressive. And that fact, too, can be illustrated by reference to the doctrine of the church itself.

St. Augustine, who lived in the fifth century A.D., was, no doubt, the greatest of the church fathers. It is truly remarkable that both Calvinists and Roman Catholics like to appeal to him. But they appeal to different — and it must be said, contradictory — elements in his teaching. Calvinists are enthusiastic about his doctrine of salvation by grace; Roman Catholics are no less enthusiastic about his doctrine of the church. Benjamin B. Warfield has said that these teachings were, so to speak, two children struggling with each other in the womb of his mind. They were at odds with each other. Augustine's doctrine of the church was in error. It was a form, albeit a mild one, of sacerdotalism, which is the view that God imparts saving grace to sinners only through the mediation of the church and that, therefore, there is no salvation apart from the church. It was not until the Protestant Reformation in the sixteenth century that the truth of evangelicalism overtook in a decisive way the error of sacerdotalism. The Reformers discovered the Scriptural teaching that, while God the Holy Spirit, in working faith in the hearts of men, employs as a means the gospel preached by the church, the actual imparting of saving grace is accomplished by Him without the mediation of the church, and that membership in the church, while indeed a normal consequence of salvation, is not prerequisite to salvation. The one prerequisite of salvation is faith in the Lord Jesus Christ.

However, in an important respect even the Reformers erred in their doctrine of the church. By way of reaction from the Romish error that the church must govern the state, they concluded that the state must to a large extent govern even the spiritual affairs of the church. That accounts for Article XXXVI of the Belgic Confession in its original form of 1561. And even the Westminster divines, nearly a century later, held that it is the duty of the civil magistrate "to take order, that unity and peace be preserved in the church, that the truth of God be kept pure and entire, that all blasphemies and heresies be suppressed, all corruptions and abuses in worship and discipline prevented or reformed, and all the ordinances of God duly settled, administered, and observed. For the better effecting whereof, he hath power to call synods, to be present at them, and to provide that whatsoever is transacted in them be according to the mind of God" (Westminster Confession of Faith, Chapter XXIII, Section III). It was not until the eighteenth and nineteenth centuries that the Scriptural teaching of the separation of church and state gained anything like broad acceptance within Protestantism.

How clear that the Holy Spirit has throughout the centuries illuminated the church progressively in its study of the Word of God! And the example just given is but one of many that might be cited.

TODAY THE CHURCH MUST BE PROGRESSIVE

The church of our day stands in crying need of conservatism. A great many forces operating both within and without the church are drawing it away from the truth. The warning addressed by the glorified Christ to the church at Philadelphia: "Hold that fast which thou hast, that no man take thy crown" (Revelation 3:11) needs to be impressed deeply upon the church of today.

The church must be reminded that the Bible presents objective, unchangeable truth, which the church is in sacred duty bound to uphold, and that the Bible lays down an objective, unalterable standard of goodness, which the church is in sacred duty bound to maintain. Nor may the church forget that since the completion of special revelation the Spirit of truth has illuminated the church in its study of that revelation, and that the products of that illumination, as embodied in the great creeds of Christendom and the writings of outstanding theologians, although not on a par with the Word of God, must be zealously guarded.

However, the duty of the church has not thus been stated fully. It is no less necessary that the church be progressive than that it be conservative. History tells us that a church is sure to lose its Christian character if it ceases to be conservative. History also tells us that a church will become extinct if it fails to be progressive.

The church's conservatism must be unto progressivism. Never may it, after the manner of liberalism, tear down the foundation that has been laid. That would mean retrogression and even destruction. But neither may it be satisfied to guard the foundation without building upon it. That would spell petrifaction. It must maintain the foundation with a view to building upon it and withal proceed to build. That is at once healthy conservatism and true progressivism.

Let no one think that by this time the church has exhausted Holy Scripture. It has done nothing of the kind. It remains the God-assigned task of the church to explore the Word of God ever more thoroughly and to bring forth from its depths ever greater riches of truth. In the words of Jesus, it must bring forth out of this treasure "things new and old" (Matthew 13:52). History teaches us that doctrinal controversy, which in our day is customarily decried as a great evil, can be exceedingly helpful to that end. Again, it is important that the church distinguish sharply between Scriptural teachings and human traditions, and it must ever stand ready, if need be, to discard the latter, no matter how ancient and firmly established they may be. Still another duty of the church which it may not neglect, but often does, is to apply the teachings of Scripture to the specific problems and peculiar needs of the times.

Reference may here be made once more to ecclesiology. Who dares to assert that the last word has been said even now on the relation of church and state? And who can deny that precisely today, when state totalitarianism is in the ascendancy, there is urgent need for further study of this matter? Again, the church has not always taken pains to distinguish sharply between a true church and a false. In these days of departure from the faith by nearly every church it is of the greatest moment that this be done. Also, ours is an age of sectarianism. New denominations spring up almost with the proverbial rapidity of toadstools and often for the most insignificant reasons. Shall we recognize all such groups as churches just because they call themselves churches? And most certainly the last word has not been said on the timely subject of ecumenicity.

There is a Latin sentence, long used by churchmen, which expresses aptly the church's duty to be progressive: *"Ecclesia reformata semper est reformanda."* That simply means that a reformed church must ever keep on reforming. It is not too strong an assertion that when a church ceases to reform itself it forfeits the right to be called reformed. And that is just another way of saying that complacency is a most heinous sin in any church. A self-satisfied church is either dead or dying. When a church boasts: "I am rich and increased with goods, and have need of nothing," the Head of the church stands ready to spew it out of His mouth (Revelation 3:16, 17).

Chapter 13

INDESTRUCTIBILITY

In outward appearance the church of Christ is far less glorious than are most dominions of the world. Nevertheless, in all essential respects the church is incomparably more glorious. One of those respects is the matter of durability. Earthly kingdoms come and go. Some of the greatest and mightiest world empires vanished very quickly after their founding. But the church continues from age to age and will outlast the ages. The Christian church is indestructible.

THE MEANING OF INDESTRUCTIBILITY

There is serious trouble, let us assume, in a particular church. It is threatened with extinction. On a certain Sunday morning the pastor announces as his text Matthew 16:18 — "Upon this rock I will build my church, and the gates of hell shall not prevail against it." He consoles his audience with the assurance that according to this declaration of the Son of God the congregation cannot be destroyed. Or let us suppose that a denomination is in danger of disruption. At the general synod, **general conference**, or general assembly the moderator comforts the commissioners with Isaiah 54:10 — "For the mountains shall depart and the hills be removed; but my kindness shall not depart from thee, neither shall the covenant of my peace be removed, saith the Lord that hath mercy on thee." He affirms that the future of the denomination is as sure as are the promises of God.

Those ministers have misinterpreted and misapplied the Word of God. Scripture does not guarantee the permanence of a particular church. Christ Himself threatened the church at Ephesus with destruction. He had the apostle John write to this church: "Repent, and do the first works; or else I will come unto thee quickly, and will remove thy candlestick out of his place, except thou repent" (Revelation 2:5). And history shows that it is not unusual for a whole denomination to pass out of existence.

What, then, is the meaning of such Scripture passages as Isaiah 54:10 and Matthew 16:18? The answer is obvious. The Christian church in its entirety will never perish. The body of Christ will never be destroyed. To the end of time there will be a communion of true believers on earth. The answer to our Lord's rhetorical question: "When the Son of man cometh, shall he find faith on the earth?" (Luke 18:8) may very well be that He will find but little; it cannot be that He will find none.

The exegesis of Jesus' saying that the gates of hell shall not prevail against His church has occasioned considerable debate. Likely the best interpretation is that given by Geerhardus Vos in his excellent little book *The Teaching of Jesus Concerning the Kingdom of God and the Church*. He says: "Probably . . . the correct rendering is 'the gates of Hades shall not surpass it.' The gates of Hades seem to have been a figure for the highest conceivable strength, because no one can break through them. On this rendering our Lord simply means to say that the church will not be excelled in strength by the strongest that is known; the figure is a further elaboration of the idea that the church is built upon a rock" (p. 154). Because of its strength the church will prove invincible.

The question is sometimes asked whether indestructibility is an attribute of the invisible church only, or also of the visible church; in other words, whether Scripture teaches merely that there always will be believers on earth or also that there ever will be an *organization* of believers. On this matter there need be no doubt. The context in which occurs the promise, "The gates of Hades shall not surpass it," settles it unmistakably. Christ here speaks of the church as a house, of its builder and its foundation;

for He says: "Upon this rock I will build my church." He makes mention of the keys of this house when He says: "I will give thee the keys of the kingdom of heaven." He refers to church discipline in the words: "Whatsoever thou shalt bind on earth shall be bound in heaven, and whatsoever thou shalt loose on earth shall be loosed in heaven." It is clear that, when asserting the indestructibility of the church, Christ was conceiving of the church as, in the words of Vos, the "external organization" or "outward embodiment" of the kingdom. Throughout the ages there will be a visible church.

THE MANNER OF PRESERVATION

The continuance of the church is not something automatic. The church is indestructible because God preserves it. It should be worth while to consider a few of the means which God employs unto its preservation.

Speaking of the church of God, Isaiah said: "No weapon that is formed against thee shall prosper" (Isaiah 54:17). Time and again the church has been violently assailed by the world. The persecution of the early church by the Roman emperors is an outstanding example. Christians were thrown to the lions, and Nero is said to have bound them in bundles, poured pitch over them, and set them on fire to illumine the imperial gardens for his nocturnal bacchanalia. Frequently the very existence of the church has been in jeopardy. But always the Almighty intervened in time to preserve His church. More than that, in His all-wise providence He overruled the attacks of the world unto the growth of the church. Driven this way and that by their persecutors, believers preached the gospel far and wide. Their unperturbed faith and radiant joy in the face of violent death commanded the admiration of their enemies. In scores of ways the blood of the martyrs became the seed of the church.

The foe that threatens the existence of the church is found at least as often within the gate as without. Not only has heresy lifted its ugly head in the church; often it has seemed to prevail. In the middle ages the pestilent error of salvation by works was almost universally accepted. That is true also today, and it has been supplemented with the no less pestilent error of salvation by character. Nearly all the large denominations of our day, and many small ones besides, have been invaded by theological liberalism, which denies the Bible as the very Word of God, Christ as the very Son of God, supernatural regeneration as the very essence of salvation. When considering the history of heresy one can hardly help wondering how it is that the church was never completely overwhelmed by error. That it was not, is indeed a most amazing fact. The explanation is that the great Head of the church, at the right hand of God, has ever kept His promise to guide the church into the truth by the Spirit of truth (John 16:13). Even when the overwhelming majority in the church turned their backs upon the truth, God caused His church to continue as guardian of the truth. Unbelievable though it may seem, He even led the historic church into the truth *progressively*.

A third method by which God preserves the church deserves much more attention than it ordinarily receives. It is bound up inseparably with the thoroughly Scriptural, yet much neglected, doctrine of the covenant of grace. In His counsel of predestination God might conceivably have elected to eternal life none in certain periods of history. Concretely, He might have elected no one who would live, let us say, in the tenth century after Christ. In that case there obviously would have been no true church on earth in that century. Or God might sovereignly have elected no one who would live in the last century before the second coming. Then the church would of necessity cease to exist a hundred years before Christ's return. As a matter of fact, however, God has His elect in every age, and that fact is tied up with the truth that in the counsel of predestination God took family ties into account. God decreed to impart saving grace from generation to generation. Therefore He said to Abraham: "I will establish my covenant between me and thee and thy seed after thee in their generations for an everlasting covenant, to be a God unto thee and to thy seed after thee" (Genesis 17:7). This does not mean that godly parents will without exception have godly children. Least of all does it mean that saving grace is an heirloom handed down by parents to children, for only when Christian parents are diligent in providing a Christian training for their children may they confidently expect them to grow up to fear and love the Lord. What does follow is that it is certain that God will at all times have a covenant people, a church, on earth. The flow of covenant mercy will never be interrupted.

Still another means which God employs for the continuation of the church is the preaching of the gospel by the church to those who are without. Ours is an age of rapid dechristianization of the Christian nations. It might seem that the inevitable outcome will be the ruination of the Christian church. Not so. The faithful covenant God has promised that at least a remnant will be preserved. That remnant will never fail to proclaim the glad tidings of salvation to a lost world. And God will see to it that His Word does not return void, but that through it sinners are continuously delivered from the power of darkness and translated into the kingdom of His dear Son (Colossians 1:13). Thus God will keep adding to the church until all His elect from every nation shall have been brought in.

> O, where are kings and empires now
>   Of old that went and came?
> But, Lord, thy church is praying yet,
>   A thousand years the same.
> Unshaken as eternal hills,
>   Immovable she stands,
> A mountain that shall fill the earth,
>   A house not made by hands.

Chapter 14

THE GLORIOUS HEAD OF THE CHURCH

The relationship of Christ to the church is so varied and rich as to defy adequate description. To name but a few of the numerous aspects of this relationship, He is both its founder and its foundation, its savior and its owner, its preserver and its hope, its lover and its beloved, its righteousness and its holiness, its Head and its King.

Without fear of contradiction it may be said that no aspect of Christ's relationship to the church looms larger in Holy Writ than the fact that He is its Head. As such He is transcendently glorious. And His body, the church, cannot but partake of His glory.

ITS FEDERAL HEAD

At the beginning of history God forbade Adam to eat of the tree of the knowledge of good and evil and threatened him with death if he did eat (Genesis 2:17). The unmistakable implication was that, in case he remained obedient, he would be permitted to eat of the tree of life and thus would be rewarded with life eternal. Theologians have these facts in mind when they say that God established with Adam the covenant of works. Not for a moment may it be thought that it was a covenant between God and Adam as a mere individual. In this covenant Adam was the representative, the federal head, of all his descendants. Therefore his first sin affected the whole human race. God imputed the guilt of that sin to all men. "By the offense of one, judgment came upon all men to condemnation" (Romans 5:18).

Long before man fell, even before the foundation of the

world, the God of all grace had made provision for his salvation. In the quietude of eternity He ordained the covenant of grace. In this covenant He provided another Adam, another representative or federal head, to accomplish all that was necessary for the redemption of His elect. Not only was the second Adam to make full atonement for their sin, He was also to do all that the first Adam should have done but failed to do. By His perfect obedience to the divine law He was to merit eternal life for those whom the Father had given Him. God would impute to them His righteousness. By the obedience of one would many be made righteous (Romans 5:19).

How much more glorious is the second Adam than the first. The first was of the earth earthy; the second was the Lord from heaven (I Corinthians 15:47). The first, although created good and in the image of God, was capable of sinning; the second, although sorely tempted, could not sin. The first did sin and thus brought death upon the race of humanity; the second became obedient unto death, even the death of the cross, and thus guaranteed eternal life for the new humanity, the church of God. The first was made a living soul; the second was made a quickening spirit (I Corinthians 15:45). It may well be for these reasons that Scripture speaks of the Saviour as the *last* Adam rather than the *second*. He did all that the first Adam failed to do. He wrought perfect righteousness and life eternal. No additional Adam was needed or ever will be.

Its Organic Head

Scripture tells us repeatedly that Christ is the Head of the church and that the church is His body. The apostle Paul reminded the Ephesian Christians of their duty as members of Christ's body, the church, to "grow up into him in all things, which is the Head, even Christ" (Ephesians 4:15). And the same apostle, after telling the believers at Colosse that "the body is of Christ," warned them against "not holding the Head, from which all the body by joints and bands having nourishment ministered, and knit together, increaseth with the increase of God" (Colossians 2:17, 19). The gist of these passages is that the relationship between Christ as the Head and the church as His body is organic.

Our Lord gave expression to the same truth by means of another metaphor. He spoke of Himself as "the vine" and of the members of His church as "the branches" (John 15:5). It goes without saying that the relationship of the vine to the branches and of the branches to the vine is organic.

The organic union of Christ and His church is a profound mystery. Therefore he who seeks to describe it must exercise the greatest care to speak soberly. On the one hand he must indeed aim to do justice to the intimacy of this union, but on the other hand he must beware lest he completely identify Christ and the church.

C. G. Trumbull, a modern mystic and advocate of The Victorious Life once wrote these words: "At last I realized that Jesus Christ was actually and literally within me; and even more than that: that He had constituted Himself my very being . . . my body, mind, soul and spirit. . . . My body was His, my mind His, my spirit His, and not merely His, but actually a part of Him. . . . Jesus Christ had constituted Himself my life — not as a figure of speech, remember, but as a literal, actual fact, as literal as the fact that a certain tree has been made into this desk on which my hand rests" (*The Life That Wins,* pp. 13, 14).

This is amazing language and a gross exaggeration. It does away with the distinction between Christ and the Christian. It asserts that the Christian's individuality has been abolished and that he has become a part of Christ. Applied to the church, this can only mean that the church has ceased being the communion of believing men and women and has become Christ Himself.

What, then, does it mean that Christ is the organic Head of His church? It means that the church has no life apart from Christ and receives from Christ whatever life it has. It means that the church was originated not only by Christ, but also from Him, and cannot continue to exist for even a moment apart from Him. It means that the church in all of its members lives and operates only through Christ. It means that one and the same Spirit, even the Holy Spirit of God, dwells both in Christ and in His church. It means that the life which Christ has imparted to the church and keeps imparting to it is His very own.

What glory for the church!

Its Ruling Head

Implicit in the Scriptural teaching that Christ is the Head of the church is His rule over the church. This appears clearly in the words: "For the husband is the head of the wife, even as Christ is the head of the church: and he is the saviour of the body. Therefore, as the church is subject unto Christ, so let the wives be to their own husbands in everything" (Ephesians 5:23, 24). For that reason Scripture speaks of Christ as the King of the church. Referring to Christ and the church, God declared: "Yet have I set my king upon my holy hill of Zion" (Psalm 2:6). And Paul described the church as the kingdom of God's dear Son (Colossians 1:13).

How does Christ rule His church?

He does it through the instrumentality of men, the officers of the church. Ministers, elders and deacons represent Christ as prophet, king and priest respectively. Particularly to the ruling elders has Christ committed the government of His church. However, it is a fact of the greatest moment that, while He does *delegate* authority to them, He never *transfers* to them the authority which is His. After all it is Christ Himself who governs the church through its officers. Therefore those officers may never

presume to legislate for the church. Their sole task is
to declare and apply the laws of Christ without ever
adding to them or subtracting from them.

Christ governs the church by His Word and His Spirit.
This is not to say that no member of the church ever
violates His Word or resists His Spirit. Sad to say, that
happens all too often. However, Christ does keep adding
members to His church by the irresistible grace of His
Spirit operating in their effectual calling through the
Word. And it is also true that He so controls the living
members of the church by His Word and Spirit that, in
spite of their many remaining imperfections, they delight
in His law after the inner man and render to Him the
beginning of perfect obedience.

Not only is Christ Head of the church, He is Head over
all things. God "gave him to be the head over all things
to the church" (Ephesians 1:22). As such He is in a
position to protect the church against the onslaughts of
the world, to fulfill His own promise that the gates of
hell will not prevail against the church, and even to cause
the wrath of its enemies to contribute to its final triumph.
Satan himself cannot so much as stir without His permission, and He will see to it that all the machinations of
the prince of darkness against the church redound to its
glory. Therefore the church sings:

> Did we in our own strength confide,
> 　Our striving would be losing,
> Were not the right man on our side,
> 　The man of God's own choosing.
> Dost ask who that may be?
> Christ Jesus, it is He;
> Lord Sabaoth His name,
> From age to age the same;
> 　And He must win the battle.

This glorious Head of the church Scripture describes
as seated "on the right hand of the Majesty on high"

(Hebrews 1:3). And the seer on the isle of Patmos saw Him in the midst of the seven golden candlesticks "like unto the Son of man, clothed with a garment down to the foot and girt about the paps with a golden girdle. His head and his hairs were white like wool, as white as snow; and his eyes were as a flame of fire; and his feet like unto fine brass, as if they burned in a furnace; and his voice as the sound of many waters. And he had in his right hand seven stars: and out of his mouth went a two-edged sword: and his countenance was as the sun shineth in his strength" (Revelation 1:13-16).

How glorious a Head! What glory to be His body!

Chapter 15

THE HARMONIOUS MEMBERS OF THE CHURCH

The church is the body of Christ. He is its Head, and all who believe in Him are its members. The church is glorious because of the resplendent majesty of its Head. It is glorious also because of the beautiful harmony of its members.

THE IMPERATIVE OF HARMONY

To all outward appearances the church frequently presents a picture of dissension rather than harmony. Nor are such appearances altogether deceiving. As a matter of plain fact, there is at all times considerable disharmony within the visible church.

For that reason Scripture enjoins church members to manifest their harmony "with all lowliness and meekness, with long-suffering, forbearing one another in love; endeavouring to keep the unity of the Spirit in the bond of peace" (Ephesians 4:2, 3). For the same reason, when the apostle Paul was informed that there were parties in the church at Corinth, he wrote to that church: "Now I beseech you, brethren, by the name of our Lord Jesus Christ, that ye all speak the same thing, and that there be no divisions among you; but that ye be perfectly joined together in the same mind and in the same judgment" (I Corinthians 1:10).

What accounts for disharmony in the church? Two factors especially. There are always those in the church who are not of it. Inevitably they occasion division. With reference to such members Paul wrote to the Galatians: "I would they were even cut off which trouble you"

(Galatians 5:12). The faithful exercise of discipline is definitely in the interest of harmony within the church. And those who are truly of the church are still at best very poor Christians. The frequent disobedience of the members of the church to its Head drives them apart.

The obvious reason why the members of the human body normally act so harmoniously is that all of them alike obey the head. If only all the members of the body of Christ would obey the Head, who has enjoined them with all the emphasis at His divine command that they love one another as He has loved them, what harmony the church would display! Instead, church members indulge so often in the twin sins of pride and jealousy. So few of them have learned to "esteem other better than themselves" (Philippians 2:3). Time and again they must be told to lay aside "all malice, and all guile, and hypocrisies and envies, and all evil speaking" (I Peter 2:1). Like the disciples of old, who disputed with one another which of them was greatest in the kingdom of heaven, they need to be reminded of the Master's telling words: "Verily I say unto you, Except ye be converted, and become as little children, ye shall not enter into the kingdom of heaven" (Matthew 18:3). Those who fail to repent of the sin of wanting to be first will not even be last.

THE SEMBLANCE OF HARMONY

Often the church is harmonious only in outward appearance, not in reality. Then harmony is a mere sham.

That occurs whenever the church forgets or declines to be militant against whatever evil dwells in its midst. There is flagrant sin, let us say, among prominent members of a given church. To combat such sin will unavoidably disturb the peace. The offender is excused with the trite remark that there is not a church member who does not sin. Thus the storm that threatened to break is dissipated. Peace is maintained. But a malignant disease keeps gnawing at the vitals of the church.

Or let us assume that there is controversy in a church on an important doctrine. There are two opposing groups or wings. It is practically a foregone conclusion that many members will refuse to take sides. They pride themselves on striking "the golden mean." Although the doctrine at issue is of such moment that Christianity stands or falls with it, they opine that this particular doctrine is relatively insignificant. Although one side is essentially right and the other essentially wrong, they insist on the obvious fact that neither is infallible. They are certain to condemn both sides for the "bitterness" that mars their debate, and often they have a point here; but they forget that they themselves are guilty of the heinous sin of doctrinal indifference. They boast of their zeal for the church's peace, but the sad fact is that they are working overtime for its destruction. Middle-of-the-road pacifism in significant doctrinal controversy has ruined many a church.

The prophet Zechariah exhorted the Jews of his day: "Love the truth and peace" (Zechariah 8:19). He did not urge them to seek peace at the expense of truth, for he realized that peace purchased at that price is not really peace at all. No, he regarded truth as an absolute prerequisite of peace that is truly peace. He also knew that the way of truth is the *sure* road to peace.

THE REALITY OF HARMONY

There is much disharmony within the church. There is also a great deal of simulated harmony. These are sad facts. But they do not alter the truth that the church of Jesus Christ is characterized by a very real harmony.

The book of Acts paints a beautiful picture of the early church at Jerusalem: "All that believed were together, and had all things common; and sold their possessions and goods, and parted them to all men, as every man had need. And they, continuing daily with one accord in the temple, and breaking bread from house to house, did eat their

meat with gladness and singleness of heart, praising God
and having favor with all the people" (Acts 2:44-47).
Although the New Testament nowhere commands other
churches to imitate the "communism" of the Jerusalem
church, every true church of Christ is characterized by
a goodly measure of the same harmony, for the same
Spirit indwells it.

Shortly a difficulty arose in the church at Jerusalem. The
Grecians murmured against the Hebrews because, as they
supposed, their widows were neglected in the daily min-
istration (Acts 6:1). It was then that under the guidance of the apostles a new office was established in the
church. It was the diaconate, the office of mercy. It is a
permanent office in which throughout the centuries the
love of the members of the church for one another, particularly for the poor and needy, comes to tangible expression.

In the same letter in which he berated the Corinthian
Christians for divisions among them, the apostle Paul
strongly stressed the truth that believers are members
of one body. And not only did he exhort them to behave
toward one another as members of the same body should,
he also declared boldly that in essence harmonious co-
operation of the members of the church is as much a
fact as is the harmonious co-operation of the members of
the human body. The church *is* the body of Christ. Believers *are* the members of that body. They *are* controlled
by one Head. Therefore they *do* act harmoniously. All
that is plainly implied in the assertion: "For by one Spirit
are we all baptized into one body" (I Corinthians 12:13).

The harmony that prevails among the members of
Christ's body is made to stand out strikingly in relation
to their diversity. Harmony presupposes diversity. When
identical voices sing identical notes, no one thinks of
harmony. But when different voices singing different
notes blend with one another, the product is harmony. If
the human body consisted of several parts, all of the same

size and shape, harmony would be out of the question. Now that it consists of many widely differing members, all aiding one another, the quality of harmony is outstanding. There is much diversity among the members of Christ's church. Some have five talents, others but one. Some have attractive characters, others are relatively unattractive. Some are leaders, others followers. Some are rich, others poor. Some are highly educated, others unlearned. Some are strong in the faith, others weak. But each needs all the others. They complement one another. They co-operate with each other. Collectively they constitute one body. And all are bound together by the greatest of Christian virtues — love.

That is harmony indeed. And such harmony is of the essence of the church. Where it is wanting there is no Christian church. It is found in every true church. For the church is undeniably the body of Christ.

Chapter 16

THE CHURCH AND THE TRUTH

In his *Institutes of the Christian Religion* John Calvin teaches that the first and foremost mark of the true church is faithfulness to the Word of God. Adherents of the Reformed faith have ever taken the same position. If that position is correct, the relationship of the church to the truth of God's special revelation must of necessity be exceedingly close. As a matter of fact it is so close that to do full justice to it is next to impossible. The following paragraphs will indicate that relationship from a few of its many angles.

PRODUCT OF THE TRUTH

The church was brought into being by the revelation of truth.

When man fell into sin in the garden of Eden, God at once appeared on the scene. He pronounced judgment on the man and the woman as well as the serpent. But He also gave to fallen humanity a promise which has come to be known as the protevangelium, the first announcement of the gospel. Said God to the serpent: "I will put enmity between thee and the woman, and between thy seed and her seed; it shall bruise thy head, and thou shalt bruise his heel" (Genesis 3:15). That promise spoke of the victory of Christ crucified over Satan, sin and the world. It may be taken for granted that Adam and Eve embraced it in faith. If so, they constituted the first Christian church, for the church consists of the believers of all ages.

In the days of Abraham God established His church in a more formal way, and again He did it by the revelation of truth. His numerous revelations to Abraham culminated in the promise: "I will establish my covenant between me and thee and thy seed after thee in their generations for an everlasting covenant, to be a God unto thee and to thy seed after thee" (Genesis 17:7). Abraham believed and became "the father of all them that believe" (Romans 4:11), whether of the old or the new dispensation. Collectively they constitute the church of God.

The church in its New Testament aspect was founded when the Holy Spirit was given on the day of Pentecost. Numerous souls were added to the church from every part of the inhabited world. That also came to pass through the revelation of truth, particularly through the inspired preaching of the apostle Peter.

From the fall of man to the end of time God builds His church. And His invariable method of doing it is by His Word of truth and the Spirit of truth. The Heidelberg Catechism says: "The Son of God, from the beginning to the end of the world, gathers . . . to Himself by His Spirit and Word, out of the whole human race, a church chosen to everlasting life" (Lord's Day XXI, Question 54).

Surely, the church is a product of the truth.

CONVEYOR OF THE TRUTH

On rare occasions God has used angels to convey His truth to men. For instance, angels first proclaimed the Saviour's birth and His resurrection. Ordinarily, however, God has reserved this honor for human beings.

The men whom God employed as conveyors of the truth in the old dispensation are commonly called prophets. It has been said aptly that their task was not so much to fore-tell as to forth-tell. God first spoke to them and then they told men what God had told them. They were God's messengers to men. Therefore they did not present their own opinions but declared authoritatively: "Thus saith the Lord." That expression or its equivalent actually occurs hundreds of times in their writings. Peter tells us: "The prophecy came not in old time by the will of man: but holy men of God spake as they were moved by the Holy Spirit" (II Peter 1:21).

The men through whom God conveyed His truth in the new dispensation are known as apostles. They were instructed in the truth by the Lord as they walked with Him during His public ministry. When He was about to leave, He promised them "another Comforter . . . even the Spirit of truth" (John 14:16, 17). Controlled by this Spirit, they, too, proclaimed not their own wisdom but the wisdom of God. When the apostle Paul came on the scene as one born out of due season, he certified that the gospel which he preached was not after man and that he had not received it of man but was taught it by the revelation of Jesus Christ (Galatians 1:11, 12). All the books of the New Testament were written either by the apostles themselves or by others under their guidance or influence.

Not every one whom the Bible calls a prophet or an apostle was a true child of God. Balaam, for instance, was not, nor was Judas Iscariot. Nevertheless, the prophets and apostles by and large bore the closest relationship to the church of God. They were members of the church. They constituted the foundation of the church, and the foundation is an integral part of a building. By virtue of their office they represented the church. Therefore it may be asserted without hesitation that God has been pleased to employ His church as the conveyor of special revelation.

CUSTODIAN OF THE TRUTH

To the church of the old dispensation "were committed the oracles of God" (Romans 3:2). Its task was the keeping, the guarding, the conserving of special revelation. That such is likewise the task of the church of the new dispensation is unmistakably explicit in Paul's description of the church as "the pillar and ground of the truth" (I Timothy 3:15). The function of pillars is to uphold structures. One important function of the ground is to uphold numberless things. If the earth failed to perform that task, this planet would obviously be chaos. The function of the church as the pillar and ground of the truth is to uphold the truth.

There have been times in the history of the church when it took that task seriously. During the first centuries of the Christian era and again in the age of the Protestant Reformation the church was much more concerned about the truth than about its own immediate peace and prosperity. The truth was dearer to the hearts of men than were their possessions, their lives, even their wives and children. In comparison, how sad is the church's plight today! The cancer of doctrinal indifference is gnawing at its vitals. The insistent and widespread demand for church union and the truly tremendous emphasis on ecumenism are in many instances symptoms of that disease. And instead of casting out deniers of such cardinal Christian truths as the Holy Trinity, the deity of Christ and the substitutionary atonement, the church often bestows upon them its highest honors. Thus it has come to pass that in numerous instances the church, having ceased to contend for the faith once for all delivered to the saints, has ceased being the church.

Will the church pass out of existence and the truth fail? No, never! The Spirit of truth will abide with and in the church forever (John 14:16). One denomination after another may become a false church, but there will always be a remnant according to the election of grace. The pillar and ground of the truth cannot be destroyed. Not even the gates of hell surpass it in strength. God Almighty Himself will see to it that His church continues to the end of time as custodian of the truth. Martin Luther was right when he sang:

And though this world with devils filled
. Should threaten to undo us,
We will not fear, for God hath willed
His truth to triumph through us.

INTERPRETER OF THE TRUTH

Rome teaches that special revelation is not complete in the Bible and that it is the church's task and privilege to add to it. Therefore it places the teachings of the church on a par with — and sometimes above — Holy Scripture. It is as certain of the immaculate conception of the virgin Mary and her assumption into heaven, neither of which has the slightest basis in Scripture, as it is of the unmistakably Scriptural teachings of the virgin birth of Jesus and His ascension. The Protestant Reformers rejected this view of revelation as grievous heresy and insisted on the sufficiency of Scripture. At the same time they strongly stressed the duty of the church to *interpret* the Word of God. How right they were! In order that the church may rightly divide His Word, God has given to it the Spirit of truth.

Some Protestants of the Reformation age stressed the individual believer's right of private interpretation out of all proportion to the church's function of interpreting the Word of God. But most of the Reformers had the good sense, while insisting on the right of private interpretation, to hold high the honor of the church as divinely appointed interpreter of Holy Writ.

How the churches of the Reformation worked at that task! The energy displayed by them in its performance was truly prodigious. Numerous confessions and catechisms were the result. And almost all of them are masterpieces of Scripture interpretation.

Today there are a few Christians — very few in fact — who regard the creeds as practically sacrosanct and hesitate exceedingly either to add to them or to subtract from them. They overlook the fact that the church of all ages must continue active as interpreter of God's truth. All the creeds of Christendom put together do not nearly exhaust the truth of Holy Writ. Nor are they infallible. However, those who hold the creeds in contempt are far more numerous. They are also more vocal. Most modernists laugh the creeds out of court as outdated and outmoded products of "the pre-scientific age," while many fundamentalists keep repeating the vapid phrase "No creed but Christ." Both belittle, not only the church, but a most significant work which the Spirit of truth has accomplished through the church.

PROCLAIMER OF THE TRUTH

The church has no more important task than that of preaching the Word of God.

Some would have the Word preached by individuals rather than the church. There have been in the past, and there are today, evangelists and other preachers so called who have never been ordained to the ministry or sent out by the church. That savors of unwholesome individualism. While no one has the right to say that God will not use the labors of such men, it may be asserted without hesitation that their position is far from ideal. Most assuredly, all Christians must witness for their Lord, but the preaching of the truth of special revelation is the official task of the church. For a bit of Scriptural proof, were not Paul and Barnabas sent out as missionaries by the church of Antioch with the laying on of hands, and did not that church send them out at the express command of the Holy Spirit (Acts 13:1-3)?

How stupendous a task is preaching! Not only isolated portions of the Bible but "all the counsel of God" (Acts 20:27) must be declared. Preaching involves both explanation and application of the Word of God. And the Word must be applied, not merely to the needs of the individual hearers, but to all those social problems that have a religious import. The truth of God must be pro-

claimed to all men: to those who are nigh and to those who
are afar off, to rulers and subjects, to rich and poor, to
adults and children, to the learned and the ignorant, to
the cultured and the uncultured, to the converted and the
unconverted, to men of every race, nation and language.
That stupendous task the exalted Christ has committed
to His church.   And on its performance hangs the salvation of the world.

*   *   *   *

Much more might be said on our theme, but enough has
been said to make it clear that the relationship of the
church to the truth is exceedingly intimate.   Some conclusions are now in order.

The church that has grown indifferent to the truth is,
to put it mildly, on its way out.   And the church that
knowingly tolerates in its midst denial of the basic truths
of the Word of God is itself guilty of such denial and by
that very token has ceased being a true church.

A church with a large membership, an imposing edifice,
an elaborate ceremonial, an efficient organization and dignified vestments, but without the truth, is not a church.
On the other hand, a church with a numerically negligible
membership, with no building other than a lean-to, with
the simplest order of worship, with a minimum of organization and with no clerical vestments at all, is a church of
Jesus Christ if only it is loyal to the truth.

In this world, which under the spell of the liar from
the beginning has become a dark den of falsehood and
deception, there is one institution whose sole concern is
to hold high the torch of God's special revelation.   That
distinction belongs to the Christian church.

Chapter 17

THE CHURCH AND SALVATION

The Christian church is usually defined as the communion of believers. That amounts to saying that those who are saved are its living members.

On this view of the church there is considerable agreement in Christendom. But when it comes to the question precisely what is the relationship of the church to salvation, there is much disagreement. Can the church impart saving grace to men? Is church membership essential for salvation? Or does the Scriptural teaching of justification by faith alone imply that membership in the church is of little importance? To such questions various answers have been given.

TWO EXTREME VIEWS

The teaching of the Roman Catholic Church on this score is arrogant in the extreme. It says that Christ has indeed wrought salvation by His atoning death, but that He has committed the dispensing of salvation to the church. As a Leyden jar is used to store electricity, so, it is said, the church is a storehouse of saving grace, and but for this storehouse there is no way for one to receive the blessings of salvation. To change the metaphor, the church is a middleman between Christ, the author of salvation, and the sinner as the recipient of salvation, and God has ordained that the sinner can obtain salvation only through this middleman. In a word, the church has a monopoly on saving grace. Particularly through the instrumentality of the sacraments the church is said to impart saving grace. Therefore no one, not even an infant, who dies without the benefit of baptism can be saved; and without the use of the Eucharist, or holy supper, no adult may expect to be saved.

In fairness it must here be remarked that this teaching of Rome is not altogether equivalent to asserting that no one can be saved who is not enrolled as a member of the Roman Catholic Church. Especially in recent decades leading Roman Catholic theologians have become concessive in their interpretation of the ancient tenet *Extra ecclesiam nulla salus;* that is to say, Outside the church there is no salvation. For example, the possibility is said to exist that one may belong to the "soul" of the church without belonging to its "body."

The historic teaching of Rome on this score can be understood only in the light of its basic error concerning the church — that the church is divine. It is said to be nothing less than Jesus Christ Himself in His earthly form, a reincarnation of Christ to the end of the continuation and completion of His redemptive work.

However, it can hardly be denied that the church consists of human beings. That being the case, Rome places a human mediator between God and the sinner. It denies Christ as the one and only Mediator. It causes the sinner to fall into the hands of faulty and fallible men rather than the hands of the God of all grace.

Over against this teaching of Rome, the theological term for which is *sacerdotalism,* the Protestant Reformers placed the doctrine of *evangelicalism.* In its simplest terms it is that God imparts the benefits of salvation to men directly, without the mediation of the church.

Rome's position is quite extreme. However, many otherwise conservative Protestants go to the opposite extreme. They teach that, if one believes on the Lord Jesus Christ, it matters little or nothing whether one is a member of the church. They like to play up Christianity against "churchianity." Sometimes they go so far as to refuse to name a communion of believers a church. In their evangelistic preaching they are less than insistent that converts unite with a church.

There is another large group that goes under the Protestant name and conceives of the connection between the church and salvation as exceedingly loose. Modernists ridicule as quite outmoded the notion that church membership and salvation go hand in hand. While they do not deny that by and large it is a good thing to be a church member, they insist that the one requirement for entrance into the kingdom of God is nobility of character, and they are very certain that a host of men and women who have never committed themselves as undone sinners to the Christ crucified and have no desire to be members of His church, yet are loyal citizens of the kingdom. That certainly is rank heresy.

Two Scriptural Truths

What does Holy Scripture teach concerning the relationship of the church to salvation? Two truths stand out prominently.

In the first place, Scripture teaches unmistakably that all who are saved should unite with the church.

The view that membership in the visible church is requisite to salvation has no basis whatever in Scripture. When the Philippian jailer asked what he should do to be saved, Paul said only: "Believe on the Lord Jesus Christ, and thou shalt be saved, and thy house." The apostle did not command him to join the church. However, when he did believe he was at once baptized (Acts 16:31-33). As soon as the Ethiopian eunuch confessed Christ he likewise was baptized (Acts 8:36-38). So were all who were converted at Pentecost. Now according to Paul's words, "By one Spirit are we all baptized into one body" (I Corinthians 12:13), baptism signifies reception into the church. It is clear that in the days of the apostles it was universal practice to receive believers into the visible church.

What could be more logical? He who believes in Christ is united with Christ. Faith binds him to Christ. He is a member of Christ's body, the invisible church. But the visible church is but the outward manifestation of that body. Every member of the invisible church should as a matter of course be a member of the visible church.

Extremely significant in this connection is Acts 2:47 — "And the Lord added to the church daily such as should be saved." Not only does the Lord Christ require of those who are saved that they unite with the church; He Himself joins them to the church. And the reference is unmistakably to the *visible* church.

Does it follow that he who is outside the visible church is necessarily outside Christ? Certainly not. It is possible that a true believer because of some unusual circumstance may fail to unite with the church. Conceivably one may, for instance, believe in Christ and die before receiving baptism. But such instances are exceptional. The Scriptural rule is that, while membership in the church is not a prerequisite of salvation, it is a necessary consequence of salvation. Outside the visible church "there is no ordinary possibility of salvation" (Westminster Confession of Faith, Chapter XXV, Section II).

A second teaching of Holy Writ on this subject is that it is the God-assigned task of the church to dispense the means of grace — the Word and the sacraments.

Rome is in grievous error when it asserts that the church dispenses *saving grace itself.* But so are they in error who overlook the fact that the church must dispense *the means of saving grace.*

God employs but one means to impart faith to men. It is His Word, the Bible. "Faith cometh by hearing, and hearing by the word of God" (Romans 10:17). It is the sacred duty of the church to proclaim that Word. When it pleases the Holy Spirit to call sinners effectually by the Word as preached by the church, believers come into being. It is because of this important role of the church in

the birth of believers that the church deserves to be denominated *the mother of believers*. Believers are born
of God through the church. To that truth the apostle Paul
gave expression when he said: "Jerusalem which is above
. . . is the mother of us all" (Galatians 4:26).

It is the function of a mother also to feed her children.
By the preaching of the Word and the administration of
the sacraments the church nurtures her members and
builds them up in the faith. And that, too, is an integral
part of their salvation. To be sure, for results the
church here again is utterly dependent on the grace of
the Holy Spirit. Only when God blesses the means of
grace will they prove effective. But the fact remains
that God has committed to the church the means for
spiritual growth.

We conclude that all the glory for man's salvation
belongs to God and that none belongs to the church. But
it is also true that it has pleased God to honor the church
highly by committing to it the means of saving grace.
The church plants and waters, but it is God that gives the
increase. On the one hand, neither he that plants is
anything nor he that waters, but God that gives the increase. On the other hand, the church has the glorious
distinction of laboring together with God unto the salvation of men (I Corinthians 3:6-9).

Chapter 18

AN ORGANISM AND AN ORGANIZATION

A very good dictionary defines an organism as "a body composed of different organs or parts performing special functions that are mutually dependent and essential to life." The same dictionary defines an organization as "the systematic union of individuals in a body whose officers, agents and members work together for a common end." An organism is something that is alive, as a plant, an animal, or the human body. An organization, although consisting of living beings, is not itself alive.

Is the Christian church an organism and not an organization? Or is it an organization and not an organism? Or is it both an organism and an organization?

THE TEACHING OF SCRIPTURE

There cannot be the slightest doubt as to the Scriptural answer to those questions. The Bible speaks unmistakably of the church as both an organism and an organization.

The apostle Paul wrote to the church at Rome: "So we, being many, are one body in Christ, and every one members one of another" (Romans 12:5). To the church at Corinth he wrote: "For by one Spirit are we all baptized into one body" (I Corinthians 12:13). In these and many other passages Scripture likens the church to a living human body. Obviously it conceives of the church as an organism.

It is just as clear that the Bible regards the church as an organization. Therefore it speaks repeatedly of the church as a building. A building, in distinction from the human body, is not alive. When Jesus said: "Upon this

114

rock I will build my church" (Matthew 16:18), He was
thinking of the church in that way. Hitherto an internal,
invisible kingdom had loomed large in His teaching; now
He went on to speak of His church as an external organization. It was the practice of the apostles to form an
ecclesiastical organization wherever there was a group of
believers. For instance, when Paul and Barnabas, on
their way homeward from their first missionary journey,
visited the various places where they had recently preached
the gospel, they "ordained them elders in every church"
(Acts 14:23).

Scripture is not at all careful to distinguish between the
church as an organism and the church as an organization.
Often it speaks in one breath, as it were, of the church
in both capacities. For but one example, church members
are told: "Ye, as lively stones, are built up a spiritual
house" (I Peter 2:5). As a *stone house* the church is an
organization, as a *spiritual* house, consisting of *lively*
stones, it is an organism. Nowhere does Scripture speak
of an unorganized group of Christians as a church. Therefore it is hardly proper to suppose that one group of
believers constitutes the church as an organism, while
another group of believers constitutes the church as an
organization. A voluntary association of Christians con-
ducting a Christian day school, constituting a Christian
labor union, or establishing a Christian recreation center,
is sometimes denominated the church as an organism, but
such language does not excel in precision. It has no basis
in Scripture. Strictly speaking, such an association is
not a church. The truth of the matter is that one and
the same group of believers is at once the church as an
organism and the church as an organization. The church
is both in one.

AN EXTREME VIEW

Throughout the history of the Christian church there
have been within it numerous individuals and several

sects which stressed the truth that the church is an organism to the practical exclusion of the truth that it is an organization. To name but one of such groups, the Plymouth Brethren make that error. The only tie that binds them together, say they, is their common faith in Christ, not an external organization. They have no ordained ministers or other officers. Of church government they will have nothing. In view of the organizational connotation of the word *church*, some go so far as to refuse to call their communion by that name.

In line with this one-sided conception of the church is the so-called pure church idea. Since only those who have been born again are living members of the body of Christ, it is affirmed that all others should by all means be excluded from their fellowship. The practical impossibility of doing this does not keep those who hold this view from insisting that it must be done. [In consequence, it is not unusual for them to presume to be able to tell well-nigh infallibly who are born again and who are not.]

A logical consequence of this unbalanced view is an almost total disregard of the ideal of organizational unity for the Christian church as a whole. Scripture teaches that all believers the world over are one in Christ. They constitute His one body. Ideally this unity ought to manifest itself in oneness of organization. In other words, the visible church should manifest the unity of the invisible church. This important truth is lost sight of by those who exalt the church as an organism out of all proportion to the church as an organization. They say that, since all believers are united spiritually, it matters little whether they are in one church or in many churches or in no church at all. An undenominational church is said to have as much and as little right to exist as any denomination. Schism is not a sin, for the simple reason that ecclesiastical organization is of no account. For the same reason attempts to reform a denomination have little or no value. The only thing, it is held, that really counts is the fact of the spiritual unity of all true believers constituting the church as an organism.

There are those who hold this extreme view in a less extreme way than do others. These are perfectly willing to grant that a particular church is an organization as well as an organism, but the church in a broader sense they regard exclusively, or nearly so, as an organism. That conception underlies what is known as Independency, according to which each congregation is a law unto itself and is independent of every other congregation. Congregations may confer with one another, it is held, for mutual counsel, but such conferences have no authority over the particular churches. A logical consequence of this view is that only the needless disruption of a congregation is schism and that each particular church is to all intents and purposes undenominational. In a word, this less extreme view still puts a premium on the organizational disunity of the Christian church.

THE OPPOSITE EXTREME

Others there are who stress the fact that the church is an organization out of all proportion to its being an organism. The prevalence of this view within the church of our day is one of its most flagrant faults.

Many a pastor is much more concerned about the size of his church than about its purity. Therefore he receives with open arms into the church anyone who professes to be a Christian. Because the church is unable to look into the hearts of men, he considers himself excused from attempting to ascertain the credibility of an applicant's profession. He offers the same excuse for the church's failure to discipline its erring members. He is more interested in church management than in teaching the Word of God, and he would rather be known as a good organizer than as a faithful shepherd.

The organization complex is not confined to particular churches and their pastors. Many a denomination prides itself on well-oiled and smoothly running ecclesiastical machinery while it largely, or even completely, neglects sound doctrine. Literally hosts of church members boast of their loyalty to a denomination without ever inquiring whether the denomination is loyal to the Word of God. One reason why church union is so very popular is that it results in bigger and supposedly stronger organizations. A temptation besetting all federations of churches is that they will do too much thinking in terms of size, and there is evidence that several of them have yielded to that temptation. It does not seem to occur to the World Council that the smallest church which contends uncompromisingly for the truth once for all delivered to the saints is contributing incomparably more to the coming of the kingdom of God than is a globe-encircling federation of churches that darkens the truth by ambiguous words. Nor does it realize that the former is a manifestation of the body of Christ, while the latter is not.

A BALANCED POSITION

Only he who holds to the Scriptural teaching that the church is both an organism and an organization can maintain a balanced view of the church.

The fact that the church is an organism and an organization makes imperative both the purity and the unity of the church.

The church that is conscious of being both an organism and an organization will be careful not to judge the hearts of men and will thus avoid extremes in discipline, but it will also be zealous for discipline with a view to keeping the church as pure as is humanly possible.

From the fact that the church is both an organism and an organization it follows, on the one hand, that its spiritual unity is a fact, but also, on the other hand, that it may never cease striving toward the ideal of organizational unity.

The truth that the church is an organization as well as

an organism demands its organizational unity, not only on the congregational level, but also on the denominational level, and even on the universal level.

Because the church is at once an organism and an organization, it is supernatural without being unnatural, invisible but also visible, heavenly and therefore not of the world, yet for the present definitely in the world.

Chapter 19

EXALTED OFFICES

Every organization has its officers. So does the church. However, at this point there emerges a striking difference between the church and man-made organizations. The officers of the church occupy an incomparably more exalted position than do the officers of such organizations. Whatever the two may have in common, only the officers of the church have the high honor of representing the Lord Jesus Christ, the great Head of the church.

And yet it may not be thought for a moment that the officers of the church are on a par with Christ Himself. To all intents and purposes Rome takes that position. Therefore, it ascribes to the church the infallibility which belongs only to its divine Head. It maintains that whatever the church declares officially, Christ declares. The pope is said to be Christ's vicar. The truth of the matter is that, while on the one hand the officers of the church represent Christ, on the other hand their authority is restricted by Christ, and they are definitely subordinate to Him.

REPRESENTATIVE OF CHRIST

The name Christ means *Anointed*. Christ was anointed with the Holy Spirit to a threefold office — that of prophet, priest and king. In this threefold capacity He rules the church. But He sees fit to exercise His rule through the instrumentality of men. Small wonder that the very same offices are found within the church. Christ clothes some in the church with prophetic authority, some with priestly authority, some with royal authority; and those whom He thus honors represent Him in His three-fold office.

The work of a prophet is to deliver messages from God to men. Therefore those who proclaim the Word of God represent Christ as prophet. The apostle Peter says of the Old Testament prophets that it was "the Spirit of Christ which was in them" that "testified beforehand the sufferings of Christ and the glory that should follow" (I Peter 1:11). Because the Spirit of Christ spoke through them they prophesied in Christ's name. It was the resurrected Christ who said to His disciples: "As my Father hath sent me, even so send I you" (John 20:21) and commissioned them — and in them the church of succeeding ages — to go and "teach all nations" (Matthew 28:19). Time and again the apostle to the gentiles called himself "an apostle of Jesus Christ," and he insisted that he was an apostle "not of men, neither by man, but by Jesus Christ" (Galatians 1:1). All who preach the gospel may declare with him: "Now then we are ambassadors for Christ, as though God did beseech you by us: we pray you in Christ's stead, be ye reconciled to God" (II Corinthians 5:20).

An important task of a priest is to show mercy. Therefore, those whose work it is to help the poor and needy in the church represent Christ as priest. In the old dispensation the priests and the Levites had to share with "the stranger, the fatherless, and the widow" the tithes which they received from the Israelitish people (Deuteronomy 14:29, 26:12). It is as meaningful as interesting that the men who, in the parable of the good Samaritan, first saw the victim of violent robbery lying by the roadside but passed by without rendering aid, were a priest and a Levite (Luke 10:31, 32). They of all men should have shown mercy. When the apostles were kept so busy preaching the Word that they could hardly take proper care of the poor in the church at Jerusalem, deacons were chosen for this task, and they were ordained by the apostles (Acts 6:1-6). In the New Testament church the diaconate is the office of mercy. Very significantly, "to do good and to communicate" are denominated by the author of Hebrews as "sacrifices" (Hebrews 13:16). As the bringing of sacrifices is a priestly activity, so are doing good and communicating. It is clear that those whose special task it is to perform works of mercy in the church perform this task as representatives of Him whom Scripture calls "a merciful high priest" (Hebrews 2:17), even Jesus Christ.

The business of a king is to rule. Therefore those who rule the church represent Christ as king. When Paul enjoined the elders of the Ephesian church to "take heed unto the flock," he reminded them not only that the Holy Spirit had made them overseers over the church, but also that the Lord Jesus Christ had purchased it with His own blood (Acts 20:28). From the fact that the church belongs to Christ it follows that those whom He has charged with overseeing it do so in His name. The same apostle besought the believers at Thessalonica to know them which labored among them and were over them "in the Lord"; namely, the Lord Christ (I Thessalonians 5:12). The author of Hebrews exhorted his readers: "Obey them that have the rule over you, and submit yourselves: for they watch for your souls, as they that must give account" (Hebrews 13:17). He to whom they must give account can be none other than the King of the church, on whose behalf they rule. And when Peter told the elders of the churches to which he was writing that the chief Shepherd would reward their faithfulness in feeding the flock and exercising the oversight thereof (I Peter 5:2-4), that apostle obviously conceived of the elders as under-shepherds representing the "great Shepherd of the sheep" (Hebrews 13:20).

SUBORDINATE TO CHRIST

Great is the glory of the offices in the Christian church. Far be it from us, however, to equate their authority with the authority of Christ. A few respects in which the latter far transcends the former may be named.

The authority of Christ is original, that of the offices in His church is derived. As the authority of a monarch surpasses that of his ambassador, so the authority of the Head of the church is incomparably greater than is that of His representatives.

The authority of Christ is sovereign, that of the offices in His church is only ministerial. To be sure, in the days of His flesh Christ declared that He, too, came "not to be ministered unto but to minister" (Matthew 20:28), but when God "raised Him from the dead and set Him at His own right hand in the heavenly places," He exalted Him "far above all principality and power and might and dominion and every name that is named, not only in this world, but also in that which is to come" and "put all things under His feet, and gave Him to be the head over all things to the church" (Ephesians 1:20-22). Most assuredly, that cannot be said of the officers of Christ's church. Contrariwise, they need to be admonished not to be "lords over God's heritage" (I Peter 5:3). And the great apostle Paul assured the Christians of his day: "We preach not ourselves, but Christ Jesus the Lord; and ourselves your servants for Jesus' sake" (II Corinthians 4:5).

Christ is the Lawgiver of His church, but its officers, instead of making laws for the church, must be content with declaring to it the law of Christ. In order that all things may be done decently and in order, the officers of the church may indeed make certain regulations, but such regulations are never comparable to the law of Christ. Christ's law is perfect, and nothing may at any time be added to it. Speaking of "matters of faith and worship," concerning which the officers of the church may conceivably presume to legislate, the Westminster Confession of Faith says not only: "God alone is lord of the conscience, and hath left it free from the doctrines and commandments of men which are in any thing contrary to his word," but it advisedly adds: "or beside it" (Chapter XX, Section II).

Christ is infallible in the exercise of His authority, the officers of His church are fallible in the exercise of theirs. According to Rome certain passages in the New Testament ascribe infallibility to the church and its officers. Prominent among these are Matthew 16:19, in connection with 18:18, and John 20:22, 23. In the first of these passages the Lord, having described Peter as the recipient of a special revelation from the Father in heaven, says to him: "I will give unto thee the keys of the kingdom of heaven, and whatsoever thou shalt bind on earth shall be bound in heaven, and whatsoever thou shalt loose on earth shall be loosed in heaven." That these words were addressed to Peter, not as an individual, but as representative of the twelve, becomes clear from Matthew 18:18, where precisely the same authority is assigned to all the apostles. In the John passage the risen Christ, after breathing on the apostles and saying to them: "Receive ye the Holy Ghost," adds: "Whose soever sins ye remit, they are remitted unto them; and whose soever sins ye retain, they are retained." It is clear that these passages speak of specifically apostolic prerogatives which do not belong to the church of succeeding times. Meyer's famous *Commentary on the New Testament* insists that those addressed in Matthew 18:18 are "the apostles, but not the *disciples in the more comprehensive sense of the word,* nor the Church, nor its *leaders*"; and in commenting on John 20:23 the same standard work speaks of "the peculiar authority of the apostolical office." The apostles in their official pronouncements were infallible, but they have had no successors.   The infallibility of the church and its officers is a myth.

From every conceivable viewpoint the officers of the church are subordinate to Christ.   Yet the fact that they represent Christ remains.   And that is an exceedingly great honor.   A greater is hardly imaginable.

Chapter 20

THE UNIVERSAL OFFICE

Organizations have officers. The church, too, has its officers. However, at this point, as at so many others, appears the unique glory of the church. Whereas in other organizations a limited number of persons is wont to hold office, in the church every single member is an officer.

Nor is that the whole truth. There are in the church three offices. They represent Christ, the Head of the church, as prophet, as priest and as king. Now each church member holds not merely one or even two of these offices, but all three. Every single church member is at once a prophet, a priest and a king. That surely spells glory.

We shall consider how this truth is taught in Scripture and how it has fared in the history of the church.

IN SCRIPTURE

The doctrine of the universal office of believers is revealed progressively in Holy Writ. Consequently it is taught much more clearly and fully in the New Testament than in the Old. Yet, beyond all doubt it has been true from the very founding of the church that every one of its members was a prophet, a priest and a king.

Man was created in the image of God. That image consisted chiefly of knowledge, righteousness and holiness (Ephesians 4:24, Colossians 3:10). By virtue of his knowledge man was a prophet, for knowledge is a prime requisite in a prophet. By virtue of his righteousness he was a king, for righteousness is a prime requisite in a king. And by virtue of his holiness he was a priest, for holiness is a prime requisite in a priest. When he fell into sin man lost these aspects of the image of God. However, they are restored in the new birth. It follows that every regenerated person is a prophet, a king and a priest. But that is only another way of saying that every true church member holds that threefold office, for the membership of the church is made up of the regenerate.

The universal *prophethood* of believers is taught repeatedly in Scripture. The eleventh chapter of Numbers tells a most interesting story bearing directly on this matter. Seventy men of the elders of Israel were chosen to assist Moses in governing the people. At an appointed time they were to gather at the tabernacle in order to receive the Spirit. Sixty-eight of them did so; the Spirit came upon them, and they prophesied. The remaining two, whose names were Eldad and Medad, did not put in their appearance at the tabernacle; nevertheless the Spirit came upon them also, and they prophesied in the camp. When this irregularity was reported to Moses, his servant Joshua protested: "My lord Moses, forbid them." But, believe it or not, Moses, instead of administering a rebuke to Eldad and Medad, replied: "Would God that all the Lord's people were prophets, and that the Lord would put his Spirit upon them." The fulfillment of that prophetic wish was predicted by the prophet Joel when he said: "And it shall come to pass afterward that I will pour out my Spirit upon all flesh; and your sons and your daughters shall prophesy, your old men shall dream dreams, your young men shall see visions: and also upon the servants and upon the handmaids in those days will I pour out my Spirit" (Joel 2:28, 29). This prophecy was fulfilled when, at Jerusalem, the believers "were *all* with one accord in one place," cloven tongues as of fire "sat upon *each* of them," and "they were *all* filled with the Holy Ghost, and began to speak with other tongues" (Acts 2:1-4).

The universal *priesthood* of believers is taught no less clearly in Holy Scripture. Perhaps the most striking

instance of this teaching is the rending of the veil of the
temple at the time of the Saviour's death on the cross. The
veil separated the holy place from the holiest of all, where
God dwelt between the cherubim.   In the old dispensation only one man, the high priest, was permitted once a
year, on the day of atonement, to pass through the veil,
and when he did so he had to sprinkle atoning blood upon
the mercy seat.   But when the great High Priest, Jesus
Christ, entered into the heavenly sanctuary with His own
blood, God rent the veil from top to bottom (Matthew
27:51).   And that meant that henceforth every believer
in Christ would be privileged to come into the presence
of God without the mediation of a priest after the order
of Aaron.   In a word, every believer is now a priest.

The universal *kingship* of believers is taught, for one
example, in the opening sections of the book of Revelation.   Addressing the seven churches in Asia Minor, John
wrote: "Unto him that loved us and washed us from our
sins in his blood, and hath made us kings and priests unto
God and his Father; to him be glory and dominion for
ever and ever. Amen" (Revelation 1:5, 6).

In one sentence the apostle Peter ascribed to believers
all three offices.   Said he: "Ye are a chosen generation, a
royal priesthood, a holy nation, a peculiar people; that ye
should show forth the praises of him who hath called you
out of darkness into his marvelous light" (I Peter 2:9).
Believers are a priesthood of kings and a royalty of priests.
And their work is to proclaim the praises of God, their
Saviour.   That is the task of prophets.

IN HISTORY

As was just indicated, in the apostolic age the universal
office of believers received much emphasis.   Sad to say,
very soon this doctrine came to be obscured, and after
some time it was lost out of sight almost completely.

This office is foreign to the very genius of Roman
Catholicism.   Rome draws a sharp line of demarcation

between the clergy and the laity. The former are said to
be spiritual in a sense in which the latter are not. The
former are to rule, the latter are to be ruled. The former
are to teach, the latter are to be taught. The latter must
accept in implicit faith what the former teach and must
bow unreservedly before their authority. Of the pope,
who is the very personification of the church's authority,
someone has aptly said: "The pope plus the church equals
the pope minus the church." In that equation the church
cancels out, which is a way of saying that the pope is
everything. As recently as 1907 pope Pius X in an en-
cyclical against modernism described Presbyterianism as
modernism because it gives the laity a voice in the government of the church.

One of the most significant accomplishments of the
Protestant Reformation was that it restored the universal
office of believers to the place of honor which it deserves.
Already in the twelfth and thirteenth centuries the Wal-
denses revived this truth of Scripture, and so did certain
subsequent forerunners of the Reformation. But in the
sixteenth century it became a distinctively Protestant
doctrine.

The Reformers stressed particularly the universal priesthood of believers. The reason for their singling out this
office for special emphasis is apparent. Rome had an order
of priests which lorded it over the membership of the
church. Luther, Calvin and the other Reformers taught
that every believer is a priest. But they also stressed
the universal prophethood of believers and their universal
kingship. Every believer, they insisted, has the right,
yes the duty, to apply the touchstone of Holy Scripture to
the teachings of the church and, in case these teachings
cannot stand that test, to raise his voice in protest. And,
instead of merely being governed, the members of the
church must, said they, have a voice in its government.

The Heidelberg Catechism, which was written in the
Reformation age, answers the question, "Why are you

called a Christian?" thus: "Because I am a member of
Christ by faith, and thus a partaker of His anointing, that
I may confess His name, present myself a living sacrifice
of thanksgiving to Him, and with a free and good conscience fight against sin and the devil in this life, and
hereafter reign with Him eternally over all creatures"
(Lord's Day XII, Question 32). That is a beautiful way
of saying that every Christian is a prophet, a priest and
a king.

Today there is a crying need for another revival of this
doctrine. Protestantism, which once extolled it, now
largely neglects it. To name a number of specific instances
of such neglect is not at all difficult.

How few church members today are serious students
of Holy Scripture! In how few supposedly Christian
homes is the family altar held in honor, at which parents
pray with and for their children and teach them the Word
of God! How few, on returning home from a preaching
service, follow the example of the Bereans and search the
Scriptures whether these things are so (Acts 17:11) ! How
few churches find it possible to maintain an active organization of their men! How few organizations of women
in the churches, besides sewing and raising money for
the church, engage in Bible study! How few church
members are capable of leading in prayer in public! How
few of the communicant members of the church are qualified to serve as elders or deacons! How few church members realize that it is their solemn duty to admonish their
erring fellow members! How few are able to teach the
youth of the church! How few, in times of doctrinal or
other controversy, refuse to follow the clergy blindly and
insist on studying the issues for themselves! How few
engage actively in evangelistic effort!

Much might be added, but enough has been said to make
it clear that the universal office of believers is not being
exercised nearly as it ought to be.

Nevertheless this office remains a reality. In every age every living member of the body of Christ is undeniably a partaker of Christ's anointing and hence a prophet, a priest and a king.

The glory of the Christian church is often veiled but ever present.

Chapter 21

SPECIAL OFFICES

Every member of the Christian church is an officer. In fact, every member holds three offices. He is at once a prophet, a priest and a king. However, it does not follow that every member is a minister, a deacon and a ruling elder in the technical sense of those terms. The great majority of church members do not hold so much as one of these offices. And because these offices are held by only a few they are properly designated *special offices*.

WARRANTED BY SCRIPTURE

The universal office of believers was strongly emphasized over against Roman Catholicism by the Protestants of the Reformation age. That was most commendable. But there were certain extremists among the Protestants who stressed the universal office to the detriment of the special offices in the church. They took the position that the universal office renders special offices superfluous.

The history of Protestantism cannot be understood unless it be remembered that practically all Protestant churches down to the present day have been influenced more or less by that extremism, and that very few of them, if indeed any, have ever succeeded in purging out that leaven completely. And so it is not at all strange that disrespect of the special offices in the church has been a frequent phenomenon in Protestantism. One specific instance must be named.

John Nelson Darby, who had taken orders in the Church of Ireland, broke with that communion in 1827. His most important reason was that, under the influence of a strong

reaction from high church ecclesiasticism, he had come
to doubt the Scriptural authority for church establish-
ments in general and for an ordained ministry in particular. In 1830 Darby visited Cambridge and Oxford in
England, and soon thereafter his followers began to hold
regular meetings at Plymouth, a fact which gave rise to
the name Plymouth Brethren. Their most distinctive pe-
culiarity is their refusal to recognize any form of church
government or any office of the ministry. They insist on the
equal right of all male members of the church to prophesy
or preach. Today the Brethren are numerous on this conti-
nent as well as in Europe. And, although Darby died in
1882, his soul goes marching on, and Darbyism is in evidence in many denominations.

While it is not difficult to sympathize with Darby in his
protest against certain evils prevalent in the established
church of his day and land, neither is it difficult to show
that the view that the universal office in the church rules
out special offices is erroneous. Special offices have plain
Scriptural warrant. The Word of God tells us that Christ
"gave some, apostles; and some, prophets; and some, evangelists; and some, pastors and teachers; for the perfecting of the saints, for the edifying of the body of Christ"
(Ephesians 4:11, 12). Paul and Barnabas, on their first
missionary journey, "ordained . . . elders in every church"
(Acts 14:23). The apostle Paul exhorted: "Let the elders
that rule well be counted worthy of double honor, especially they who labor in the word and doctrine" (I Timothy
5:17). The same apostle enjoined the elders of the church
at Ephesus: "Take heed unto yourselves and to all the
flock over which the Holy Ghost hath made you overseers,
to feed the church of God, which he hath purchased with
his own blood" (Acts 20:28). The apostles instructed
the believers at Jerusalem to choose deacons for the care
of the poor. This was done, and they set them "before
the apostles; and when they had prayed, they laid their
hands on them" (Acts 6:6).

How clear that the apostles recognized special offices in the church! Granted that, because of conditions peculiar to the apostolic church, some functionaries were intended only for that day and age, it is evident that through the apostles God ordained certain permanent ecclesiastical offices. They are those offices by which Christ as prophet, priest and king continues to govern His church.

Rooted in the Universal Office

Quite naturally the question arises how the special offices in the church are related to the universal office.

That the two are closely related to each other is self-evident. Christ means *Anointed.* He was anointed with the Holy Spirit to the threefold office of prophet, priest and king. Every Christian, too, is anointed with the Holy Spirit to the selfsame threefold office. But it is also true that the special offices in the church represent Christ as prophet, priest and king. The minister or teaching elder represents Him as prophet, the deacon represents Him as priest, and the ruling elder represents Him as king. It follows that the universal office and the special offices are inseparable. Precisely expressed, the special offices are rooted in the universal office.

For that reason the members of the church choose, or ought to choose, their own officers. In such churches as the Roman Catholic and the Greek Catholic the officers are not ordinarily chosen from below but are appointed from above. The simple explanation is that these churches deny to all intents and purposes the universal office of believers. A church which gives full recognition to the universal office of believers will insist that its members choose their own officers.

For the same reason the membership of the church is governed by its officers, or should be, *with its own consent.* No human being or group of human beings has the right to force rule upon the membership of the church against its will. No bishop, no archbishop, no metropolitan, no patriarch, no church council, no college of cardinals, no pope may do that. When it is done, that amounts to a denial of the universal office of believers.

Again, for the same reason, the members of the church choose their officers, or ought to choose them, *from their own number*. A particular church will elect its elders and deacons from its own membership. Ordinarily a particular church will choose its pastor from the pastors of its denomination. And if occasionally it calls a pastor from another denomination, it ought not to be possible for him to become the pastor of that church without his previously becoming affiliated with the denomination of which it is a constituent part.

That the members of the church choose their own special officers, that they are governed with their own consent by these officers, and that they choose their officers from their own number — all this exemplifies the truth that the special offices in the church are rooted in the universal office.

RESPONSIBLE TO CHRIST

In the sense and to the extent just indicated the Christian church may be said to be a democracy. In another sense, however, it is not at all a democracy. Although the special officers of the church govern with the consent of the membership and are chosen by the membership from its own number, yet their ultimate responsibility is not to the congregation but to Christ, the divine Head of the church. That makes the church a monarchy.

A great many Protestant churches fail to get this point. They regard the people as the final source of authority. That is the underlying error of Congregationalism. Nor is Congregationalism confined to the churches that go by that name. Another name for it is Independency, and this type of church government is in vogue in several denominations. Sometimes one meets with this error even in a Presbyterian or Reformed church. A sharp difference of opinion arises within the session, perhaps between the minister and the ruling elders or between two groups of elders. A congregational meeting is called, and it is agreed that whatever the congregation, as the ultimate court of appeal, decides will stand. Or, let us say, the session lacks the courage to make an important decision. So it calls a congregational meeting and asks the congregation to make up its mind for it. In such ways the session is in great danger of becoming the servant of the congregation and of ceasing to be the servant of Christ.

In a limited sense the church is, to be sure, a democracy. It is a democracy in the sense of not being a hierarchy. Ultimately, however, it is a monarchy. Christ is its one sovereign Head. Christ's law is its only law. Its special officers are not to please men but Christ. After all it was Christ who, through the instrumentality of the universal office of believers, appointed them to their several offices. It was Christ who clothed them with authority. It is Christ as prophet, priest and king whom they represent. And their ultimate responsibility is to Christ alone.

It follows that the special offices in the church are truly glorious. Far from being subservient to men, they function in Christ's name.

Chapter 22

THE OFFICE OF THE MINISTER

The glory of the Christian church appears both in the universal office of believers and in its special offices. Every member of the church is a prophet, a priest and a king; and its ministers, elders and deacons represent Christ in its government.

The consideration of the peculiar function of each of the special offices will serve to bring out further the glory of the Christian church. It is fitting and proper that the function of the ministry be considered first.

ITS SPECIAL DIGNITY

Much dignity attaches to all three of the church's offices, but the ministry excels in dignity. According to the Form of Government of several Presbyterian churches, the office of the minister is "the first in the church for dignity." That is true for at least two reasons.

In the first place, the ministry, in distinction from the eldership and the deaconship, is a full-time office. Elders and deacons ordinarily give only a relatively small part of their time to their offices, but the minister must devote all of his time to his office. There are ministers who have an additional occupation, farming for instance, and often it is difficult to tell which is their vocation, and which their avocation. It also happens that ministers become so deeply interested in some hobby or other that their proper work suffers from neglect. Granted that the minister is entitled to a reasonable amount of relaxation, such conditions are far from ideal. Even in the smallest church there is an abundance of work to occupy all of his time, if only he does his work faithfully.

137

A second reason why the office of the ministry is the first in dignity is that the minister, in distinction from the ruling elder and the deacon, holds not merely one office, but two offices. He is both a teaching elder, representing Christ as prophet, and a ruling elder, representing Christ as king. There is good Scriptural ground for this position. Paul exhorted: "Let the elders that rule well be counted worthy of double honor, especially they who labor in the word and doctrine" (I Timothy 5:17). It is clear that there were two kinds of elders in the apostolic church. It is equally clear that they are not accurately distinguished as elders who only ruled and elders who only taught. On the contrary, both ruled. But some did little else than rule, while others both ruled and taught.

In this connection something may be said about the overlapping of the work of the various offices in the apostolic church. It was not unusual for ruling elders and deacons to bring the Word of God to men. Paul enjoined the ruling elders of the church at Ephesus to "feed the church of God" (Acts 20:28). The food that they were to supply can have been only the Word of God. And hardly had the church at Jerusalem chosen deacons to care for the poor when one of them, namely Stephen, declared the Word of God (Acts 6, 7). There is nothing strange about such overlapping. It is more correct to say that Christ, whom the special officers in the church represent, holds one threefold office than to say that He holds three separate offices. It must also be borne in mind that the special offices in the church are rooted in the universal office of believers, by virtue of which every church member should function at once as a prophet, a priest and a king. It follows that every prophet in the church is also a priest and a king, that every priest is also a prophet and a king, and that every king is also a prophet and a priest.

But this overlapping of the tasks of the special offices in the church is something quite different from the holding of more than one office by one person. In the absence of the minister, a ruling elder may well read a sermon to the congregation or even deliver a discourse of his own making, but the precise name for such activity is *exhorting*, not preaching. Likewise deacons should remind the distressed of the consolations of Holy Scripture, but by so doing they do not become ministers. The minister, on the other hand, is not only a teaching elder but also a ruling elder. He, and he alone of the special officers in the church, holds two offices.

ITS CENTRAL TASK

Although the minister is both a ruling and a teaching elder, for good reason he is usually denominated a teaching elder. His central task is to teach men the Word of God. That is incomparably his most important business.

How colossal a task that is! He must teach the Word of God to the youth as well as to the adult members of the church. He must teach the Word, not only to those who are within the church, but also to those who are without, in order that they may be brought in. He must teach the Word, not only publicly in the pulpit, but also privately in pastoral counseling. He must teach the Word, not just in the abstract, but by way of practical application to concrete situations, and he must apply the Word not merely to personal difficulties but also to communal problems. He must teach the Word both constructively and controversially; that is to say, he must set forth the truth positively, to be sure, but also contrast it with error, particularly with contemporaneous error. He must declare "all the counsel of God" (Acts 20:27). It goes without saying that he cannot possibly do all this without being and continuing a diligent student primarily of the Word itself, but also of human nature, current events and thought, and the problems of society.

It is clear that by far the greater part of the minister's time will be taken up by his duties as teaching elder. In fact, if he performs those duties faithfully, it is difficult to see how he can find time for much besides. Therefore, if he is wise, he will relate his work as ruling elder directly to his work as teaching elder. The most valuable contribution that he can make to the rule of the church is to inform himself and the other ruling elders concerning the teaching of Holy Scripture on the subject of church government.

It has been said that of the three special offices in the church that of the minister is first, not only for dignity, but also for usefulness. That is altogether correct. The ministry is especially useful, not only because the minister performs the duties of two offices and devotes all his time to them, but also for another very significant reason. The supreme task of the Christian Church is to proclaim the Word of God. Everything else that the church does ought to be subsidiary and auxiliary to that task. Nothing is more important, and all else is important only in the measure in which it contributes to the declaration of the Word. But precisely the preaching of the Word is the minister's business. It follows that his task is identical with the supreme task of the church. It is no exaggeration to assert that his office represents the very reason for the church's existence. What office could be more useful? No other office in the church can be as useful.

Its Peculiar Perils

He who holds the ministerial office is beset by certain perils that are properly described as peculiar for the reason that they spring from the special dignity and the great usefulness of his office. It may seem strange that such virtues as dignity and usefulness should present temptations, but that may very well be the case, and in this instance actually is. The depravity of human nature often turns assets into liabilities.

Many a minister, conscious of the dignity of his office, has forgotten that he is a man of like passions with others and has become pretentious and pompous. Popularly put, it is not at all unusual for a minister to become "a stuffed shirt." A man gifted with a considerable measure of good sense once said of his two brothers, both of whom were pastors: "One of my brothers has entered the ministry, the other has remained a human being." What is even more serious, the sin of egotism is sadly common among those who hold this office.

Because he is both a teacher and a ruling elder, many a minister assumes a domineering attitude and presumes to lord it over God's heritage. More than a few ministers are autocrats. Often the minister regards himself as the commander-in-chief of his church. He insists that his word be honored as law, hardly less binding than the laws of the ancient Medes and Persians. As a certain monarch once said: "I am the state," so a minister sometimes says in effect: "I am the church."

Because his duties are manifold, there is great danger that the minister will fail to put first things first; that he will "spread himself thin," as the popular saying has it; that he will attempt to do so many things that he does nothing well. Perhaps he will be an administrator rather than a teacher. The finances of the church may interest him more than do the spiritual riches of the Word of God. The numerical growth of the church may concern him more than does its spiritual growth. Instead of concentrating on the central task of the ministry, teaching the Word of God, he may make the erection of a new church edifice his chief ambition. He may even turn into the proverbial "jack of all trades," comprising chauffeur, messenger boy and assistant housekeeper. Because he tries to do too much, he may accomplish next to nothing.

How can these perils be avoided? The answer is simple. The minister must always remember that the dignity of his office adheres not in his person but in his office itself. He is not at all important, but his office is extremely important. Therefore he should take his work most seriously without taking himself seriously. He should preach the Word in season and out of season in forgetfulness of self. He should ever have an eye single to the glory of Christ, whom he preaches, and count himself out. It should be his constant aim that Christ, whom he represents, may increase while he himself decreases. Remembering that *minister* means nothing but *servant,* he should humbly, yet passionately, serve the Lord Christ and His church. The words of the apostle Paul should be his very own: "Whose I am and whom I serve" (Acts 27:23).

Such a minister is sure to enhance the glory of Christ's church.

Chapter 23

THE OFFICE OF THE RULING ELDER

Of the three special offices in the church that of the ruling elder represents Christ as king. Nations that have a king customarily speak of him as "His Majesty." And anyone at all familiar with Holy Scriptures knows that it, too, associates much majesty, dignity, honor and glory with kingship. Small wonder that the glory of the Christian church is reflected brightly in the office of the ruling elder.

Its Momentous Duties

The New Testament has two names for ruling elders. Sometimes they are called presbyters, which simply means older men or elders; at other times they are called bishops, which means overseers. It is significant that these are two names for the same men. Nowadays the term bishop is ordinarily used to denominate a clergyman who stands above other clergymen in both dignity and authority. But such is not at all the Biblical usage of that term. When Paul, on his way to Jerusalem at the conclusion of his third missionary journey, arrived at Miletus, he sent to Ephesus and called the *presbyters* of the church (Acts 20:17). When they had come, he spoke to them and said: "Take heed unto yourselves, and to all the flock, in which the Holy Spirit hath made you *bishops*" (Acts 20:28, ASV). It is clear that according to Scripture every presbyter is a bishop. And that is a way of saying that the work of the elder is to oversee the church.

Usually church members regard ruling elders less highly than ministers. In so doing they are not altogether mistaken, for it is true that a special dignity attaches to the ministerial office in virtue of the fact that the minister,

143

being both a teaching and a ruling elder, holds two offices
in one, which two offices take up, or ought to take up, all
his time. On the other hand, there is great danger that
the dignity of the ruling elder's office in comparison with
that of the minister's office will be underestimated.

Frequently the work of the ruling elder and that of the
minister overlap. The ruling elder may not leave the
comforting of the distressed and the correcting of the
erring exclusively to the minister, for he himself, too, is
a shepherd or pastor. When, in Acts 20:28, Paul exhorted
the Ephesian elders to take heed to the "flock," he evidently
thought of the members of the church as sheep and of the
elders as shepherds. So the ruling elder is a pastor, for
pastor means *shepherd.* He is also a teacher. When, in
the same verse, Paul enjoined the Ephesian elders to
"feed" the church he undoubtedly had reference to the
Word of God, for it is the only spiritual food that God
has provided for His people. Therefore, when the minister is absent, it is highly proper for a ruling elder to
read a sermon in a service of public worship or to "exhort"
the congregation with a discourse of his own making.

In a very real sense the ruling elder even stands above
the teaching elder. One of his most solemn duties is to
oversee the life and work of the minister. If the minister
fails to lead an exemplary life, the ruling elders of the
church must correct him. If he is not as diligent in his
pastoral work as he ought to be, they should spur him on
to greater zeal. If his preaching is lacking in that passion
which must characterize all preaching of the Word of God,
they should take steps to overcome that defect. And if
his preaching in any respect, whether great or small, is
not according to the Scriptures, they may not rest until
that evil has been remedied.

If that makes the work of the ruling elder both important and difficult — and it most certainly does — he has
other duties that are nothing short of momentous. It is
his task either to accept or to reject applicants for church

membership and to exercise judicial discipline upon the erring members of the church.

What a responsibility, when someone expresses the desire to become a communicant member of Christ's church, to accept him as such! Likewise, what a responsibility it is to reject him! Well may these tasks be performed with fear and trembling. Because the elders cannot look into the hearts of men, they can never be altogether certain of the proper course. The applicant who uses pious terminology glibly may be a hypocrite, whereas the applicant who has to be "pumped" to say anything at all may be a true child of God. Because of this difficulty, which is truly insuperable, it is not unusual for elders to let the matter go at taking the applicant's word for it that he believes in the Lord Jesus Christ. But obviously that will never do. Almost any modernist will vow that he believes in Jesus, and even among self-styled evangelicals there is no perfect unanimity as to what is saving faith. The applicant should be closely questioned concerning three matters. First, the elders must find out whether he possesses the doctrinal knowledge that is prerequisite to saving faith. For but one example, if he does not know that Jesus is God, he must certainly be rejected. In the second place, the elders must seek to discover whether the faith which he claims to have is truly saving faith. For instance, if he trusts at all in his own works or character for salvation, he must be refused. Thirdly, the elders must ascertain whether he brings forth the fruits of faith in his life; in other words, whether he honors Christ not only as Saviour but also as Lord. In brief, the elders must do all that is humanly possible to determine whether or not the applicant is a Christian.

No less heavy is the responsibility of exercising judicial discipline. Also in this matter the elders do not dare to claim infallibility. Therefore many neglect this duty altogether and salve their consciences by referring to the well-known but little understood parable of the tares. The truth is that this parable is not at all meant to discourage the exercise of discipline but is a warning against *excesses* in discipline. Scripture teaches most emphatically that church members who err in either doctrine or life must be disciplined. How unpleasant, how onerous, a task! Is it altogether certain that the member who is charged with an offense is guilty? If that is certain, who can determine the precise degree of his guilt? And who possesses the wisdom to choose the most just and appropriate mode of censure? Sometimes the elders must resort to excommunication. Then they not only exclude the offender from the particular church or congregation concerned, or for that matter from the denomination, but they solemnly declare that they can no longer regard him as a child of God. Seldom, if ever, can elders resort to such action without some slight misgiving, unless indeed they mistakenly believe in an infallible church. And every time they do take such action they do it with bleeding hearts.

It might be thought that the elders are kept so busy with spiritual matters that they have neither time nor energy left for the material interests of the church. For that reason a number of churches have trustees to attend to the church's finances. Perhaps it is for the same reason that many churches have charged their deacons, not only with caring for the poor, but also with managing all the other financial aspects of the church's work. The latter is a mistake, and it may never be forgotten that the trustees are responsible to the elders for all they do. It is simply impossible to sever from each other the spiritual and the material affairs of the church. The finances of the church must always be managed in business-like fashion, to be sure, but also in a spiritual way and to a spiritual end. And so this matter, too, falls under the overseeing of the church with which Scripture charges the elders.

Well may any ruling elder exclaim: "Who is sufficient for these things?" (II Corinthians 2:16)

Its Exacting Requisites

As one might expect, the qualifications for the office of the ruling elder are commensurate with the duties of this office. If its duties are truly momentous, its requisites must be truly exacting. That this is actually the case will appear as a few of these requisites are named.

It is a great American fallacy that a man who is successful in business or a profession is qualified for pretty nearly any position of responsibility. That accounts for it that so many churches have a decided preference for men of that type for the eldership. Seldom is a relatively poor laboring man elected to this office. And yet he may possess the qualifications for this office in a higher degree than does the president of a bank or a college.

A prime requisite for the office of ruling elder, as well as for that of teaching elder, is godliness. That should go without saying but is sometimes forgotten. In choosing elders church members often have more regard to popularity than to godliness. In his first letter to Timothy, and also in his letter to Titus, the apostle Paul enumerated several requisites for this office, and most of them fall under the head of godliness. He said, "A bishop then must be blameless, the husband of one wife, vigilant, sober, of good behavior, given to hospitality . . . not given to wine, no striker, not greedy of filthy lucre, but patient, not a brawler, not covetous" (I Timothy 3:2, 3). Incidentally, the word "striker" denotes the quick-tempered man who is inclined to come to blows over almost any difference. It may also be remarked that there is some difference of opinion as to the meaning of the expression "the husband of one wife." It is likely that in the apostolic church polygamy was in some instances and for the time being tolerated, although never approved of, in recent converts from paganism. If that was the case, Paul says that to have a polygamist serve as elder in the church is entirely out of the question even under the most unusual circumstances.

A Christian virtue on which Scripture puts special em-

phasis as a requisite for the office of elder is humility. This
emphasis is not difficult to account for. Just because the
office is so exalted and honorable, only the humble man is
fit to hold it. Any other man, if chosen to this high office,
will almost certainly be overcome by pride. For that reason Paul instructed Timothy that no "novice" should be
made an elder, "lest being lifted up with pride he fall
into the condemnation of the devil" (I Timothy 3:6). For
the same reason Peter admonished the elders in the
churches for which his first epistle was intended to do their
work not "as being lords over God's heritage" (I Peter
5:3). There is an old saying that in the church there are
two kinds of elders: those who rule, namely the ruling
elders, and those who are ruled, the ministers. It is intended as a jest, but in some instances it is sad reality.
In many sessions there is a "leading" elder. Almost invariably he is a hindrance to the pastor and a detriment
to the church.

That every teaching elder should be a theologian is a
matter of course, but that every ruling elder should be
a theologian is just as true. How can a ruling elder do
his duty in checking up on the soundness of the minister's
preaching unless he is himself well versed in theology?
How will he be "able by sound doctrine both to exhort and
to convince the gainsayers" (Titus 1:9) unless he knows
his Bible? Every ruling elder should be a diligent student
of the Word of God, have, and frequently use, a reliable
commentary on Holy Scripture, possess an intimate
acquaintance with the doctrinal standards of his church,
and own, and often consult, some sound book setting forth
the salient points of Christian theology. How many elders
meet that requirement? Rather, how few!

It was for good reason that James said: "If any of you
lack wisdom, let him ask of God, that giveth to all men
liberally and upbraideth not; and it shall be given him"
(James 1:5). For wisdom is exceedingly rare. Not only
is it better than rubies but also far more scarce. Yet

it is indispensable for the ruling elder. It presupposes knowledge but is much more than knowledge. It is the ability to make the proper use of knowledge, to employ the best means to the best end. It is sanctified common sense, which is a gift of God and far from common. Because it grows through experience, older men usually possess it in greater measure than the young, and that is one reason why Scripture ordinarily commits the rule of the church to its older members. One way in which it manifests itself is in good judgment in dealing with men. Therefore Scripture stipulates that an elder must be "one that ruleth well his own house" and that he "must have a good report of them that are without" (I Timothy 3:4, 5, 7). But that is not all. Sometimes church members for lack of good judgment do not rule their own houses well and do not have a good reputation with outsiders, but at least as often the underlying cause of these failures is a paucity of godliness. "The fear of the Lord is the beginning of wisdom" (Proverbs 9:10). Godliness is of the essence of wisdom. Ruling elders must needs possess it to a high degree.

Chapter 24

THE OFFICE OF THE DEACON

Of the three special offices in the Christian church that of the deacon usually commands the least respect. The average church member holds the ruling elder in lower esteem than the minister, and the deacon in lower esteem than the ruling elder. Some churches do not even bother to have deacons. They feel they can get along very well without them.

Of all possible reasons for that unhealthy attitude two stand out prominently. On the one hand, from the fact that it is the task of deacons to care for the poor it appears that their office directly concerns the natural, and it is a common fault among Christians to underrate the importance of the natural. On the other hand, the fact is often overlooked that the work of deacons has important spiritual aspects. The consideration of the natural and the spiritual aspects of this office should, therefore, be conducive to upholding its honor.

ITS NATURAL ASPECT

The sixth chapter of the book of Acts tells of the origination of the diaconate in the apostolic church. It was instituted early in the church's history, practically at the very beginning.

The members of the church at Jerusalem had all material things in common. It hardly needs to be said that this communism was something quite different from the communism for which so many clamor today. It was communism among Christians only. It was local in its scope, there being no evidence in the New Testament that it was practiced in any church other than that at Jerusalem. Even in the Jerusalem church it was a temporary arrangement. There was nothing compulsory about it, for when a member of the church sold a possession and pretended to give the whole price to the church, although actually he gave but part, Peter said to him: "Whiles it remained, was it not thine own? and after it was sold, was it not in thine own power?" (Acts 5:4). And the spirit behind this communism was radically different from that which often comes to expression in present-day communism. Someone has aptly said: "The Christians at Jerusalem said, 'All mine is thine'; communists today say, 'All thine is mine.'"

At first the distribution of material things among the members of the Jerusalem church according to their several needs was made by the apostles. As there were many poor, this task was burdensome. And when the number of the disciples was multiplied it became so onerous that the apostles, busy as they already were with preaching, could no longer discharge it properly. A murmuring arose of the Grecians, Hellenistic Jews who had the Greek national character and spoke Greek as their native language, against the Hebrews, Palestinian Jews who had the Jewish national character and spoke the Hebrew language, because the widows of the former were thought to be neglected in the daily ministrations. The apostles called a congregational meeting. Addressing this meeting, they said: "It is not reason that we should leave the Word of God and serve tables. Wherefore look ye out among you seven men of honest report, full of the Holy Ghost and wisdom, whom we may appoint over this business. But we will give ourselves continually to prayer and to the ministry of the Word." This saying pleased the congregation. Seven men were chosen to serve as deacons. They were set before the apostles, who ordained them with prayer and the laying on of hands (Acts 6:1-6).

How clear that the office of the deacon concerns the physical, the temporal, the material, the natural!

Throughout the history of the Christian church there have been those — many of them pious souls — who took an unwholesome view of the relation of the natural and the spiritual, and in their exaltation of the spiritual belittled the natural. This has ever been one of the outstanding characteristics, and, it must be added, one of the basic errors of Rome. Hence its insistence on the perpetual virginity of Mary, its teaching that there is special merit in taking the vows of celibacy and poverty, and its prescription of fasting on Fridays and during Lent. But some Anabaptists of the Reformation period and subsequent times went even farther in their disparagement of the natural. While Rome taught that the natural is sure to become evil unless it is held in check by the spiritual as a bridle, the most extreme of the Anabaptists taught that there is something inherently wrong about the natural. Therefore they virtually denounced as sin all physical pleasure. They frowned upon such pleasure as is afforded, for instance, by the playing of games, the wearing of ornaments, and the attraction of boy and girl to each other. Let no one think that by this time the leaven of Roman Catholicism and Anabaptism has been purged from Protestantism. The truth is that it is still working in practically every Protestant church. It is no exaggeration to assert that there exists a decided strain of Anabaptism in American evangelicalism. The prevalent powerful prejudice against certain things the use of which should be left to the individual conscience, and the too strong insistence sometimes at young people's Bible conferences that they devote themselves to "full-time" Christian service rather than engage in so-called secular vocations, are just two bits of evidence.

Scripture teaches that the natural was created by God as well as the spiritual and that as a divine creation it is entitled to the Christian's high regard. It also tells us that the natural constitutes the background of the spiritual. Before God established the covenant of grace with Abraham He made the covenant of nature with Noah. Thus He first guaranteed the continuity of the human race, subsequently the continuity of the church. Inseparable from, and in a sense previous to, the spiritual blessings which God promised to Abraham and his spiritual seed was the natural blessing of the promised land for his natural descendants. Jesus first asked the Samaritan woman for a drink of ordinary water and then shifted the conversation to the water of life. He opened the physical eyes of the man born blind before opening the eyes of his soul. Many of Jesus' sermons were parables, natural or earthly stories with a spiritual or heavenly meaning. Somewhat as the woof of a rug is woven into the warp, so the spiritual is woven into the natural. The natural is, no doubt, patterned after the spiritual, not *vice versa,* but it is also true that in this present world the spiritual needs the natural.

The fact, then, that the diaconate concerns itself primarily with the natural is no good reason for disparaging that office. The Directory of the Orthodox Presbyterian Church for the Public Worship of God says: "The office of deacon is based upon the solicitude and love of Christ for His own people. So tender is our Lord's interest in their temporal needs that He considers what is done unto one of the least of His brethren as done unto Him. For He will say to those who have ministered to His little ones: 'I was hungry, and ye gave me to eat; I was thirsty, and ye gave me to drink; I was a stranger and ye took me in; naked, and ye clothed me; I was sick, and ye visited me; I was in prison, and ye came unto me.'" (See Matthew 25:35, 36.) In the light of those words of the Lord, who will dare to say that the office of the deacon is relatively unimportant? It is supremely honorable.

Its Spiritual Aspect

Let no one think that the deacons of a church have done their full duty when they have gathered from the members of the church gifts for the poor among them and have distributed those gifts to the poor. The directory for public worship which was just quoted tells us that their duty extends also to such spiritual activities as praying with the distressed and reminding them of the consolations of Scripture. There is abundant ground for that statement. Deacons represent Christ in His office of mercy, and the exercise of mercy certainly entails the consoling of the distressed. It is not unusual for charity so called to be administered in a cold and even haughty manner. Then it is merciless. How often Jesus Himself coupled words of comfort with deeds of mercy. When He was about to raise from the dead the young man of Nain, He looked at his heartbroken mother, had compassion on her and said: "Weep not" (Luke 7:13). And to the woman with an issue of blood He said: "Daughter, thy faith hath made thee whole; go in peace, and be whole of thy plague" (Mark 5:34).

It is sometimes said that, while both the minister and the ruling elder have considerable authority, the office of the deacon is not one of authority but of service, and when this is said it usually represents an attempt to belittle the dignity of the diaconate. As a matter of fact that statement is not precise, and whatever truth it does contain is not by Christian standards disparaging. There is a measure of authority bound up with this office. By Christ's authority the deacons are to remind the members of the church of their duty to help the needy. And in Christ's name the deacons are to give aid to those who need it, for which reason this aid should be accepted humbly as well as gratefully. Nevertheless the aspect of service is most prominent in this office. The primary meaning of the Greek word from which the English *deacon* is derived is *servant,* and repeatedly that word occurs in the New Testament in the simple sense of *servant* without any reference to an office in the church. But, surely, the fact that the diaconate is pre-eminently the office of service does not detract from its dignity. Contrariwise, that fact may truthfully be said to enhance its dignity. Did not Jesus say to the twelve: "Ye know that the princes of the gentiles exercise dominion over them, and they that are great exercise authority upon them. But it shall not be so among you: but whosoever will be great among you, let him be your minister; and whosoever will be chief among you, let him be your servant: even as the Son of man came not to be ministered unto but to minister, and to give his life a ransom for many" (Matthew 20:25-28) ?

The whole moral law of God can be summed up in the one demand of love. "Love is the fulfilling of the law" (Romans 13:10). When Jesus was about to return to the Father, He commanded His disciples above all else to love one another. He said: "A new commandment I give unto you: that ye love one another; as I have loved you, that ye love also one another" (John 13:34). And the apostle Paul climaxed his famous encomium on love with the words: "But now abideth faith, hope, love, these three; and the greatest of these is love" (I Corinthians 13:13, ASV). The diaconate is accurately described as the office of love, the greatest of Christian virtues. This is not to say that love does not play an important role in the other offices in the church. It most certainly does. But Christian love comes to its most tangible expression in the office of the deacon. This office is pre-eminently that of love. Love is its beginning and its end.

Because of its spiritual character the office of the deacon draws a sharp line of demarcation between the church and the world. It stresses the antithesis of the two. By virtue of the common grace of God the world exercises a sort of charity. Many philanthropists are worldly persons. Many charitable organizations and institutions are not at all Christian, but of the world. Often the state extends aid to the needy, but not in the name of Christ. The Christian church, however, has a benevolence all its own. This benevolence is in a class entirely by itself and differs qualitatively from the charity of the world. In the name of Christ and actuated by the love of Christ the church of Christ dispenses mercy to Christ's very own. It does this through the office of the deacon.

If a particular church has no poor of its own, it should by all means through its deacons come to the assistance of other churches that have many. In such cases churches of the same denomination will naturally receive first consideration, but they need not be the only ones that are aided. Particularly in these days the Christian churches of America should contribute generously to the relief of countless suffering saints in many churches and many lands. In that way the diaconate will give expression to a beautiful Biblical ecumenicity.

Does it follow that deacons should never extend aid to needy persons outside the fold of the church? The answer must be negative. Did not the merciful Christ heal the daughter of a Syrophenician woman and thus permit a Greek to eat the crumbs that fell from the table of God's covenant people (Mark 7:24-30)? By following that example deacons may sometimes engage in effective evangelism.

Will the reader pardon a brief personal reference? The head of a poor family living within a city block from the church which the writer served as pastor was taken critically ill. Although this family did not belong to his church and never attended its services, he called repeatedly on the sick man. From the physician he learned that, humanly speaking, the patient's one hope for recovery lay in a very costly drug. The deacons of the church were persuaded to pay for the drug. The man recovered, and after a while he and his entire family confessed Christ and united with the church. Significantly Scripture tells us that of the seven deacons chosen by the church at Jerusalem two — Stephen and Philip — were active also as evangelists.

Truly, the office of the deacon is richly spiritual as well as exquisitely natural.

Chapter 25

THE DOUBLE RESPONSIBILITY OF THE CHURCH

It is not at all unusual for human beings mistakenly to regard certain matters as absolute opposites. The technical name for that sort of thing is *false antithesis*. Every once in a while Christians err in that way in matters of religion. For instance, there are those who teach that the people of God in the old dispensation were under law whereas we today live under grace, and that law and grace are mutually exclusive. But in reality the Old Testament saints were saved by grace as we are, and we are no less obligated to obey the moral law of God than were they. Again, how often the distinction is made between saints and sinners with the implication that each individual is one or the other! The truth is that, while not nearly all sinners are saints, every saint on earth is a sinner.

In like manner, when the question arises whether the task of the church is to build up its members in the faith or to bring the gospel to those who are outside the church, some choose for one of these to the practical exclusion of the other. But that betrays a serious lack of balance. The church must do both.

ITS RESPONSIBILITY TO THOSE WITHIN

Some time ago the wife of a minister said in the hearing of the writer that in her opinion the sole task of the church is to preach the gospel to those who are outside the fold. There are whole denominations, some of them large, which have impressive missionary programs but do next to nothing for the building up of their own membership in the faith.

Not only is this view of the church's task extremely one-sided, it is decidedly pernicious. At least two serious errors underlie it. It fails to take into account the children of the covenant, who are members of the visible church and beyond all doubt are in need of Christian nurture, an important phase of which is their indoctrination by the church. And it loses sight of the significant truth that salvation is not merely a momentary occurrence but a continuous process as well. It is true that a person who has been born again is saved and is sure to persevere to the end of his earthly life, but it is also true that every saved person is still in need of salvation and will be to his last breath. Sanctification, which is a most important aspect of salvation, is a tedious process that is completed only at death. Therefore the church must zealously proclaim to its members the truth of God, for through it God is wont to sanctify His own (John 17:17).

He who would evangelize those without the church while neglecting the building up of those within the church is a good deal like the head of a family who is moved with deep compassion for the emaciated children of his neighbor but neglects to feed his own, forgetting the startling warning of the inspired apostle: "If any provide not for his own, and specially for those of his own house, he hath denied the faith and is worse than an infidel" (I Timothy 5:8).

To change the simile, he is like a general who leads his army forth to conquer other lands but fails to keep strong the base of operations in his own land. The danger is far from imaginary that after a little that general will no longer have an army. The church that neglects the teaching of the Word of God to its members cannot long have a constituency that is zealous for Biblical missions. And the church that fails to indoctrinate its youth will soon have no missionaries to send out, most assuredly no missionaries that proclaim the only true gospel.

Its Responsibility to Those Without

It has often been said that the churches of the Protestant Reformation were not interested in missions. But that is hardly a fair representation. They were zealous for the evangelization of Europe, which is a way of saying that they engaged actively in home missions. And let it never be forgotten that home missions are no less worthy than foreign missions. The churches of the Reformation had a genuine interest in foreign missions also. To name but a few facts, as early as 1555 there was a French Reformed mission in Brazil; the Dutch East India Company, which was founded in 1602, was bound by its charter "to help convert the heathen in the countries with which it traded"; and in 1622 there was founded at the University of Leyden a seminary for the training of missionaries.

Nevertheless it must be admitted that there have been churches in the past which were considerably less zealous for missions than for the edification of their own members. As late as 1790 a certain church is said to have adopted the resolution that "to spread abroad the knowledge of the gospel amongst barbarous and heathen nations seems to be highly preposterous, in so far as philosophy and learning must in the nature of things take the precedence, and that, while there remains a single individual at home without the means of religious knowledge, to propagate it abroad would be improper and absurd." Nor is that altogether as strange as it might seem. Not until the nineteenth century did Protestantism as a whole wax truly enthusiastic about missions. Sad to say, even today there are sporadic instances of churches that are lukewarm toward that great cause.

The Word of God puts tremendous emphasis on the duty of the church to preach the gospel to those beyond the fold. It is not at all true, as some suppose, that the missionary note is lacking in the Old Testament. At the very time when God called Abraham in order that he might become the father of His peculiar people Israel, God told him: "In thee shall all families of the earth be blessed" (Genesis 12:3). The old Testament fairly teems with such predictions of coming universalism as: "All nations whom thou hast made shall come and worship before thee, O Lord, and shall glorify thy name" (Psalm 86:9). God commanded Jonah to preach the gospel of repentance to the wicked inhabitants of Nineveh, capital of the Assyrian empire. Several converts from paganism were taken into the church of the old dispensation. In the New Testament the missionary command rings out clear and loud. In the appearances of the risen Christ to His disciples missions were the chief subject of conversation. The great commission of Matthew 28:18-20 falls in this period. The last words that the Lord spoke to His apostles before He ascended into heaven were these: "Ye shall receive power after that the Holy Ghost is come upon you: and ye shall be witnesses unto me both in Jerusalem, and in all Judea, and in Samaria, and unto the uttermost part of the earth" (Acts 1:8).

At Pentecost and immediately thereafter the church began to discharge the missionary task in earnest. It did not postpone this task until the mother churches at Jerusalem and Antioch in Syria had grown large and strong, but it undertook missions when these churches were still relatively small and weak. The most highly educated of the apostles was set aside by God Himself as missionary to the gentile world. His name was Paul. He was the greatest missionary the church has ever had, but countless missionaries have followed in his train, and this will continue until the earth is full of the knowledge of the Lord as the waters cover the sea (Isaiah 11:9).

There is an old illustration which drives home rather well the importance for the church itself of the faithful performance of its evangelistic task. In Palestine are two large lakes, the Sea of Galilee in the north and the Dead Sea in the south. Water flows from the mountainous region of Hermon and Lebanon into the Sea of Galilee and out of it through the river Jordan into the Dead Sea. The Sea of Galilee is a fresh-water lake and has much life in it. The Dead Sea is said to be so dead that no living creature can possibly survive in its briny waters. Why this difference? The answer is that the Sea of Galilee gives as well as takes, while the Dead Sea only takes. The question aside whether this is the sole cause of the difference, the point illustrated is an excellent one. The church that only takes and never gives is sick unto death. On the other hand, here, too, the words of Scripture apply: "The liberal soul shall be made fat, and he that watereth shall be watered also himself" (Proverbs 11:25).

*   *   *   *

The church must maintain a proper balance between its task to the inside and its task to the outside. But this does not mean that it should do a little of each. It rather means that it must do much of both.

As proper balance is essential for architectural beauty, so this particular balance will greatly enhance the glory of Christ's church. Each of these tasks is glorious; combined in proper balance they are supremely glorious.

Chapter 26

THE SUPREME TASK OF THE CHURCH

The church's task is to teach and preach the Word of God. Whatever else it may properly do is subordinate and subsidiary to that task. This is its supreme task.

On that truth the creeds of Protestantism are in complete agreement. For a few examples, the famous Augsburg Confession of 1530, which is Lutheran but was held in high esteem also by Calvin, defines the church as "the congregation of saints wherein the Gospel is rightly taught"; and Article XIX of the no less famous Thirty-nine Articles of the Church of England says: "The visible Church of Christ is a congregation of faithful men, in the which the pure Word of God is preached."

AN HONORABLE TASK

The church's task is truly honorable, for in its performance the church delivers a message which it has received from none other than God. Therefore the preachers of the church may properly appropriate the apostolic boast: "Now then we are ambassadors for Christ, as though God did beseech you by us: we pray you in Christ's stead, be ye reconciled to God" (II Corinthians 5:20).

According to such dialectical theologians as Karl Barth and Emil Brunner it is more correct to say that the Bible *witnesses to* the Word of God than to assert that the Bible *is* the Word of God. In consequence they take the position that the Christian preacher cannot really proclaim the Word of God but at best can only witness to it. But the prophets of old did not hesitate to preface their message with the unqualified declaration: "Thus saith the Lord"; and the apostle Paul solemnly enjoined his spir-

itual son Timothy: "I charge thee before God and the
Lord Jesus Christ, who shall judge the quick and the dead
at his appearing and his kingdom: Preach the word" (II
Timothy 4:1, 2).

In a very real sense the church has the distinction of
being a mediator between God and man. To be sure, when
saying that, we must be on our guard against a most serious error. Rome teaches that the church is the *conveyor*
of salvation. The truth of the matter is that the church
is but the God-ordained *preacher* of salvation. But even
that is an exceedingly great honor. Scripture tells us
that Moses, in receiving the law from God and transmitting
it to God's people, acted as a "mediator" (Galatians 3:19).
In much the same sense the church as preacher of the
gospel mediates between God and man.

AN URGENT TASK

It is the specific task of the organized church to declare
to men the truth of God's special revelation as given in
Holy Scripture. Now the Bible is the book of salvation.
To be sure, not every detail of its content bears directly
on salvation, but the central message of Holy Scripture is
what the God of sovereign grace has done and is doing
through His Son and His Spirit for the salvation of sinners. General revelation, valuable though it is, does not
tell men how they may be saved from sin and death; special revelation tells them all they need to know on that all-
important subject.

Adherents of the Reformed faith are wont to insist that
the Bible is God-centered. In doing that, they are altogether right, for the Bible is God's revelation of Himself.
Yet it may also be said that Scripture is salvation-centered.
The Scriptural doctrine of salvation is itself God-centered.
The whole teaching of the Word of God on salvation may
be summed up in the phrase *salvation by grace*. And
salvation by *grace* is nothing else than salvation by *God*.
When we say that salvation is of grace, we mean that the

sinner cannot possibly save himself and that, if he is to be saved, God will have to do it.

So the task of the church is to proclaim *salvation*. That is indeed an urgent task. Every day on every hand men are passing on into eternity without having heard that blessed name which is the only one given under heaven by which they must be saved (Acts 4:12) and without the slightest acquaintance with Him who declared: "I am the way, the truth, and the life: no man cometh unto the Father but by me" (John 14:6). Besides, a host of human beings who have heard the gospel reject the one and only Saviour in unbelief; and, if they persist in that course, the wrath of God will abide on them (John 3:36). No wonder that Richard Baxter, that great Puritan preacher, spoke of himself as "a dying man preaching to dying men." The church's task is a matter of life and death, even of eternal life and eternal death.

From another viewpoint, too, the church's supreme task excels in urgency. Beyond all doubt, the time of Christ's return is unchangeably determined in God's eternal counsel. However, the divine plan includes also the entire complex of events leading up to that great day. Therefore Scripture teaches that the end will not come until the gospel has been preached in all the world for a witness to all nations (Matthew 24:14). It follows that, when Christ makes the comforting announcement: "Surely, I come quickly," the church, in addition to responding: "Even so, come, Lord Jesus" (Revelation 22:20), must labor to that end. Although the divinely foreordained date of the second coming is unalterable, it nevertheless is quite correct to say that by the diligent proclamation of the gospel the church contributes to the *hastening* of the consummation of Christ's glorious kingdom.

A Comprehensive Task

The church must declare "all the counsel of God" (Acts 20:27). Obviously, this does not mean that in the course

of thirty or forty years of service a minister must preach
a sermon on every book and chapter and verse of Holy
Writ.   The Bible is not a collection of countless isolated
truths but a revelation of truth as a unit.   It is a self-
consistent whole.   Every part must be understood in the
light of all other parts.   Therefore preaching of "all the
counsel of God" will excel in balance.   For a few examples,
the church must proclaim both God's infinite love and His
perfect justice; both what is true and what is good; and
sin, salvation and service — all three.

Once in a long while one meets a person who takes the
position that the sole purpose of preaching is to build up
believers in the faith.   Every once in a while one hears
the opinion expressed that the sole purpose of preaching
is the conversion of the unsaved.   Scripture teaches unmistakably that the church must direct its preaching, not
to one or the other of those ends, but to both.   The same
apostle who strove to preach the gospel, not where Christ
was named, lest he should build upon another man's foundation (Romans 15:20) also taught that the ascended
Christ provided various functionaries in the church "for
the perfecting of the saints . . . for the edifying of the
body of Christ" (Ephesians 4:11, 12).   The church which
stresses missions and evangelism to the neglect of its
members is, harsh as it may sound, committing suicide.
The church which neglects the great commission of its
divine Head is also, to say the least, in process of dying.

Ordinarily preaching is directed to adults only.   Few
and far between are the churches which take seriously
the task of presenting the Word of God to children.   To
be sure, almost all churches make an attempt at it in
Sunday school, but that attempt usually excels in feebleness.   The same description often applies to the sermon-
ettes which ministers preach to the little tots in the
Sunday morning service.   Would that ministers might
learn in all their preaching to present profound truth
in so simple a way that children of school age could be

benefited! Then, as a wise teacher once remarked, even college graduates might possibly understand. And would that the church everywhere might restore to its rightful place of honor the good old custom of giving catechetical instruction to its children! Such instruction is not a whit less necessary than is congregational preaching. In manner the two naturally differ, but not in importance.

In still another respect the task of the organized church is comprehensive. In recent decades many liberal preachers have substituted the so-called social gospel for the gospel of individual salvation. Many conservative ministers, on the other hand, preach only the gospel of individual salvation and insist that social problems have no place in the Christian pulpit. Both these views are in serious error. While they err in opposite directions, both alike detract from the comprehensiveness of the church's message. The gospel primarily concerns the salvation of individuals, but it undoubtedly has its social implications. The church must call upon men, not only to receive Christ as Saviour, but also to honor Him as Lord. And they must be told to honor Him as Lord, not only in their private lives, but in all human relationships, for Christ is indeed "the head over all things" (Ephesians 1:22).

AN EXCLUSIVE TASK

In two senses the preaching of the Word of God is the exclusive task of the organized church. On the one hand, this task has been assigned by God to the church as to none other. On the other hand, the church must beware of undertaking any other task.

In those circles which tend to belittle the importance of the organized church and its offices the distinction between *preaching* by an ordained minister and *exhorting* by an unordained church member is often laughed out of court, and by the same token it is not at all unusual for voluntary associations of Christians to take over the church's task of sending out missionaries. That every believer is

in duty bound to witness for Christ is indisputable, and
it may even be granted that under unusual circumstances
boards which are independent of ecclesiastical control
may conduct missions. But the position must be firmly
maintained that *normally* the preaching of the Word is
to be regarded as a God-given prerogative of the organized
church.

It goes without saying that the church must conduct
public worship. But it may never be forgotten that the
preaching of the Word is central in public worship. It
may not even be supposed that the administration of the
sacraments is another task of the church in addition to
the preaching of the Word. Least of all may the church
give so much prominence to the sacraments as virtually
to crowd out the Word. The fact is that the sacraments
are subsidiary to the Word. They add nothing to the
gospel but merely reinforce its message. In a very real
sense the administration of the sacraments is a way of
declaring the gospel. Scripture teaches in so many words
that whenever the members of Christ's church celebrate
the holy supper they "proclaim the Lord's death" (I Corinthians 11:26, ASV).

It cannot be denied that the organized church must
care for its poor. Beyond all doubt, that is an important
function of the church. But this task, too, is subordinate
to the preaching of the Word. That is indicated by what
the apostles told the church at Jerusalem when the office
of deacon was about to be instituted. Said they: "It is
not reason that we should leave the Word of God and
serve tables" (Acts 6:2). It may even be said that by
caring for the poor the church in some sense preaches the
gospel. Francis of Assisi is said to have invited a monk
to assist him in bringing the gospel to a certain village.
They spent the whole day in works of mercy and never got
around to preaching. Toward evening his companion inquired of Francis when they were going to begin to preach.
Francis replied that they had been preaching all day.

That story is easily misapplied. Let no one think that good deeds may be substituted for the gospel. That simply is not so. The one and only means by which God is pleased to bring sinners to saving faith is His Word. But it is true that works of mercy serve admirably to reinforce the gospel message.

Again, it must be granted that the church is required to discipline its erring members. But also that task is inseparable from teaching the Word. It is an important aspect of "teaching them to observe all things whatsoever I have commanded you" (Matthew 28:20). Significantly, the preaching of the gospel and the exercise of discipline are the two keys of the kingdom of heaven, and these two may not be put asunder.

Just because the preaching of the Word is so great a task the church must devote itself to it alone. For the church to undertake other activities, not indissolubly bound up with this one, is a colossal blunder because it inevitably results in neglect of its proper task. Let not the church degenerate into a social club. Let not the church go into the entertainment business. Let not the church take sides on such aspects of economics, politics, or natural science as are not dealt with in the Word of God. And let the church be content to teach special, not general, revelation. Let the church be the church.

If the church attempts to be something else than the church, it denies itself and detracts from its own glory. If it is satisfied to be the church, its glory will shine forth.

Chapter 27

PREACHER OF REPENTANCE

The God-assigned task of the church is to proclaim the Word of God. One important aspect of that task is the preaching of repentance.

REPENTANCE AND THE WRATH OF GOD

It is highly significant that the inspired preachers of Bible history put a truly tremendous emphasis on repentance. Repentance was the very first thing they demanded of their hearers.

Noah, "a preacher of righteousness" (II Peter 2:5), called upon his contemporaries to repent of their evil deeds. In all the writings of both the major and the minor prophets there is not a note more prominent than that of repentance. In season and out of season they pleaded with the erring people of God to repent. Ezekiel, for instance, cried out: "Thus saith the Lord God, Repent and turn yourselves from your idols; and turn away your faces from all your abominations" (Ezekiel 14:6), and "Turn ye, turn ye from your evil ways; for why will ye die, O house of Israel?" (Ezekiel 33:11).

John the Baptist thundered at the Pharisees and Sadducees: "O generation of vipers, who hath warned you to flee from the wrath to come? Bring forth therefore fruits meet for repentance" (Matthew 3:7, 8). Scripture tells us that he preached "the baptism of repentance" (Mark 1:4). The very first note sounded by the Son of God in His public ministry was that of repentance. It is said significantly: "From that time Jesus began to preach and to say, Repent: for the kingdom of heaven is at hand" (Matthew 4:17). In the application of his Pentecostal sermon Peter exhorted: "Repent, and be baptized every one of you in the name of Jesus Christ for the remission of sins" (Acts 2:38). The apostle Paul told the Athenians that God "commandeth all men everywhere to repent, because he hath appointed a day in which he will judge the world in righteousness" (Acts 17:30, 31), and he summarized his career as a preacher by asserting that he had "showed first unto them of Damascus, and at Jerusalem, and throughout all the coasts of Judea, and then to the gentiles, that they should repent and turn to God, and do works meet for repentance" (Acts 26:20). The letters which the glorified Christ commanded the apostle John to write to the seven churches of Asia Minor abound in commands to repent (Revelation 2:5, 16; 3:19).

It can hardly be denied that the call to repentance does not resound nearly as loudly from the pulpits of our day as from Scripture. From modernist pulpits it is seldom heard, and even from many relatively conservative pulpits it comes but feebly.

What accounts for this notable difference between the preaching contained in the Bible and the preaching of today? One explanation, and certainly a correct one, is that the Word of God takes sin incomparably more seriously than does the modern pulpit. But underneath that fact lies another. The reason why Scripture takes sin so much more seriously than does present-day preaching is that it takes God so much more seriously. What makes all sin exceedingly sinful is that it constitutes an affront to the completely sovereign, perfectly holy and absolutely just God. For that reason sin causes the wrath of God to burn hotly, and for the sinner to fall into the hands of the living God, who is a consuming fire, becomes a fearful thing (Hebrews 10:31, 12:29). If he does not repent, there awaits him a certain fearful looking for of judgment and fiery indignation which will devour him (Hebrews 10:27). The unrepentant sinner is on his way to the place where, in the words of Jesus, "shall be wail-

ing and gnashing of teeth" (Matthew 13:42) and where
"their worm dieth not and the fire is not quenched" (Mark
9:44, 46, 48).

Scripture's call to repentance is rooted in Scripture's
conception of God as the Sovereign One who will brook
no resistance to His will, as the Holy One who hates sin
with an infinite hate, and as the Righteous One who demands that sin be punished with death, even death eternal.
Only when the church has returned to the *theology* of the
Bible will it once more assign to the call to repentance
that prominence which God has given it in His Word.

REPENTANCE AND THE LAW OF GOD

Repentance is a gift of God. Except the Spirit of God
work in the sinner's heart, he will not repent. But the
truth may never be neglected that, in performing this
work and imparting this gift, the Holy Spirit is wont to
employ means. The means is the preaching of the Word
of God by the church, more particularly the preaching of
the law of God. For, as Scripture says, "by the law is
the knowledge of sin" (Romans 3:20).

The law of God has been compared to a mirror. If a
mirror is not bent or soiled or marred, it will present an
exact picture of him who stands before it. The law of
God as a perfect mirror shows up the sinner with all his
blemishes and in all his filthiness. As he sees himself
in this mirror he will, if he be not blind, be not only
greatly shocked, but will utterly abhor himself. That
is a sign of repentance.

The law of God may also be compared to a mountain.
It is a mountain which the sinner is in sacred duty bound
to scale but cannot possibly scale. The law requires that
the sinner love God with all his heart, with all his soul,
with all his mind and with all his strength (Mark 12:30).
But who is sufficient for that? The law of God demands
that the sinner be perfect even as God is perfect (Matthew
5:48), but to meet that demand is infinitely far beyond

his powers. Confronting, as he does, an utterly impossible task, he stands helpless and his case is hopeless. Sinking into the slough of despond, it behooves him to cry: "Woe is me, for I am undone." That is a cry of repentance.

Again, the law of God may be compared to an executioner. But that language, strong though it may seem, is really far too weak. Not only does the law *resemble* an executioner, it *is* an executioner, it is *the* executioner *par excellence*. Not only does it threaten its transgressor with death, saying: "If thou break me, I will break thee," but it carries out that threat. When God ordained that the wages of sin would be death (Romans 6:23), He did not lay down an arbitrary rule, but He stated an inescapable law. That he who violates the law of God must die is itself a law of God, for to sin is to turn from God, and to turn from God is to die. Thus the law of God not only pronounces the sentence of death upon the sinner, but it puts that sentence into effect. The apostle Paul had that in mind when he said: "The commandment, which was ordained to life, I found to be unto death" (Romans 7:10). The law of God slays the sinner. Confronting that executioner, what can he do but cry aloud to God for mercy? That is repentance.

REPENTANCE AND THE GRACE OF GOD

If the church preached only the law of God, it would drive men to despair. But the church is under orders to preach especially the good news of the grace of God. Therefore, having preached the law unto repentance, it must go on to preach repentance unto salvation.

The apostle Paul has told us that "the law has become our schoolmaster unto Christ" (Galatians 3:24). He had in mind God's progressive revelation to the church of the two dispensations. The emphasis on the law in the Old Testament was intended by God to teach His people that they were sinners incapable of saving themselves and thus to prepare them for the reception of salvation by faith in Jesus Christ, which is indeed taught in the whole of Scripture but is fully revealed in the New Testament. However, for the individual sinner, too, the law becomes a pedagogue to Christ. In the words of Luther, "the law reveals and amplifies sin, humbling the proud to desire Christ's aid." Thus the law prepares for grace.

The call to repentance is indeed a divine command, but it is also a most urgent and cordial divine invitation. Swearing by Himself, God declares: "As I live, I have no pleasure in the death of the wicked; but that the wicked turn from his way and live"; and then He pleads with the wicked: "Turn ye, turn ye from your evil ways; for why will ye die?" (Ezekiel 33:11). And the apostle Peter assures us that God is "not willing that any should perish, but that all should come to repentance" (II Peter 3:9). In comment on that sweeping assertion Calvin has said: "So wonderful is His love towards mankind that He would have them all to be saved, and is of His own self prepared to bestow salvation on the lost. But the order is to be noticed, that God is ready to receive all to repentance, so that none may perish; for in these words the way and manner of obtaining salvation is pointed out. Every one of us, therefore, who is desirous of salvation must learn to enter in by this way." Repentance is indeed prerequisite to salvation; but not only does God invite all penitents to salvation, He lovingly invites all sinners to repentance.

When the preaching of the law is applied by the Holy Spirit to the heart of the sinner, he is brought under conviction of sin. When the Spirit of God proceeds to apply the preaching of the gospel to his heart, the convicted sinner throws himself upon the mercy of God. With the publican of the parable he smites upon his breast and gasps: "God, be merciful to me a sinner," and the God of all grace justifies him (Luke 18:13, 14). With the prodigal son of another parable he returns to the Father with the confession: "Father, I have sinned against heaven and in thy sight, and am not worthy to be called thy son," and even before he has finished his confession the Father has compassion on him, falls on his neck and kisses him (Luke 15:20, 21). And the Saviour, mindful of His promise, "Him that cometh to me I will in no wise cast out" (John 6:37), calls the penitent His very own.

True repentance never comes too late. Two malefactors were crucified with our Lord. In the closing hours of his criminal career one of them repented. He confessed that he was deserving of crucifixion and, turning to the Saviour, he prayed: "Lord, remember me when thou comest into thy kingdom." Jesus replied: "Verily I say unto thee, today shalt thou be with me in paradise" (Luke 23:41-43). Presently the gates of paradise swung open, and hand in hand his Lord and he entered in. That morning he was scorned by men; that evening the angels of God welcomed him. That morning he was utterly vile; that evening, washed in the crimson flood, he was whiter than snow. That morning he was naked; that evening he was clothed in white raiment. That morning he was a criminal; that evening he was numbered among the spirits of just men made perfect. That morning he stood on the very threshold of hell; that evening he found himself in Jerusalem the golden. That morning he was in the clutches of Satan; that evening he was safe in the arms of Jesus. That morning he hung on an accursed cross; that evening he sat with the Son of God in His throne.

Wonderful grace of God!

Chapter 28

PREACHER OF GOOD TIDINGS

In a great many churches only the gospel of "be good and do good" is proclaimed. To it applies Paul's scathing description: "another gospel which is not another" (Galatians 1:6, 7). It is a wholly different kind of gospel and therefore does not rate as a second gospel alongside the gospel which the apostle preached. In reality it is no gospel at all.

The word *gospel* means *good news*. That which is preached as gospel in so many churches is not even news, let alone good news. A man has been found guilty, shall we say, of a heinous crime and has been sentenced to death. He is now in prison, awaiting the day of his execution. A friend comes to visit him. This friend calls out: "I have good news for you!" Eagerly the condemned man asks: "What is it?" The answer comes: "Be good." In that message there is not so much as a shred of good news. It is most cruel mockery. Yet many a self-styled minister of Christ holds forth to sinners under the sentence of eternal death a precisely equivalent message as gospel.

The gospel contained in Holy Writ does not primarily tell sinners what they must do, but, contrariwise, *what God has done and is doing for them.*

To be the bearer of those good tidings — a few glimpses of which follow — is the inestimably great honor of the Christian church.

"GOD SO LOVED THE WORLD"

John 3:16 has often been said to be "the gospel in a nutshell." "God so loved the world," we are told, "that he gave his only begotten Son, that whosoever believeth in him should not perish, but have everlasting life."

The term *world* as it occurs here has often been interpreted quantitatively. Some have said: "The love of God is so great that it embraces all the elect, and they are a throng which no man can number." Others have said: "The love of God is so great that it embraces not only the elect but all human beings that have ever lived on the face of the earth, all that live there now, and all that remain to be born." Still others have said: "The love of God is so great that it embraces not only all men but the sum total of things created, the whole of the universe." But all three of these interpretations attempt to measure the infinite in terms of the finite, and that is something which cannot be done. God is infinite in all His attributes, also in His love. In comparison with the infinite the sum total of finite things is precisely nothing.

Benjamin B. Warfield was, no doubt, right when, in a sermon on John 3:16, he insisted that *world* must here be interpreted qualitatively. The *holy* God loves *sinful* humanity — that is the amazing truth here revealed. Amazing it is. God is the Holy One of Israel, the Perfection of Holiness, in whose presence the very seraphs cover their faces as they cry out: "Holy, holy, holy is the Lord of hosts: the whole earth is full of his glory" (Isaiah 6:1-3). That holy God looks down to earth and there sees sinful men, veritable lepers, covered with spiritual leprosy from the crowns of their heads to the soles of their feet. And unbelievable though it may seem, He loves them.

 How that is possible no mortal will ever comprehend. Only this do we know: divine love differs from human love in that, while the latter is dependent on its object, the former is not. God loves sinners for reasons that reside, not in them, but in God Himself.

An old legend has it that the only thing that can melt adamant is the blood of a lamb. So, it has been said, the blood of the Lamb of God was required to melt the adamantine heart of God. But John 3:16 teaches quite the opposite. God loved sinful men long before the blood of His Son was shed on Calvary. It was God's infinite love that moved Him to send His Son into the world that He might die for the ungodly.

God had a Son, an only-begotten Son. He loved that Son with all the love of which the heart of God is capable. But so unsearchably great was His love for hell-deserving sinners that He willingly gave the Son of His eternal and infinite love to suffer the anguish and torment of hell in their stead. As we contemplate that truth, it behooves us to bow our heads in adoration and to whisper: "Lord God, we cannot understand; we do not begin to comprehend; but, because Thou sayest it, we believe."

On the ground of the finished work of His Son, God offers everlasting life to sinners everywhere, and He does so freely. Salvation is a gift of purest grace. Man need neither work nor pay for it. He may have it for the taking. Not even by taking it does he merit it. All he needs to do is look away from self and every other creature and look to Christ crucified. In that look there is life, even life eternal, for it is the very essence of saving faith.

Such are the good tidings of John 3:16, and these stammering remarks give but an inkling of the infinite love of God which it declares.

"CHRIST DIED FOR THE UNGODLY"

Another summary statement — and no less profound — of the good tidings which the church is honored to bring to sinful men is contained in Romans 5:6, 8 — "In due time Christ died for the ungodly" and "God commendeth his love toward us, in that, while we were yet sinners, Christ died for us."

Christ's death on the cross constituted at once the very nadir of His humiliation and the very zenith of His obedience to the Father, who had sent Him. Paul tells us: "He humbled himself and became obedient unto death, even the death of the cross" (Philippians 2:8). It was the zenith both of His passive obedience, manifest in His suffering, and of His active obedience, manifest in His keeping the law of God.

Men are ungodly sinners. For such the justice of God demands death in its most comprehensive sense. They are hell-deserving. But Christ "descended into hell" in sinners' stead. When He was hanging on Calvary's cross He bore the curse that was due to the ungodly. When He cried out with a loud voice: "My God, my God, why hast thou forsaken me?" (Matthew 27:46) He was at the very bottom of the bottomless pit, where man deserved to be, and all the waves and billows of the divine wrath against man's sin rolled over His head and crushed His soul. In consequence there is now no condemnation for those who believe on His name. So far as they are concerned, the justice of God is satisfied and His wrath is appeased. God so declared by raising His Son from the dead.

From the beginning God decreed that eternal life would be the reward of perfect obedience to Him. Implicit in His threat to Adam, the representative head of our race: "In the day that thou eatest thereof thou shalt surely die" (Genesis 2:17), was the promise of life as the reward of obedience. Adam became disobedient and thus brought death upon himself and all his descendants. And ever since the fall human nature has been so corrupt that no man is able to keep God's commandments. But, lo and behold, in the fullness of time there appeared upon the scene of history another Adam, the last Adam, even Jesus Christ. He kept the law of God to the point of perfection. And to all who believe on Him God imputes His perfect righteousness as their very own. "As by one man's disobedience many were made sinners, so by the obedience of one shall many be made righteous" (Romans 5:19). The believer may jubilantly sing: "I will greatly rejoice in the Lord, my soul shall be joyful in my God; for he hath clothed me with the garments of salvation, he hath

covered me with the robe of righteousness, as a bridegroom decketh himself with ornaments and as a bride
adorneth herself with her jewels" (Isaiah 61:10). Wearing the robe of Christ's righteousness, he may pass through
the gates of pearl into the golden city and enter the palace
of the King.

Thus Christ by His death on the cross made provision,
not only for paying the debt of sinners to the uttermost
farthing, but also for procuring for them the riches of
eternal glory.

"The Lord Is Not Willing that Any Should Perish"

The puny minds of men often insist that the gospel
should tell us that in the end all men will be saved. "That,"
they say, "would be good news indeed." And not a few
have distorted Holy Scripture so as to make it teach that
very thing. Today we are witnessing a mighty resurgence
in several churches of the ancient heresy of universal
salvation. But the undeniable teaching of the Word of
God is that only God's elect will enter through the gates
into the city.

However, let no one conclude that the Word of God contains good news only for the elect. The same Bible which
teaches election also contains an abundance of good news
for each and every sinner. As striking a paradox as any
in Holy Writ is that the very God who from eternity
elected a limited number of men to eternal life invites
in perfect sincerity to life eternal all to whom the gospel
comes. No theologian has ever succeeded in harmonizing
the elements of that paradox before the bar of human
reason, but the greatest theologians have humbly accepted
both as the very truth of God.

John 3:16 and Romans 5:6, 8 were not written for the
elect alone. And Scripture tells of a universal love of
God which comes to expression, not only in the gifts of
rain and sunshine to the evil as well as the good, the unjust as well as the just, but also in the sincere offer of

salvation to all who hear the gospel. Swearing by Himself, God says: "As I live, I have no pleasure in the death of the wicked; but that the wicked turn from his way and live" (Ezekiel 33:11). And the apostle Peter assures us that "the Lord is not willing that any should perish, but that all should come to repentance" (II Peter 3:9).

In the light of such passages of Holy Scripture the greatest teachers and preachers of the Christian church have proclaimed the glad tidings that God will not only be pleased to save all who repent and believe, but also that He will be pleased to have all to whom the gospel comes repent and believe and thus be saved. Commenting on Ezekiel 18:23, which parallels Ezekiel 33:11, Calvin said: "God desires nothing more earnestly than that those who were perishing and rushing to destruction should return into the way of safety." The Canons of Dort, which are a precise formulation by the Reformed churches of Europe of the so-called five points of Calvinism, insist: "As many as are called by the gospel are unfeignedly called. For God has most earnestly and truly declared in His Word what will be acceptable to Him: namely, that all who are called should come unto Him" (Heads of Doctrine III and IV, Article 8). Herman Bavinck, that prince of Dutch theologians, has asserted that the call of the gospel "is for all without exception proof of God's infinite love" (*Gereformeerde Dogmatiek*, Vol. IV, p. 7).

That, too, is a significant aspect of the glorious gospel the proclamation of which is the glorious task of the glorious church. God Himself charged His church with that task when He cried: "O Zion, that bringest good tidings, get thee up into the high mountain; O Jerusalem, that bringest good tidings, lift up thy voice with strength; lift it up, be not afraid" (Isaiah 40:9).

Chapter 29

PREACHER OF SALVATION BY GRACE

The glorious message of the Christian church has numerous aspects. It is like a precious stone with many sparkling facets. To name but a few of those facets: it is an urgent and loving call to repentance; it brings the glad tidings of what God has done in human history for sinners; it is the gospel of salvation by grace.

Christians do much talking and singing about salvation by grace, but not nearly all of them have a clear conception of its meaning. A very simple and correct definition of salvation by grace is *salvation by God.* No more urgent question confronts the race of sinful men than this one: how they may be saved from sin and death. Every religion under the sun gives an answer to that question, but only one religion gives the correct answer. Christianity alone replies that salvation is of God; all other religions reply that the sinner must save himself. In brief, only Christianity offers salvation by grace.

Exceedingly sad to say, the churches that preach the gospel of salvation by grace in all its Scriptural purity are few and far between. There are churches so called that deny it altogether. They boldly substitute salvation by works or character for salvation by the grace of God. But by so doing they forfeit every claim to Christianity. A great many churches compromise the issue. They would divide the work of salvation between God and man, ascribing certain parts to each. Such churches detract immeasurably from the beauty of their God-given message.

It is the glory of the Christian church that it has been commissioned by its divine Head to proclaim the unadulterated gospel of the grace of God. A few glimpses of that gospel follow.

GOD THE FATHER PLANNED SALVATION

"According as he hath chosen us in him before the foundation of the world, that we should be holy and without blame before him in love: having predestinated us unto the adoption of children by Jesus Christ to himself, according to the good pleasure of his will" (Ephesians 1:4, 5): On this passage of Scripture, together with a great many others, is founded the doctrine of divine election. Modernists will have nothing of it, and many fundamentalists strongly dislike it; but it is unmistakably taught by God in His Word.

Admittedly, election presents great difficulties, even unfathomable mysteries, to the mind of man. Yet a number of statements can be made concerning it with complete certainty.

God did the electing, not man. Scripture affirms that in so many words, and the fact that election occurred "before the foundation of the world" leaves no other possibility. Man did not yet exist except in the counsel of God. A rather widespread popular conception of election must here be refuted. There is an election going on, it is said, concerning the salvation of men. God votes for the salvation of every individual, and Satan votes for the damnation of every individual. So the vote stands a tie in the case of each individual, and it is for him to break the tie. If he votes with God, he is elected. That presentation of election is far from innocent. In transferring election from God to man, it flagrantly contradicts the Scriptural teaching of salvation by grace.

God was under no obligation to choose unto eternal life any member of the lost human race. If God had permitted all sinners to perish everlastingly, all would have received their just due. The popular notion that God owes every man at least a chance of salvation is an expression of human arrogance and dishonors God. The only thing that God owes sinners is damnation. It follows that God's choice of some to life eternal was a matter of purest grace.

Why God elected certain persons to everlasting life we cannot say. But this we know: the reason lay in God, not in man. God did not choose a given individual because He foresaw that that individual would believe, but God chose him "according to the good pleasure of His will." That can only mean that He chose him sovereignly. Faith is a consequence of election, not its ground. This, too, we know: God chose a certain person because He loved him, for Scripture tells us: "Whom he did foreknow, he also did predestinate to be conformed to the image of his Son" (Romans 8:29). *To foreknow* here means *to love from eternity.* But why God should have loved him from eternity is far beyond our comprehension. All we can say is that God loved him in Christ.

It may not be inferred that God brings the elect to glory by external force and that likewise by force He thrusts the non-elect into perdition. That is not at all the case. God does not lift men up to heaven nor cast them down to hell as so many "stocks and blocks." Contrariwise, He deals with them as rational and moral, hence responsible, beings. Impossible though it is for our puny minds to reconcile human responsibility with divine sovereignty, the Word of God upholds both uncompromisingly. Therefore, when a sinner perishes, he perishes because he is unwilling to be saved, and he himself must bear all the blame; and when a sinner is saved, he is saved by the grace of God alone, which has made him willing to be saved, and to God belongs all the glory.

GOD THE SON MERITED SALVATION

The third chapter of Galatians contains two quotations from the Old Testament in both of which occurs the word *cursed.* The tenth verse says: "Cursed is every one that continueth not in all things which are written in the book of the law to do them." That applies to sinners. The thirteenth verse says: "Cursed is every one that hangeth on a tree." That applies to Christ crucified. Between these curses there exists the closest relationship. On Calvary's cross Christ bore the curse that was due to sinners. A famous Reformed catechism states: "He bore the wrath of God against the sin of the whole human race" (Heidelberg Catechism, Lord's Day XV, Question 37). More particularly, by His accursed death Christ designed to deliver the elect from the curse of God. And that design He accomplished.

Christ did much more than that for the elect. Not only did He deliver them from the curse of God, He also gained for them the divine blessing. Not only did He pay their debt, He also procured for them infinite riches. It is this that theologians have in mind when they say that Christ not only delivered the elect from eternal death by His passive obedience, manifest in His suffering, but also procured for them eternal life by His active obedience, manifest in His perfect observance of the divine law.

Some one has no assets whatever, let us say, but is in debt to the extent of a million dollars. A good and rich friend pays his debt. Surely he has reason for profound gratitude. But just how rich is he now? Obviously he is still as poor as the proverbial church mouse. Christ not only paid our great debt to the last farthing; in addition, He merited for us the infinite riches of life eternal.

It is clear that Christ has merited full salvation for sinners and that there is precisely nothing left for them to merit.

That precious truth is denied by the teaching of Rome that the sinner is saved by a combination of Christ's merits and human merits. It is denied even more emphatically by the teaching of liberal Protestantism that the sinner is saved, not by the merits of Christ at all, but solely by his own works and character. And, sad to say, even some Bible-believing Protestants are inclined to compromise this truth by their teaching of "evangelical obedience." In fact, not one of us is without the heinous sin of self-righteousness.

No one is saved by doing his best, for "all our righteousnesses are as filthy rags" (Isaiah 64:6). Tears of repentance are no substitute for the blood of Christ. Could our tears forever flow, they would not atone for as much as one of our transgressions. The most zealous worker in Christ's church is not saved by his labors. Men are saved not by works but by faith, and not even their faith merits salvation. As a beggar reaching out his hand to receive an alms does not thereby earn the alms, so the sinner merits nothing by the acceptance in faith of the offered salvation. The Christian's "evangelical obedience," consisting of a life of faith and love, can never take the place of the smallest part of Christ's passive or active obedience. To repeat one of Spurgeon's illustrations, he who would get to heaven by his works or his character is like a man who tries to climb into the sky on a ladder of sand, and so is he who substitutes faith and love for works or character as a ground of salvation. The same preacher of the grace of God has said: "If there be but one stitch in the celestial garment of our righteousness which we ourselves are to put in, we are lost." In the words of the Westminster Shorter Catechism, "Faith in Jesus Christ is a saving grace whereby we receive and rest upon him *alone* for salvation" (Question 86).

GOD THE HOLY SPIRIT APPLIES SALVATION

On the basis of the finished work of His Son, God in all sincerity offers eternal life to all to whom the gospel comes, and all who accept that offer in faith are saved.

That not all believe is nothing strange. The total depravity of natural man explains it. He loves death rather than life. The wonder is that any believe. How to account for that, is a question of prime importance.

Here a great many who claim to be conservative depart

far from the truth. They say that at this point salvation is no longer of God who shows mercy, but of him that wills. Here, it is asserted, God's part of the work of salvation ends and man's part begins. Even unregenerate man is said to have the ability to receive Christ in faith, and whether or not he will make the proper use of that ability is said to depend on him. In other words, God has made salvation possible for every man by the death of His Son, and now it is for each man to make his salvation actual by accepting Christ of his own free volition.

That teaching, which is of the essence of Arminianism, particularly of that brand of Arminianism known as Wesleyan, and regrettably is proclaimed by many sincere and zealous evangelists — among them Billy Graham — cannot be reconciled with the Scriptural doctrine of salvation by the grace of God. Having identified coming to Him with believing on Him, Jesus said: "No man can come to me except the Father which hath sent me draw him" (John 6:35, 44). Lydia, one of several women who heard Paul preach at Philippi, believed the gospel. What accounted for her doing so? The Word of God answers that question by saying, not that *she* opened her heart, but that *the Lord* opened her heart (Acts 16:14). Paul told the Christians at Philippi that it was *given* to them both to believe on Christ and to suffer for His sake (Philippians 1:29). And he informed the Corinthians: "No man can say that Jesus is the Lord but by the Holy Ghost" (I Corinthians 12:3). According to Scripture faith does not precede the new birth, the divinely wrought momentary transition from death to life, but follows it; and that means that faith is a gift of God the Holy Spirit before it can become an act of man. Here, too, salvation is of God.

Is it true, perhaps, that the sinner is dependent on the grace of the Holy Spirit to set him on the way of life, but that, once on the way, he can travel onward in his own strength? Not according to the Word of God. It insists that he remains completely dependent on the grace of God to his very last step.   Significantly, that is taught in a passage which strongly emphasizes the responsibility of believers.   Paul enjoined the Christians at Philippi: "Work out your own salvation with fear and trembling, for it is God which worketh in you both to will and to do" (Philippians 2:12, 13).   The exact sense of the second clause is: for it is God who right along keeps working in you both to will and to do.   The continued operation of the grace of the Holy Spirit within him both obligates and enables the believer to work out his own salvation.

Conscious of his utter dependence on the grace of God in the whole process of salvation, the Christian prays with Augustine: "Command, Lord, what Thou wilt; give what Thou commandest." And he sings:

> I sought the Lord, and afterward I knew
>   He moved my soul to seek Him, seeking me;
> It was not I that found, O Saviour true;
>   No, I was found of Thee.
>
> I find, I walk, I love; but O the whole
>   Of love is but my answer, Lord, to Thee,
> For Thou wast long beforehand with my soul;
>   Always Thou lovedst me.

*   *   *   *

What an honor to proclaim such a gospel!

It is the one and only gospel that meets the sinner's needs, for he cannot possibly save himself.   And it honors God as does no other gospel, for it ascribes to Him all the glory for man's salvation.

It alone is truly gospel.

Chapter 30

PREACHER OF CHRISTIAN GRATITUDE

A certain catechism asks the question: "How many things are necessary for you to know, that you . . . may live and die happily?" And it replies: "Three; the first, how great my sins and misery are; the second, how I am delivered from all my sins and misery; the third, how I am to be thankful to God for such deliverance" (Heidelberg Catechism, Lord's Day I, Question 2).

These three things are so many aspects of the message which God has commissioned His church to proclaim. And it is to proclaim the third as well as the other two. Did not the Lord Jesus in His great commission charge the church to make disciples of all nations, "teaching them to observe all things whatsoever I have commanded you" (Matthew 28:20)?

GRATITUDE AND THE GRACE OF GOD

The Scriptural doctrine of salvation by grace has often been abused. In the apostolic church there seem to have been those who recommended continuing in sin in order that grace might the more abound (Romans 6:1). In the history of the Reformed churches one reads of those who stressed the truth of the believer's complete dependence on the grace of God for godly living to the detriment of the complementary truth of his unqualified responsibility for godly living. This writer has known a man who was at once a member of a Christian church and a drunkard. When admonished to break with his sin, he invariably replied: "Salvation is by grace, not by works," and, having said that, went merrily on his way.

More illogical reasoning is hardly imaginable.

No one who has been saved by grace can possibly be content to live in sin. He who willingly serves sin, by that very token gives conclusive evidence of not having been saved. To the query: "Shall we continue in sin that grace may abound?" the apostle Paul retorted: "How shall we that are dead to sin live any longer therein?" (Romans 6:2)

Scripture teaches salvation by faith, not by works; and salvation by faith alone is the exact equivalent of salvation by grace. But nowhere does Scripture teach salvation by a faith that does not work. On the contrary, it denounces such faith as dead and therefore utterly worthless. James says emphatically in his epistle: "As the body without the spirit is dead, so faith without works is dead also" (James 2:26). And when Paul insists with utmost strenuousness on justification by faith only, he has in mind living faith; in his own words, "faith that worketh by love" (Galatians 5:6). [Paul and James are in complete agreement.]

Salvation by grace presents the purest motive for godly living. While all other religions tell men to do good in order that they may be saved, Christianity commands Christians to do good because they have been saved. Every other religion says: "Do and live." Christianity alone says: "Live and do." Thus the Christian is motivated in his actions by love for God and gratitude to God. And the ultimate aim of his life is not his own good, not even his own highest good, but the glory of God, his Saviour.

Salvation by grace, far from serving as an excuse for godlessness, offers the strongest incentive for godliness. Salvation by grace is nothing else than salvation by God, and God does all the saving. Even when the regenerate work out their own salvation with fear and trembling, as they most certainly must, they do so only because God first worked in them, and right along keeps working in them, both to will and to do (Philippians 2:12, 13). Thus God is entitled to all the credit for man's salvation. This has

a most direct and important bearing on the life of him
who is saved. If God had done, let us say, fifty percent
of the saving and he himself had done the other fifty percent, he might reasonably devote half of what he is and
has to God and half to himself. If God had done ninety
percent of the saving and he himself had done the remaining ten percent, then he should in fairness devote to God
ninety percent of what he is and has, and might well re-
serve the remaining ten percent for himself. But the fact
is that God has done the entire work of saving him, and
therefore it behooves him to say:

> Were the whole realm of nature mine,
> That were a present far too small;
> Love so amazing, so divine,
> Demands my soul, my life, my *all*.

GRATITUDE AND THE LAW OF GOD

Just how is the Christian to show his gratitude to God
for the gift of salvation?

There are those who at this point divorce the guidance
of the Holy Spirit from the Word of God, particularly
from the law of God contained in His Word. That is one
of the outstanding characteristics of Mysticism, which
time and again in the history of the church has lifted its
ugly head in the guise of exceptional piety. There is
much of it in Christendom today. The followers of the
Oxford Group Movement, also known as Buchmanism and
Moral Re-armament, seek to discover the will of God by
praying to God and then listening to Him in silence with
pen and paper at hand to jot down what He may reveal.
Modern dispensationalism distinguishes sharply between
the dispensation of law and that of the Spirit and insists
that the Christian, controlled as he is by the Spirit, is not
bound to obey the decalogue. Yet that school of thought
must be credited with teaching that nine of the ten commandments — the fourth excepted — are in substance

repeated in the writings of the apostles, to which the Christian is subject. Barthianism denies that the Bible contains the objective revelation of the will of God for man's behavior in all times, places and circumstances, and teaches that the Christian in his behavior is free from law, program and pattern, free to do the will of God, as he is guided by His eye from day to day. And how many Christians in their search for the will of God substitute a mysterious sort of subjective leading for the objective guidance of Holy Scripture!

The will of God expressed in His Word, particularly in the moral law, is the one and only infallible guide for the Christian life of gratitude. With the Spirit shining upon the Word and bringing its truth to light, it is also a completely sufficient guide. In the words of the Westminster Confession of Faith, "The whole counsel of God concerning all things necessary for his own glory, man's salvation, faith, and life, is either expressly set down in Scripture, or by good and necessary consequence may be deduced from Scripture; unto which nothing at any time is to be added, whether by new revelations of the Spirit or traditions of men" (Chapter I, Section VI).

It may never be forgotten that the strictest obedience to the letter of the law, if it be not at once obedience to the spirit of the law, is actually disobedience. That is a way of saying that only he who is motivated by love for God in the keeping of God's commandments is keeping them at all. And that applies to the second table of the law as well as the first. The first table requires love for God, the second demands love for neighbors; but only he who loves his neighbors for God's sake loves them as God would have him. True love for neighbors springs from love for God. That is plainly implied in the admonition of the apostle of love: "Beloved, let us love one another, for love is of God; and every one that loveth is born of God and knoweth God" (I John 4:7).

Christians should love God because He first loved them.

Christians actually do love God because He first loved them. "We love him because he first loved us" (I John 4:19) is not a command but a statement of fact. With that fact in mind Jesus said: "If ye love me, keep my commandments" (John 14:15).

GRATITUDE AND THE LORDSHIP OF CHRIST

It is impossible to receive Christ as one's Saviour without at once acknowledging Him as one's Lord. He who claims Christ as his Saviour but refuses to obey His commands is deceiving himself. The simple fact is that he is as yet unsaved.

Jesus declared: "If any man will come after me, let him deny himself, and take up his cross, and follow me" (Matthew 16:24). Once upon a time, when great multitudes followed Him, He turned and said: "If any man come to me and hate not his father and mother and wife and children and brethren and sisters, yea, and his own life also, he cannot be my disciple" (Luke 14:26). Repeatedly He admonished those who would be His followers not to act rashly but first to consider the demands of discipleship. When a certain man vowed enthusiastically, "Lord, I will follow thee whithersoever thou goest," Jesus held him in check by reminding him that "foxes have holes and birds of the air have nests, but the Son of man hath not where to lay his head" (Luke 9:57, 58).

The very first thing Saul of Tarsus did upon experiencing the saving grace of Christ on the Damascus road was to ask: "Who art thou, Lord?" And as soon as he heard the answer he exclaimed: "Lord, what shall I do?" (Acts 9:5, 6; 22:10) He did not accept Christ first as Saviour and subsequently as Lord. He did both simultaneously. To believe in Christ and to obey Him are not two separate acts but two phases of a single act.

The blood of the Son of God which flowed on Golgotha not only atoned for the sins of the elect, it also purchased them. They are "bought with a price" (I Corinthians

6:20, 7:23). Consequently they belong to Him. They are His very property. It follows that He will never permit any man to pluck them out of His hand (John 10:28) but will certainly save them to the uttermost (Hebrews 7:25). But it also follows that they are in sacred duty bound to honor Him as their Lord and Master by obeying Him.

A colored girl was to be sold at auction in a southern slavemarket. The bids went higher and higher, until at last a benign gentleman bought her at a very great price. No sooner had he paid the price than he said to her: "I bought you to set you free; you may go wherever you please." But she clung to him and sobbed: "You have saved me from slavery; now you are my master; I want to serve you all my days."

The apostle Paul often spoke of himself as "a slave of Jesus Christ." That is an accurate description of every Christian. But, like that great apostle, he serves his Lord joyfully, from the inner compulsion of a heart aflame with loving gratitude to Him who loved him so exceedingly that He redeemed him from the abject servitude of Satan and sin with His own precious blood.

Chapter 31

PREACHER OF CHRIST'S KINGSHIP

Christ is God, and it is self-evident that as God He is King over all things eternally. Hence theologians speak of His *essential* kingship.

Scripture also teaches Christ's *mediatorial* kingship, which the Father gave to Him, the God-man, as the reward for His obedience and suffering. By virtue of this kingship Christ rules over the church, to be sure; but His mediatorial kingship also extends over the entire world.

While the church is in duty bound to preach the kingship of Christ in all of its aspects, attention may well be called in particular to the church's glorious task of proclaiming His mediatorial kingship over the whole of the universe.

A SCRIPTURAL TRUTH

Dispensationalism denies the kingship of Christ over the world as a present reality. Such influential dialectical theologians as Karl Barth and Emil Brunner also come dangerously near to denying the present reality of Christ's kingdom. While admitting that the kingdom is not merely future, because in Jesus Christ the breaking through into the historical process of the world has begun, they nevertheless insist that the kingdom is exclusively eschatological.

However, the teaching of the Word of God on this point is unmistakably clear. Although the consummation of the kingdom is reserved for the future, Scripture teaches emphatically that Christ is reigning over the universe even now. "He must reign," we are told, "till he hath put all enemies under his feet" (I Corinthians 15:25). In His command to His church to make disciples of all nations He

195

declared majestically: "All power is given unto me in heaven and in earth" (Matthew 28:18). The apostle Paul asserted that God set Christ "at his own right hand in the heavenly places, far above all principality and power and might and dominion and every name that is named, not only in this world but also in that which is to come: and hath put all things under his feet, and gave him to be the head over all things to the church" (Ephesians 1:20-22). And the seer on Patmos described Him as "the prince of the kings of the earth" (Revelation 1:5).

Deniers of the present kingship of Christ over the world often appeal to the Scriptural designation of Satan as "the prince of this world." But they overlook the evident fact that in every instance in which Scripture calls Satan by that name it teaches that Christ by His death has vanquished Satan as prince of this world. In John 12:31 Jesus says with reference to His impending crucifixion: "Now is the judgment of this world; now shall the prince of this world be cast out." In John 14:30, as death draws nearer, He tells the disciples: "The prince of this world cometh and hath nothing in me." And in John 16:11 He teaches that the coming Comforter will convict the world of judgment "because the prince of this world is judged." Whatever influence Satan may in the mysterious dispensation of the providence of God still wield in the world, the fact remains that Christ, not Satan, rules over the universe. Satan cannot so much as stir without Christ's permission.

A COMFORTING TRUTH

Scripture teaches the parallel development in human history of two kingdoms — that of light and that of darkness. Today it surely seems that the latter is far outstripping the former. While the heathen nations are slowly being evangelized and even more slowly Christianized, the Christian nations so called are rapidly reverting to paganism. In some lands the church of Christ is being crushed under the iron heel of totalitarian despots; in other instances the church is decaying from within. Not only does the church find itself in a hostile world, the hostile world is found within the church. In its determined efforts to destroy the church, the world is aided incalculably by a fifth column inside the church. Small wonder that those who constitute a faithful remnant are discouraged, almost despondent.

What comfort to know that seated at the right hand of God is an almighty King who reigns supreme, not only over His church, but also over all the forces in the universe that would destroy His holy church! Through the black darkness of the night comes His voice: "Fear not, little flock; for it is your Father's good pleasure to give you the kingdom" (Luke 12:32).

Illus.

A ship is traversing the ocean. It has a most excellent captain. Can he guarantee the vessel's safety? Certainly not, for he has no control over the winds and the waves. Together they may conceivably dash the vessel in pieces. The church of God is a ship, let us say, traversing the ocean of the world. But what a Captain it has! He is Master not only of the ship, but of all the forces that would destroy it. It is He that commanded the winds and the waves of Galilee: "Peace, be still!" — and they obeyed (Mark 4:39). His omnipotence is the absolute guarantee of the ship's safe arrival at its destination.

Nor is that the whole truth. Not merely *in spite of* the world's attacks will the church prevail, but even *through* them. As in the case of the individual believer all things, particularly life's trials, work together for good, so the King Almighty overrules unto the furtherance of His kingdom all the assaults made upon His church. Thus even the wrath of man will ultimately praise God (Psalm 76:10).

Because of the kingship of Christ over the whole of the universe the grim prince of darkness and the hostile world will not prevail against His church. The faithful members of that church exult in unison:

Wherefore do the nations rage
  And the people vainly dream
That in triumph they can wage
  War against the King supreme?
Christ, His Son, a scoff they make,
  And the rulers plotting say:
Their dominion let us break,
  Let us cast their yoke away.

But the Lord will scorn them all;
  Calm He sits enthroned on high;
Soon His wrath will on them fall,
  Sore displeased He will reply:
Yet according to My will
  I have set My King to reign,
And on Zion's holy hill
  My Anointed I maintain.

The day is dawning when Christ will cast down into utter ruin the kingdom of Satan and upon its ruins will establish His own eternal kingdom. Then the song will be heard: "The kingdoms of this world are become the kingdoms of our Lord and of his Christ, and he shall reign for ever and ever" (Revelation 11:15).

A Demanding Truth

Because Christ is King over the whole of the universe, all men must be commanded to recognize Him as King and to observe all things whatsoever He has commanded (Matthew 28:20). And it is the glorious task of the church to confront men with that obligation.

It must be confessed that by and large the Christian church has been sadly negligent in the performance of that duty.

To be sure, the liberal social gospel does much talking about the kingship of Christ, but it denies so many cardinal truths of the Christian religion that it has forfeited every just claim to Christianity. One of its most fateful errors is the divorcing of the kingship of Christ from His cross. Scripture teaches that God gave to Christ a name above every name *because* He became obedient unto death, even the death of the cross (Philippians 2:8, 9). And it is a simple fact that no sinner will ever honor Christ as Lord who has not first found Him as Saviour. By its denial of the Scriptural doctrine of the atonement the social gospel of modernism has torn the kingdom of Christ from its foundation and thus transformed it into an air-castle.

Dispensationalism, on the other hand, puts a most laudable emphasis on the atonement but, sad to say, denies Christ's kingship over the world as a present reality. Therefore it takes no interest in the salvation of society. One of its exponents has said: "The world is on fire, but I have no interest in putting out the fire; my sole concern is to rescue individuals out of the fire."

It is the church's sacred duty to call upon men to acknowledge Christ as King, not merely in their individual lives, but also in their relationships with one another. And that is a way of saying that the church may never neglect the preaching of the social implications of the gospel. A few examples may serve as elucidation.

One of the most urgent social problems of our day concerns the mutual relationship of husbands and wives. Many a modern husband laughs out of court the notion of complete fidelity to one's wife, and many a modern wife sneers at the notion of obedience to one's husband. But Christ commands: "Wives, submit yourselves unto your own husbands as unto the Lord. For the husband is the head of the wife even as Christ is the head of the church . . . . Husbands, love your wives, even as Christ also loved the church and gave himself for it" (Ephesians 5:22-25).

One of the most disruptive influences in modern society is the maladjustment to each other of employers and employees. According to Scripture the solution of this problem lies in the recognition by both of the kingship of Christ.

Says the Word of God: "Servants, obey in all things your masters according to the flesh; not with eyeservice, as menpleasers; but in singleness of heart, fearing God. . . . For ye serve the Lord Christ. . . . Masters, give unto your servants that which is just and equal; knowing that ye also have a Master in heaven" (Colossians 3:22-4:1).

At no time in the history of our race have the rulers of the nations been burdened with such staggering problems and called upon to make such momentous decisions as today. "To be or not to be" is the question confronting civilization. The human race is tottering on the brink of destruction. There are many who interpret the principle of the separation of church and state to mean that the church must keep itself strictly aloof from such matters. But the truth of the matter is that it is the solemn duty, as well as the exalted privilege, of the church to instruct civil magistrates in the law of the Lord concerning their problems, fearlessly to denounce wickedness in high places as did the prophets of old, and to demand of the presidents and potentates of the earth that they bow humbly before Christ as King of kings and Lord of lords.

The gospel has many social implications, so many that to enumerate them all is well-nigh impossible. The church must insist that Christ is indeed head over *all* things, and it must demand of all men that they honor Christ as such in every domain of their lives.

Would that the church of Christ might become conscious of its God-given dignity, cease cowering before the mighty, and "ride upon the high places of the earth" (Isaiah 58:14)!

Chapter 32

BLESSED SACRAMENTS

Rome errs in teaching that the church bestows saving grace on men. Only God Himself does that. God, not the church, saves. But it is true that God has honored His church by committing to it the *means* by which He is wont to impart saving grace to men. One of these means is the Word of God. Through His Word God both gives faith to those who have it not and strengthens the faith of those who have it. The sacraments are another means of grace by which God strengthens the faith of His people.

THEIR NUMBER

In the old dispensation God instituted two sacraments, circumcision and the passover. In the new dispensation the Lord Jesus Christ substituted baptism for circumcision and holy communion for the passover. The important reason for this substitution was that, after the shedding of Christ's own blood on Calvary, bloodless sacraments had to take the place of bloody sacraments. In both of the Old Testament sacraments blood was shed; in neither of the New Testament sacraments is blood shed. Yet the meaning of the sacraments in the two dispensations is essentially the same, and their number is identical.

To the two New Testament sacraments the Roman Catholic Church has added five. They are penance, confirmation, ordination, marriage and extreme unction. Certain Protestant communions also speak of three sacraments rather than two because they interpret literally and as a perpetual ordinance the command of Christ: "If I, your Lord and Master, have washed your feet, ye also ought to wash one another's feet" (John 13:14).

Obviously, the number of a church's sacraments is determined by its definition of a sacrament. The looser the definition, the larger will be the number; the stricter the definition, the smaller will be the number. It follows that the church which recognizes but two sacraments takes a more restricted, and also a more exalted, view of the sacraments than does the church which recognizes a larger number.

Now it is a significant fact that the whole Christian church has always been unanimous in acknowledging holy baptism and the holy supper as sacraments. And these two sacraments, like those of the old dispensation, are divine ordinances signifying the saving grace of God. But that description does not fit any of the other so-called sacraments. Penance, confirmation and extreme unction have no warrant in Scripture and therefore do not qualify as divine ordinances. Also, it cannot be substantiated that the Lord Jesus meant to require that His disciples in every age literally wash one another's feet. And, while marriage and ordination are without doubt divine ordinances, they do not signify saving grace.

We conclude that there are but two sacraments — holy baptism and the holy supper. That conclusion dignifies the sacraments, and by that very token it dignifies also the church to which the sacraments are committed.

Their Meaning

Let it be understood that the sacraments add nothing to the Word of God. There is nothing contained in the sacraments which is not contained in the Word. When the church administers the sacraments it proclaims visibly the very same gospel which it proclaims audibly in its preaching. The preaching of the Word presents the gospel to ear-gate; the administration of the sacraments presents the same gospel to eye-gate. But this is not to intimate that the sacraments are lacking in dignity. On the contrary, it means that they share in the high dignity of the Word of God.

The sacraments are means of grace. That is to say, they are means through which God the Holy Spirit is wont to convey His grace to believers. It is important to maintain that they are not more than that, and it is just as important to maintain that they are not less than that.

Rome teaches that the sacraments are more than means of grace because they themselves contain the grace which they convey. Zwingli, one of the sixteenth-century Reformers, held that the sacraments are less than means of grace, being no more than vivid reminders of the saving work of Christ. This view has many adherents in the Protestant churches of our day. Thus Rome overrates the meaning of the sacraments, while Zwingli and his followers underrate their meaning. Both Lutherans and Calvinists, on the other hand, take the balanced position that it is God, not an ecclesiastical rite, which bestows saving grace, but that it pleases God to do this through the instrumentality of the ecclesiastical ordinances which He Himself has ordained to that end. That this position is Scriptural permits of no doubt. Times without number Scripture teaches that "salvation belongeth unto the Lord" (Psalm 3:8) and is a prerogative which God has reserved for Himself. And when Peter in his Pentecostal sermon exhorted his hearers: "Be baptized every one of you in the name of the Lord Jesus for the remission of sins" (Acts 2:38), he evidently conceived of baptism as more than a mere reminder of Christ's death for sinners. So did Ananias of Damascus when he said to Saul: "Arise and be baptized and wash away thy sins" (Acts 22:16).

The sacraments have been described as signs and seals of the covenant of grace. That is a way of saying that they signify and seal to those within the covenant the benefits of Christ's redemption. Not only do they *signify* salvation, as seals they are attached to the divine promise of salvation to *authenticate* it, much as the rainbow was made a seal of the divine promise to Noah of the continuity of nature. Nor is that all. As seals they actually *convey* the grace which they signify much as a key conveys admission, a deed an estate, or the ceremony of marriage the rights of marriage.

THEIR EFFICACY

Precisely when and how do the sacraments convey the grace of God? On that matter there are serious differences of opinion. Without going into intricate details it may be said that the differences concern three questions especially.

The first question is whether or not the efficacy of the sacraments depends on the good intention of the person who administers them. Rome answers that question in the affirmative, but the position which it thus takes is a most vulnerable one. It is in line with the characteristic Roman design to make the people dependent on the priesthood. And who will say that the efficacy of the Word depends on the good intention of the preacher? Surely, God can use unto salvation the true gospel proclaimed by an unconverted man. Then let no one presume to lay down the law for God, forbidding Him to impart grace through a sacrament administered by a false minister of Christ.

A second question is whether the efficacy to confer grace resides in the sacraments themselves or in the Holy Spirit, who is wont to work through them. Rome asserts most emphatically that the sacraments contain the grace which they convey and that consequently they convey grace automatically. Lutheranism does not go all the way in rejecting that position. However, the Reformed faith insists that the sacraments have no intrinsic efficacy whatever but are made efficacious solely by the Holy Spirit, who uses them sovereignly to do His will. This view is in harmony with the unmistakable teaching of Scripture that salvation from beginning to end is a divine prerogative.

A third question is whether or not faith is necessary on the part of the recipient of the sacraments in order to be benefited by them. At this point again Rome and Calvinism are at odds with each other, while Lutheranism takes a mediating position. Rome teaches that the sacraments automatically bestow grace upon the recipient, whether or not he believes. Only when he offers active opposition does he fail to be benefited. Lutherans say that grace is objectively communicated to the recipient, whether or not he has faith, but that grace is subjectively appropriated only by him who receives it in faith. It is said by way of comparison that, although wood will not burn unless it is dry, yet the dryness of the wood does not give power to the fire burning under it. Again it is argued analogically that, although the woman with an issue of blood would not have been healed if she had not believingly touched the Lord, yet the healing power residing in Him was real, whether or not she believed. The Reformed view is simply that only those who believe receive grace through the sacraments. The plain fact that in the apostolic church faith was an indispensable prerequisite of baptism corroborates that view (e.g., Acts 2:41, 16:31). And so does the apostolic warning that those who partake of the Lord's supper in an unworthy manner eat and drink judgment to themselves (I Corinthians 11:29).

THEIR SANCTITY

The word *sacraments,* although not found in Scripture, accurately describes the ordinances under consideration. And that word designates them as *holy things.* Hence Christians generally speak of *holy* baptism and *holy* communion. It is a matter of supreme importance that the church, to which the Lord has committed the sacraments, keep them *holy.*

Therefore the sacraments may be celebrated only by the church. A group of people not organized as a church, even though they be Christians, has no right to celebrate the sacraments. Like the Word, they must be administered by an ordained minister. Nor may he administer them except in a gathering of God's people. If in an exceptional instance it is deemed proper to administer a sacrament to someone who cannot come to the church, the church must go to him. That occurs when, for instance, a pastor, accompanied by one or more elders of the church, administers the Lord's supper to a bedridden believer.

The church may never baptize an adult who does not give credible evidence of believing in the Lord Jesus Christ. Nor may the church administer the rite of baptism to any children other than those of professed Christians. In the days of the "half-way covenant" it was customary in New England to baptize the children of such parents as had themselves been baptized in their youth but had not subsequently received Christ in faith. That became a potent factor in the decadence of the church. And yet the same custom prevails in many churches today. Worse than that, there are ministers who willingly baptize any child for which baptism is requested, quite regardless of the religious beliefs or the ecclesiastical connection of the parents. Small wonder that in many communions baptism has degenerated into mere christening.

Likely the great majority of churches today practice what they proudly call open communion. By that is meant that all who happen to be in the audience on communion Sunday and regard themselves as Christians are cordially invited to partake of the sacrament. Whether or not a given stranger actually is a believer, the officers of the church make no attempt to discover. They gladly leave that matter to his own judgment. It is not at all difficult to imagine what the outcome of such procedure is going to be. Especially in these days, when there is almost hopeless confusion within the church as to what it means to be a Christian; when there is the sharpest possible division among the leaders in the church as to who Jesus is, whether a mere man, however good and noble, or the Son of God in the unique sense that He Himself is very God; when the Scriptural interpretation of Christ's death is often decried, even by self-styled Christian theologians, as "theology of the shambles"; and when the term *faith* is used so extremely loosely in religious circles that it is often emptied of all religious content — this course of action can only prove disastrous to the sanctity of the sacrament of holy communion.

The sacraments are holy. The great Head of the church has committed these holy ordinances to His holy church. There exists the most intimate connection between the holiness of the sacraments and the holiness of the church. To keep the sacraments holy is at once a God-assigned duty of the church and its God-given privilege. The church which neglects that duty and scorns that privilege cannot long continue holy. It tramples its own glory in the dust.

Chapter 33

HOLY CHILDREN

One of the consequences of the preaching of the gospel by the apostle Paul in the heathen city of Corinth was that in a number of families either the husband or the wife became a Christian while his or her spouse remained a pagan. That gave rise to the question whether in such instances the believer should continue to live in matrimony with the unbeliever. The apostle taught that ordinarily this should be done. But significantly there was no question in the church at Corinth as to the ecclesiastical status of the children of such a marriage. It was understood by all that the position of such children with reference to the church was the same as that of children both of whose parents were believers. Paul asserted that they were *holy* (I Corinthians 7:14).

Without an attempt at an exhaustive exegesis of the term *holy* in this context, it may be asserted that the children of believers are members of the holy catholic church. All of them are members of the visible church. Many of them are members also of the invisible church. Those who die in infancy are translated into the church triumphant.

By this threefold relationship of the children of believers to the church the glory of the Christian church is greatly enhanced.

Covenant Children and the Visible Church

The very least that the apostle can have meant when he described the children of believers as holy was that they are members of the visible church. To quote Meyer's commentary: "Christians' children are *not* profane, outside the theocratic community and the divine covenant and belonging to the unholy world, but, on the contrary, *holy*."

The church consists of those with whom God has established the covenant of grace, and Scripture is most insistent that this number includes not only believers, but also their children. To Abraham, the father of the faithful, God said: "I will establish my covenant between me and thee and thy seed after thee in their generations for an everlasting covenant, to be a God unto thee and to thy seed after thee" (Genesis 17:7). And the apostle Peter had in mind the same covenant of grace when in his Pentecostal sermon he pleaded with "the house of Israel": "Repent and be baptized every one of you in the name of Jesus Christ for the remission of sins, for the promise is unto you and to your children" (Acts 2:36-39).

Because the children of believers are in the covenant of grace and the church consists of those who are in the covenant, therefore these children must be received by baptism into the membership of the church. Nothing could be more logical. And so it is not surprising that the greater part by far of the Christian church from the days of the apostles to the present time has practiced infant baptism.

Exceedingly sad to say, many churches which baptize infants have long since divorced this practice from the covenant of grace. The consequences are deplorable. Rome teaches that children should by all means be baptized because, if they should die without the benefit of this sacrament, they would be assigned to a special area reserved for unbaptized children, where they do not suffer pain, to be sure, but miss the joy of seeing God. Numerous Protestant churches have on this score departed as far from the truth as has Rome. Infant baptism having become shrouded in superstition, many Protestant parents have a vague notion that in some magical way this sacrament guarantees the salvation of their little ones if they should happen to die in infancy, or at least improves their chances of being saved. Often infant baptism is regarded as a mere dedicatory rite. It is thought that in this ceremony the parents dedicate their children to God — and so they do, but the promises and obligations of the covenant of grace are forgotten. And comparatively few Protestant churches today take the membership of baptized children seriously.

That is one reason, and a potent one, why so few churches today have any hold on the children of the covenant. Many Protestant churches put their children in the same category with the children of unbelievers and pagans. If the church does not count them as members, how can they be expected to think of themselves as church members? Having no sense of belonging to the church, they drift away. And if the church regards them as heathen, small wonder if they behave like heathen.

By the grace of God there are exceptions to this rule. A few churches still take seriously the doctrine of the covenant as it relates to the children of believers, baptize these children because they are in the covenant, and actually count them as members of the church. Those churches insist, and rightly so, on their being *full* members. To be sure, they are not rated as communicant members, for the sacrament of holy communion is only for such as, having come to years of discretion, can discern the Lord's body (I Corinthians 11:29). Nevertheless they are full members, just as a child born of American parents is by that very token from the moment of its birth a full American citizen. Therefore the children are listed on the church rolls, their names appear in the church directory, they are instructed by the pastor of the church in catechism classes, they sit with their parents in the Sunday services, and, in case they err, they are admonished, not only by their parents but, in grave instances, also by the church. Such churches usually flourish because they are built not only from without, but as well from within.

COVENANT CHILDREN AND THE INVISIBLE CHURCH

All whose names appear on the church rolls are members of the visible church. But only those who by the grace of the Holy Spirit have been born again are members of the invisible church. And the reason why this aspect of the church is called invisible is that men cannot tell infallibly who are regenerated and who are not.

That not all children of believing parents are saved goes without saying. Esau and Jacob were twin sons of believing Isaac, but only Jacob was saved. By no stretch of the imagination can one come to the conclusion that all of David's sons were saved. It follows that not all children of believers are born again, for every regenerated person is sure to be saved. God, who has begun a good work in him, is certain to perform it until the day of Jesus Christ (Philippians 1:6).

The fact that not all children of believers are saved does not alter the truth that all of them are in the covenant of grace. Scripture speaks of the unbelieving children of believers as covenant-breakers (e.g., Jeremiah 31:32). They could hardly break the covenant if they were not in any sense in the covenant. Theologians correctly depict the covenant of grace by two concentric circles. The smaller one represents the covenant as a vital relationship, and only the regenerate are within it. The larger one represents the covenant as a legal relationship, and all children of believers are in it. The covenant in the latter sense can be broken, and not infrequently is.

Although not all the children of believers are regenerated, yet it is the plain teaching of Scripture that a great many of them are. Some are born again as mere babes, others as adolescents, still others as adults. Just when it may please the sovereign God to bestow the grace of regeneration upon a given child of the covenant we have no way of telling. But this we know: in the imparting of saving grace to sinners God, although not bound by family relationships, yet takes them into account. He is, and manifests Himself to be, the God of believers and their children. That truth lies at the very heart of the Scriptural doctrine of the covenant of grace. The conclusion is warranted that it may be assumed that covenant children by and large are or will be regenerated.

Scripture tells us of at least two children who experienced the spiritual birth even before their natural birth. Paradoxical though it may sound, they were born again before they were born. Said God to Jeremiah: "Before I formed thee in the belly I knew thee; and before thou camest forth out of the womb I sanctified thee" (Jeremiah 1:5). And the angel Gabriel, when announcing the birth of John the Baptist to his father Zacharias, said: "He shall be filled with the Holy Ghost even from his mother's womb" (Luke 1:15). There is no compelling reason to think that these two instances were exceptional.

It can easily be shown from Scripture that many covenant children are regenerated in babyhood. Our Lord's statement to Nicodemus: "Verily, verily, I say unto thee, Except a man be born again, he cannot see the kingdom of God" (John 3:3), was a sweeping one permitting no exceptions. Infants are no exceptions either. They were shapen in iniquity and in sin did their mothers conceive them (Psalm 51:5). Without regeneration no infant can go to heaven. But it can be shown from Scripture that those covenant children who die in infancy do go to heaven. And obviously their number is considerable. Nor is there any reason to suppose that the regenerating grace of the Holy Spirit is confined to those covenant infants the span of whose earthly life is destined to be brief. The conclusion is inescapable that a great many covenant children are born again as babes.

To base a doctrine on experience is dangerous, to say the least. All of Christian doctrine must be based squarely on the Word of God. But experience often corroborates the teaching of Holy Writ. That is true also in this instance. Countless children of the covenant as they grow up cannot recall any period in their lives when they did not fear and love the Lord. It is not unusual for covenant children to have a definite recollection of fearing and loving God at the early age of four or five.

Thus we come to the happy conclusion that in numerous instances the little lambs in Christ's flock have received new hearts. That makes them members of the invisible church.

COVENANT CHILDREN AND THE CHURCH TRIUMPHANT

Indisputably, all those within the covenant who are born again are certain, on their departure from this life, to go to heaven. It is impossible that any one should pluck them out of the hand of the good Shepherd (John 10:28). Whether they depart at the age of ninety days or ninety years, in either case they go to join the church triumphant.

At this point, however, a most important question arises. If a covenant child dies in infancy, is there any way of ascertaining whether it was born again? In other words, can believing parents be certain of the salvation of those of their children who are taken from them in infancy? It is not difficult to see that this question is one of supreme concern to all Christian parents.

A child of the covenant has died. The hearts of the parents are bleeding and bid fair to break. Their pastor seeks to console them. What shall he say?

Shall he tell the mourning parents that undoubtedly their child has gone to glory because all who die in infancy, even the children of unbelievers, are saved? That is the teaching of several Protestant churches and also of such eminent Reformed theologians as Charles Hodge, Benjamin B. Warfield and R. A. Webb. But to substantiate that position conclusively with Holy Scripture is difficult.

Shall the pastor inform the parents that their child is saved if it was numbered among God's elect? But that is a truism which holds of every deceased person. And since there is no *a priori* way of proving that any given person is elected to eternal life, that statement contains no comfort whatever for the mourning parents.

Shall the pastor assure the parents that their child is now in heaven if prior to its decease it was born again? But that saying will only cause the parents to search for evidences of regeneration in their child's behavior. And that search is almost sure to end in uncertain and deceptive subjectivism. Many a child that was thought by its parents to give proof of exceptional piety in its earliest years has grown up in unbelief.

Shall the pastor then say, not merely that the deceased child is saved *if* it was elect and regenerate, but that likely it was elect and regenerate since the covenant God in the salvation of sinners is wont to take family relationships into account? That truth might well impart a measure of comfort to the parents, but it would still leave their hearts aching, because it would render the salvation of their child only a likelihood, not a certainty.

The truth of the matter is that the pastor can and must go farther. He should base his efforts to console the bereaved parents on the objective promises of the covenant of grace. He should tell them that because of those promises "godly parents ought not to doubt the election and salvation of their children whom it pleases God to call out of this life in their infancy" (Canons of Dort, Head of Doctrine I, Article 17).

This child was a child of the covenant. God promised to be its God. It had the divine promise of eternal life. That promise is contained in God's Word and was confirmed by Him in the sacrament of holy baptism. Had the child grown up, it would have had to embrace that promise in personal, active faith. As it is, it could neither accept nor reject that promise. Therefore the promise stands. The faithful covenant God has kept and fulfilled it. He did as a matter of indubitable fact wash this His child of its sins by the blood and the Spirit of Christ. Forgiven and regenerated, it passed through the gate into the city of God. Even while the parents are bidding its wasted body a last heartbreaking farewell, the angels of God are welcoming its pure spirit. While the parents are convulsed with inward pain, the good Shepherd lifts this little lamb in His arms, holds it in His fond embrace and carries it in His bosom. While the parents would fain have their little one return to them, the Saviour whispers: "Suffer this little child to come to me and forbid it not, for of it is the kingdom of God." And lovingly He lays His hand upon its head and blesses it (Mark 10:14-16). While the parents sigh and sob, their child vies with Gabriel as it sings to the accompaniment of harps of gold the praises of its Redeemer.

Then the souls of these mourners are quieted even as a weaned child (Psalm 131:2). They say: "Jehovah gave and Jehovah hath taken away; blessed be the name of Jehovah" (Job 1:21, ASV). Like David, they rest in the assurance that, although their child will not return to them, they will go to it (II Samuel 12:23).

Chapter 34

TEACHER OF COVENANT YOUTH

The primary function of the Christian church is to teach the Word of God. The fact that preaching is its most important task in no way alters the truth just stated, for preaching is first of all teaching. But the church should teach not only from its pulpits. Its teaching function should extend beyond preaching.

That the church in the discharge of this task is to give foremost attention to its covenant children is self-evident. Nothing could be more reasonable.

A NECESSARY TASK

Scripture puts tremendous emphasis on the religious education of covenant children. For but one example, Moses commanded the people of Israel: "These words which I command thee this day shall be in thine heart: and thou shalt teach them diligently unto thy children, and shalt talk of them when thou sittest in thine house, and when thou walkest by the way, and when thou liest down, and when thou risest up. And thou shalt bind them for a sign upon thine hand, and they shall be as frontlets between thine eyes. And thou shalt write them upon the posts of thy house and on thy gates" (Deuteronomy 6:6-9). In cumulative fashion Moses drove home to God's covenant people the solemn duty to teach their children the Word of God.

The truth that God is wont to impart saving grace from generation to generation is one of the most important aspects of the doctrine of the covenant of grace. However, it must be remembered that the continuation of the covenant is not automatic. Let no one think that children receive saving grace from their Christian parents as they inherit certain physical peculiarities and traits of character from them. Horace Bushnell's famous classic *Christian Nurture,* however valid, in part at least, its criticism of the revivalism of that day and however laudable its insistence on Christian training for the children of believers, is vitiated by that error. It must also be remembered that the continuation of the covenant is not without exception. Not every child of believing parents becomes a believer. Sad to say, more than a few of them grow up to be covenant-breakers. "They are not all Israel which are of Israel" (Romans 9:6). And again it must be remembered that the continuation of the covenant is not independent of the means of grace. To be sure, God is abundantly able to impart the grace of regeneration to a child long before it can understand Holy Scripture; and beyond all doubt He often does this. But there is no reason whatever to suppose that He will impart the new life to a child that is destined to reach maturity, if the Word is not going to be present in order to sustain and nurture that life. The Scriptural dictum, "Faith cometh by hearing, and hearing by the Word of God" (Romans 10:17), applies to children of the covenant as well as to others.

If the continuation of the covenant were automatic, without exception and independent of the means of grace, covenant children would without religious education grow up as Christians. As it is, their religious education is not only desirable but essential. It is the God-provided and God-commanded means for the continuation of the covenant of grace.

That makes the church's neglect of this task unpardonable. And yet how few churches apply themselves to it! Some years ago the writer was a speaker at a large young people's conference of a comparatively conservative denomination. He soon discovered that their ignorance of Bible doctrine was abysmal, their knowledge practically nil. To his inquiry, addressed to a minister of that denomination, whether he and his colleagues were wont to give any doctrinal instruction to the youth of the church, came the answer: "We used to."

Surpassing strange to say, a number of churches which strongly stress Christian missions sadly neglect the religious training of their own children. They ought to do this and not to leave the other undone. A noted missionary once rebuked an American congregation in these words: "You are doing less for the religious education of your own children than you are doing for the religious education of Moslem children in Arabia."

William G. T. Shedd was completely right when he said in his *Homiletics and Pastoral Theology*: "In the whole range of topics in Pastoral Theology there is not one that has stronger claims upon the attention of the clergyman than the doctrinal instruction of the rising generation" (p. 407) and "The last words we should desire to address to a young clergyman, as he is going forth to his lifelong labor, would be an exhortation to make full proof of that part of his ministry to which belongs the indoctrination of the rising generation in the truths and principles of the Christian religion" (p. 429).

A Comprehensive Task

The Roman Catholic Church, a number of Lutheran churches and some other denominations think it their duty to teach the children of the church, not only God's special revelation in the Bible, but also His general revelation in nature and history. Therefore they conduct parochial schools which give instruction in reading, writing, arithmetic and all the usual day school subjects. Although Christian day schools are essential to a consistent and thoroughgoing system of Christian education for children of the covenant, such schools are the responsibility of their parents rather than the church. According to Scripture the business of the church is to teach men the Word of God. Beyond that it should ordinarily not go.

It does not follow that the church's task of teaching the children of the covenant is not a comprehensive one. Although it does not embrace the entire field of human knowledge, it is comprehensive indeed.

How often one hears it said that Christianity is not a doctrine, but a life! If that were so, all that the church would have to teach its youth would be how to lead the Christian life. But the truth is that Christianity is a doctrine as well as a life, and that prior to both of these it is a story. The church must teach its children Christianity in all three of these aspects.

In our day many historical portions of the Bible are not merely called into question but emphatically denied. That is done not only by unbelievers outside the church, but often by leaders within the church. Liberals, for instance, are wont to deny those historical accounts in which the supernatural looms large, as the creation of the universe, the virgin birth of Jesus and His bodily resurrection. And the "new orthodoxy" assigns many Bible stories to the limbo of what it calls the supra-historical. For example, it says that the story of the fall of man related in the third chapter of Genesis is not an account of what a certain man by the name of Adam did many centuries ago in a certain garden called Eden, but rather a "myth" depicting an experience that comes to every human being. Such neo-orthodox theologians as Rudolf Bultmann and Reinhold Niebuhr deem it their duty to "demythologize" the historical portions of Scripture, and Paul Tillich regards a great many of them as mere "symbols." But God's infallible Word stands or falls with Bible history. And so does Christianity. Did not the apostle Paul affirm: "If Christ be not risen, then is our preaching vain, and your faith is also vain" (I Corinthians 15:14) ?

To say that Christianity is not a doctrine is ridiculous. The Bible answers a veritable host of stupendously important doctrinal questions. To name but a few: Who is God? Where did man get his religious nature? Has

man an immortal soul? What is sin? Who is Jesus?
Must the sinner save himself or must he be saved by God?
To deny that Christianity stands or falls with the Scrip-
tural answers to such questions is the height of folly.

That Christianity is a way of living is self-evident. And
yet not all professed teachers of Christianity are agreed
on the question what the Christian life is. Many deny
that the ten commandments are an objective and abiding
standard of goodness. And, strange to say, there are
avowed conservatives within the church who would add
the precepts of men to the perfect law of God contained
in His Word.

 How necessary that the church teach its youth Christianity as a story, as a doctrine and as a life! And that
certainly is no small task.   *Story, doctrine, and a life.*

A Fruitful Task

Few if any tasks performed by the church are wont to
bear such rich fruitage as the instruction of its covenant
youth. That is accounted for by at least two reasons, a
natural one and a supernatural. The natural reason is
that this instruction concerns human beings at their most
impressionable age. It is so much easier to bend a young
tree than an old one, and as a young tree is bent so it will
continue to grow. The supernatural reason is that the
faithful covenant God is sure to bless richly the church
which diligently performs its covenant obligation with
reference to the children of the covenant.

Following are a few of the blessings with which God
will crown this work of His church.

It will insure the future of the church. Without it a
church may well pass out of existence. As a matter of
fact, many a church is suffering from pernicious anemia
and withering away for lack of the lifeblood of the rising
generation. Because they are not instructed in the teachings of Christianity, the young people have no interest in
those teachings and drift away from the church. But

the church which zealously instructs its children in the Christian religion has a guaranteed future.⌡

It will result in numerous conversions. It must not be thought that children of the covenant have no need of conversion. Even those who are regenerated in baby-hood need to be converted as they grow up. On coming to years of discretion they must experience a conviction of sin and in active faith commit themselves to Jesus Christ for salvation. At the same time they must resolve by the grace of God to fight against the devil, the world and the flesh, and in all their behavior to honor Christ as King. Proper instruction given them by the church normally results in just that. And it must be added that such conversions are usually genuine. There is little danger that in the case of covenant children persistently taught by the church for several years, the seed of the Word will, for want of depth of earth, sprout quickly and wither away just as quickly. (Compare Matthew 13:5, 6, 20, 21.)

It will tend to keep the church in the truth. One big reason why so many churches have wandered far from the truth of the Christian religion is that their members were not instructed in that truth and consequently could not distinguish between truth and falsehood. On the other hand, the membership of that church which faith-fully teaches its youth is both forewarned and forearmed against the countless heresies of the day.

It will produce intelligent and appreciative hearers of the Word. In how few churches are the members capable of digesting the strong meat of the Word! Most church members have no desire for anything but milk, preferably diluted with considerable water. The reason is that they are still babes when they ought to be teachers (Hebrews 5:12). And for this sad state of affairs the church itself is to blame. It failed to feed them properly when they were young. It is hardly an exaggeration to say that the church permitted them to grow up as spiritual imbeciles.

It will result in a church which has no dearth of men

capable of exercising the functions of its exalted offices. Many a church flounders along under the leadership, or lack of leadership, of incompetent elders. A great many churches are suffering from a shortage of pastors and missionaries. Diligent instruction of the children of the church will go a long way toward producing an adequate supply of laborers for the Lord's vineyard.

It will yield a generation of healthy Christians. Today many church members are in very poor health. Some churches closely resemble hospitals. One significant cause is the failure of religious knowledge to keep pace with religious experience. That results in such diseases as mysticism and fanaticism, both of which are rampant in the church. The most active church members often display a zeal not according to knowledge (Romans 10:2). Knowledge of Holy Scripture is the cure. It is also the preventative.

Small wonder if churches which neglect the teaching of their children are living, if at all, at a poor dying rate.

Thank God for the few churches which faithfully instruct their covenant youth in the Word of God! Their future is bright. Jehovah, the covenant God, will command His blessing there.

Chapter 35

TEACHER OF ADULT BELIEVERS

The church's duty to instruct its covenant youth is rather generally granted but often neglected. That it is the church's duty to teach also its communicant members seems to be completely forgotten by many a church. The inevitable outcome is that the membership of a great many churches is sadly ignorant of the Word of God. That is indeed a big black blot on their record. A membership that knows its Bible is essential to the glory of the Christian church.

WHY THEY MUST BE TAUGHT

The Word of God insists very strongly on the instruction of believers. By the mouth of the prophet Hosea God complained: "My people are destroyed for lack of knowledge," and He declared: "Because thou hast rejected knowledge, I will also reject thee" (Hosea 4:6). He went on to say: "I desired mercy, and not sacrifice; and the knowledge of God more than burnt offerings" (Hosea 6:6). The epistles of Paul, addressed as they were to believers, were both instructive and exhortative, but primarily instructive. That is to say, their practical portions were invariably based upon and rooted in apostolic doctrine. In his letters to Timothy the apostle stressed nothing more strongly than the necessity of teaching. He charged his son in the faith: "The things which thou hast heard from me among many witnesses, the same commit thou to faithful men who shall be able to teach others also" (II Timothy 2:2); and he berated teachers of false doctrine in no uncertain terms when he said: "If any man teacheth a different doctrine, and consenteth not to sound

words, even the words of our Lord Jesus Christ, and to
the doctrine which is according to godliness; he is puffed
up, knowing nothing" (I Timothy 6:3, 4, ASV).

One reason why so few churches attend to the teaching
of their communicant members is an obsession with the
outworn notion that Christianity is not a doctrine, but
a life.   Proceeding on that assumption, numerous present-
day ministers preach practically no doctrine but are content to tell their audiences to be good and do good.   They
assure their hearers that it makes little or no difference
what they believe or disbelieve so long as they lead good
lives.   They forget that Jesus said: "Ye shall know the
truth, and the truth shall make you free" (John 8:32).
The sad consequence is that a great many church members
lack the most elementary knowledge of the way of salvation.   Not only are they ignorant of the doctrine of salvation by grace, but they regard it a matter wholly of
course that man is to be saved by his own efforts.

A second reason why so many churches neglect teaching their communicant members is a faulty conception of
salvation.   Salvation is regarded merely as a momentary
experience and not as a continuous process.   Once a person has received Christ in faith, he is thought to have arrived.   The fact is overlooked that the same Bible which
teaches the eternal security of believers also informs us
that the best Christian is still an exceedingly poor one.
The truth is neglected that sanctification, which is an essential element of salvation, is a tedious process that
continues until the believer's last breath.   The utterly
unwarranted notion is prevalent that when Paul had finished writing Romans 7, in which he complained: "O
wretched man that I am! who shall deliver me from the
body of this death?" (Romans 7:24) and launched into
Romans 8, in which he gloried: "There is therefore
now no condemnation to them that are in Christ Jesus,
for the law of the Spirit of life in Christ Jesus made me
free from the law of sin and of death" (Romans 8:1, 2,
ASV), he "came forever out of Romans 7."   So sharp

a line of demarcation is drawn between sinners and
saints that it is forgotten that the best saint is still a
great sinner. But the Word of God puts tremendous emphasis on the believer's need of sanctification, and it
teaches that sanctification is effected by the truth. Did
not Peter exhort the believers in the dispersion: "As new-
born babes, desire the sincere milk of the word, that ye
may grow thereby" (I Peter 2:2)? And he commanded:
"Grow in grace and in the knowledge of our Lord and
Saviour Jesus Christ" (II Peter 3:18).

A third reason why the instruction of the church's communicant members is so largely neglected lies in a one-
sided conception of the church's task. Often the church's
duty to preach the gospel of salvation to the unsaved is
stressed at the expense of its duty to proclaim the whole
counsel of God to the saved. The obvious truth is overlooked that the church as "mother of believers" not only
has a duty with reference to their birth, but must also
supply them with nourishment after their birth. Forgotten is the apostolic teaching: "He gave some to be
apostles; and some, prophets; and some, evangelists; and
some, pastors and teachers; for the perfecting of the
saints, unto the work of ministering, unto the building up
of the body of Christ: till we all attain unto the unity of
the faith, and of the knowledge of the Son of God, unto a
fullgrown man, unto the measure of the stature of the
fullness of Christ" (Ephesians 4:11-13, ASV).

How They Must Be Taught

Of such importance is the instruction of its communicant members by the church that it must be done in season
and out of season. A few specific ways in which it must
by all means be done may be named.

Preaching should primarily be teaching. The preaching
of Jesus was teaching. Occasionally we are told in the
Gospels that Jesus preached; scores of times it is said that
He taught. No one who has read the Pauline epistles but

casually will care to deny that the great apostle's preaching likewise was teaching. Yet how few preachers today teach the Word of God! The great Augustine said that preaching should be directed to the intellect, the will and the emotions, all three; and he named the intellect first. Much of modern preaching is addressed to the will and the emotions, little to the intellect.

Every pastor should conduct an adult Bible class. Whether it meets on Sundays or on a week-day evening is a matter of minor concern. To combine it with the mid-week prayer meeting may in certain instances prove advisable, but in no case should less than an hour a week be devoted in this class to the study of the Word of God.

If one should say that the minister in his pastoral calls must teach the Word of God to the members of his flock, many would, no doubt, brand that statement an absurdity. The notion is prevalent that in this phase of his work the minister should speak of subjective religious experience rather than declare the objective Word, and that he should seek to console and admonish rather than to teach. But in reality all religious experience must be tested by Scripture, and only he who has knowledge of Holy Writ can receive its consolation and admonition. To be more specific, those in distress must be taught the meaning and purpose of suffering according to the Word of God, and those who stray must be taught from the selfsame Word what is the error of their way, what is godly sorrow which works repentance to salvation (II Corinthians 7:10), and what is the way in which God would have them walk.

Churches should make much more use than they ordinarily do of the printed page for the instruction of their members. In some respects the printed page is an even more effective means of teaching than is the spoken word. For instance, one can read it over and over and even memorize it. Alongside the Bible there ought to be in every family within the church an easily understood Bible commentary and also a summary — a catechism, if you will — of Christian doctrine. And all church members should be urged to study the Word of God daily, and with-al to make the use of those aids a habit.

WHAT THEY MUST BE TAUGHT

That a church should teach its members the Word of God ought to go altogether without saying. Yet that simple fact needs to be stressed today. Many churches substitute a religion of experience for God's inscripturated revelation and more than a few proclaim the opinions of the great, or supposedly great, thinkers of the past and the present rather than the eternal Word of God.

In teaching their members many churches seem to be guided by the question how little knowledge will suffice rather than the question how much knowledge they can impart. A great many church members, too, use "blon-dinizing" tactics. As a certain acrobat by the name of Blondin crossed above Niagara Falls on a tight rope when he might have used a bridge, so they would pass through the gate into the eternal city with as little knowledge as may be, rather than as much as they can possibly acquire. But Paul rebuked the believers at Corinth for their sad spiritual state which made it necessary for him to feed them with milk, not with meat (I Corinthians 3:2). And the author of Hebrews administered the stinging rebuke to his readers: "When by reason of the time ye ought to be teachers, ye have need again that some one teach you the rudiments of the first principles of the oracles of God; and are become such as have need of milk, and not of solid food" (Hebrews 5:12, ASV). The communicant members of a church should be able to profit by a sermon on divine foreordination and by a discourse which sets forth the Scriptural teaching of the atonement over against the numerous current corruptions of that doctrine.

The adult members of a church must be taught "all the counsel of God" (Acts 20:27). This means that they must be taught, not merely the various truths of Scripture in isolation from one another, but the truth of the

Word of God as a system. It means further that they must learn to accept such teachings of Scripture as are paradoxical; that is, such as seem to finite and faulty human reason to contradict each other. For instance, they must recognize both the full Biblical teaching of divine election and the full Biblical teaching of the universal and sincere divine offer of salvation. And to teach men the whole counsel of God also involves giving to different truths the same relative emphasis that they receive in God's Word. Such instruction will prove an effective safeguard against the fanatical riding of hobbies and will make for the rare virtue of theological balance.

It is a matter of the greatest concern that church members be warned against the prevalent errors of the day. If that is not done, many will certainly be swept away by the onrushing tide of modern heresies. Therefore, the truth should be presented to them by way of contrast with such heresies. That will serve not merely to forewarn and forearm them, but also to definitize their conception of the truth, for truth stands out most distinctly when contrasted with falsehood.

It is no less important that the church, in instructing its communicant membership, apply the teachings of Scripture to the peculiar conditions and pressing problems of the day. At this point modernism has substituted a false social gospel for the gospel of the Word of God, and most conservative churches have fallen far short of preaching the whole Word of God. When is war permissible or even required? What is the Scriptural solution of the race problem? Is capitalism Christian, and is communism anti-Christian? Does Scripture condemn the totalitarian state? Those are a few samples of the timely questions which the church must answer from the Word of God.

And all the time the church must keep warning its members against dead orthodoxism. Ever and anon it must tell them that the truth is not merely to be believed and confessed, but also to be done. Even the demons believe that God is one (James 2:19), but it takes a Christian to love and obey that one God. Both the Head and the body of the church are glorified when its members, in addition to talking about the truth, walk in it.

Chapter 36

CONVEYOR OF COMFORT

The supreme task of the Christian church is to bring to men the Word of God. That Word is profitable for instruction, correction and a great many other things. It also contains an inexhaustible wealth of comfort. The glorious task of conveying that comfort to troubled souls belongs to the church.

By virtue of the universal office of believers all church members should engage in the conveying of comfort. More particularly must the church dispense comfort through its special offices. Ministers, elders and deacons alike have a duty here. Most of all should the pastor comfort the disconsolate. To him especially apply the words of the prophet: "The Spirit of the Lord God is upon me; because the Lord hath anointed me to preach good tidings unto the meek; he hath sent me to bind up the broken-hearted, to proclaim liberty to the captives, and the opening of the prison to them that are bound" (Isaiah 61:1). As shepherd of the flock he must imitate the divine Shepherd, of whom it is written: "He shall feed his flock like a shepherd: he shall gather the lambs with his arm, and carry them in his bosom, and shall gently lead those that are with young" (Isaiah 40:11).

So rich is the comfort which the church is honored to convey to troubled souls that only a few samples can be cited.

COMFORT FOR SOULS TROUBLED BY SIN

Indisputably, the church must condemn unqualifiedly every form of sin. Often, too, it must rebuke sinners. Occasionally it is even called upon to excommunicate offenders. But it may never forget that the Word of God abounds in comfort for troubled sinners.

All sinners alike may be told, and must be, that, if they repent from the heart and flee to Christ crucified for washing in the crimson flood, God will remove their transgressions from them as far as the east is from the west (Psalm 103:12) and will cast all their sins into the depths of the sea (Micah 7:19). Even that is not the sum total of the message of forgiveness. The precious truths may not be neglected that God has no pleasure in the death of the wicked, but that the wicked turn from his way and live (Ezekiel 18:23), and that He is not willing that any should perish but that all should come to repentance (II Peter 3:9). The church must bring to sinners the glad tidings that God will not only abundantly pardon them *if* they repent, but also, to quote again from the comment of that prince of expounders of Holy Scripture, John Calvin, on Ezekiel 18:23 — "that God wills not the death of a sinner, but He meets him of His own accord, and is not only prepared to receive all who fly to His pity, but He calls them towards Him with a loud voice."

There are throughout the world many sinners whose consciences accuse them of having offended Deity and who now seek reconciliation by self-torture. Hindu mothers cast their babes into the waters of the Ganges. Simeon the Stylite resigned himself for the last thirty years of his earthly life to the most miserable kind of existence on a pillar in an oriental desert, where by turns he was burned by the torrid sun, soaked with rain or drenching dew, and stiffened by crackling frost. And of Martin Luther it is said that, with his bare knees on the stone floor of his cell and his back lashed with straps until the blood streamed down, he pleaded with God for mercy. But that was before the full light of the gospel of the grace of God had dawned upon him. The very heart of the gospel which the church must bring to troubled sinners is that the suffering Christ has made atonement for sin, that He was wounded for sinners' transgressions, was bruised for their iniquities, that the chastisement of their peace was upon Him, that with His stripes they are healed (Isaiah 53:5), and that consequently salvation is free.

Occasionally one encounters a serious soul who fears that he has offended the Most High too heinously and too long to be pardoned. Such need to be reminded of King David, who became guilty of the double crime of adultery and murder, but, after manifesting a broken heart and a contrite spirit, sang: "Blessed is he whose transgression is forgiven, whose sin is covered" (Psalm 32:1) ; of King Manasseh, who made the streets of Jerusalem run red with the blood of Jehovah's faithful servants and may have had the body of the prophet Isaiah sawed in two, and yet found pardon when he humbled himself greatly before the God of his fathers (II Chronicles 33:1-13) ; of Saul of Tarsus, who gladly cared for the clothes of those casting the first stones on the evangelist Stephen, consented unto his death, and himself breathed out threatenings and slaughter against the disciples of Jesus (Acts 7:58, 8:1, 9:1), but after his conversion wrote: "This is a faithful saying and worthy of all acceptation, that Christ Jesus came into the world to save sinners; of whom I am chief" (I Timothy 1:15). They must be told of the gracious promise: "Though your sins be as scarlet, they shall be as white as snow; though they be red like crimson, they shall be as wool" (Isaiah 1:18).

Of all sinners perhaps those indulging in sins of appetite must be dealt with most firmly. Mealy-mouthed advice never rescued a drunkard nor wrested from the toils of lust. To that type of sin Jesus had reference when He said: "If thy right eye offend thee, pluck it out and cast it from thee . . . . And if thy right hand offend thee, cut it off and cast it from thee: for it is profitable for thee that one of thy members should perish, and not that thy whole body should be cast into hell" (Matthew 5:29, 30). Surely, that prescription excels in severity. But, strange though it may seem, it excels no less in kindliness. For drastic measures alone are effective against sins of appetite, and summary treatment, however painful for the moment, is the one alternative to eternal gnawing of tongues and gnashing of teeth. Far from being cruel, this command of the Lord Jesus is a beautiful revelation of His matchless love for those sinners who are rated as most despicable by their fellows and whose plight seems most hopeless. These wretches must be assured that, if they will obey this command in utter dependence on the grace of God, which alone can break the shackles of sin, the Son of God will set them free indeed (John 8:36).

More than a few sincere children of God are oppressed by fear that they may have committed that sin against the Holy Spirit which Scripture tells us is unpardonable. They need to be taught from the Word of God just what that sin is. And what they need to be told above all else is that it consists in a complete hardening of heart so that for him who commits it repentance is out of the question. It follows that he who is deeply concerned about this matter and cries from the depths to God for mercy, by that very token may be certain that the grace of God has kept him from committing the unpardonable sin.

COMFORT FOR SOULS TROUBLED BY AFFLICTION

All misery and misfortune, all sickness and sorrow, all distress and disappointment, all adversity and affliction, yea and death itself, is the consequence of sin. Because of sin "man is born unto trouble as the sparks fly upward" (Job 5:7). This earth, habitat of sinful man, is rapidly being transformed into one vast cemetery. But in the midst of that burial ground stands the church of the living God, and sings:

Come, ye disconsolate, where'er ye languish,
  Come to the mercy-seat, fervently kneel:
Here bring your wounded hearts, here tell your anguish;
  Earth has no sorrows that heaven cannot heal.

While the Word of God abounds in comfort for suffering saints, it is not without a message of hope for the unsaved in the day of trouble. They may be told that, just as bodily pain is often a blessing in disguise, since it serves as a warning of present ailment and perhaps impending death, so the afflictions of the wicked may well be evidence of divine forbearance pleading with them to turn from their evil way lest they die.

No matter what may be the mediate cause of their trouble, God's children know that whatever ill betides them is controlled by the providence of a loving God and that therefore in every trial their prayer is granted: "Let me fall now into the hand of the Lord" (I Chronicles 21:13). When Job was deprived of all his possessions and servants and children by Sabeans and Chaldeans, by lightning and hurricane, or tornado, he exclaimed: "The Lord gave, and the Lord hath taken away; blessed be the name of the Lord" (Job 1:21).

A verse of Scripture which almost every Christian can repeat from memory and which throughout the centuries afflicted saints have found a source of unspeakable peace and joy is Romans 8:28 — "And we know that all things work together for good to them that love God, to them who are called according to his purpose." This is no wishful thinking. God's children know because God has spoken. Every once in a while they strikingly experience this blessed truth, as did Jacob of old when in the slough of despond he sobbed: "All these things are against me" (Genesis 42:36), but presently found himself walking in the sunshine of bliss. And even when not a ray of light seems to penetrate the encircling gloom, yet their eye of faith is not dimmed. To them tribulation resembles a chunk of hard coal which is itself black as pitch, but, when brought out into God's sunshine, sparkles like a diamond.

In his afflictions the believer finds evidence of his divine sonship. He knows that, if he were without chastisement, he would be a bastard, not a son. As it is, God is dealing with him as a son; for what son is he whom the father does not chasten? Whom the Lord loves He chastens, and He scourges every son whom He receives (Hebrews 12: 6-8). It follows that what he suffers is not punishment but chastisement. His Saviour endured the wrath of God due to him; he is experiencing the love of God. Christ atoned for his guilt; the heavenly Father is making him partaker of His holiness.

By life's trials and tribulations the child of God is both sanctified and glorified. Like gold he is refined in the fire of affliction. Like a precious stone he is cut in order that he may shine the more brilliantly. Not only is it true that "the sufferings of this present time are not worthy to be compared with the glory that shall be revealed," but he suffers with Christ to the very end that he may be glorified with Him (Romans 8:17, 18). By his afflictions he is made meet to be a partaker of the inheritance of the saints in light (Colossians 1:12). For that he gives thanks to the Father even now and will praise Him eternally.

When the angel of death enters a Christian home and flaps his wings over a child of God, there is mourning in that home, for believers are not less human, but rather more truly and fully so, than others. Yet they do not mourn as others who have no hope (I Thessalonians 4:13). Contrariwise, their grief is assuaged, and even sweetened, by the assurance that another pilgrim has completed his desert journey and reached the land of Immanuel. But what if the deceased gave no evidence of being a child of God? Then more poignant pain cannot be imagined. Yet even for hearts broken by that experience there is healing balm in Gilead. When the Saviour was about to return to heaven He promised His church "another Comforter," the Holy Spirit. And that Comforter, He said, would abide with His disciples forever, dwelling with them and even in them (John 14:16, 17). Here is the supreme comfort of the Christian, comfort that fully suffices even when he must empty the cup of woe to its bitterest dregs. It is the sense of the abiding presence of God with him and in him. When his flesh and his heart fail, he can yet glory: "God is the strength of my heart and my portion forever" (Psalm 73:26).

A saint is about to encounter the last enemy, death, and is sore afraid. A servant of God stands at his bedside, an open Bible in his hand. He reads: "Fear not; I am the first and the last: I am he that liveth and was dead; and, behold, I am alive for evermore, Amen. And I have the keys of hell and of death" (Revelation 1:17, 18). A smile of heavenly peace steals over that pallid face and it whispers: "O death, where is thy sting?" (I Corinthians 15:55) Now, like Fearful in Bunyan's famous allegory, he passes through the river "not much above wetshod." Another moment, and a sinner saved by grace has entered through the gate into the city that has no night, where God Himself wipes away all tears from the eyes of His children (Revelation 21:4), where no one complains of being sick, where sorrow and sighing shall be no more, and where the street of gold is not darkened by funeral processions — because there is no sin.

Chapter 37

ECCLESIASTICAL EVANGELISM

Today the organized church cannot be said to be highly respected. The world regards it at best as a mildly beneficent, but certainly not overly useful, institution. Even some Christians are wont to belittle it.

The fact that it is being belittled makes it the more necessary for the organized church to uphold its God-given dignity and to guard the prerogatives with which God has endowed it. Of those prerogatives none is more glorious than that of evangelizing the world. The organized church must insist on its being the God-appointed agency for evangelism.

A Divine Assignment

Nothing can be clearer than that God in His Word has designated the organized church as the agency *par excellence* for evangelism.

When Christ issued the missionary command to His disciples, He regarded them as the nucleus of His church, as representatives of the church of coming centuries to the end of the ages. About that there can be no doubt whatever. Christ was fully aware that those few men could not possibly carry the gospel "unto the uttermost part of the earth" (Acts 1:8). It would take the church more than a millennium to accomplish that. He knew full well that the apostles in their own persons would not be able to "make disciples of all the nations" (Matthew 28:19, ASV). They could only begin so colossal a task; the church of the future would be God's instrument for its completion. For that reason Christ added to the great commission the long-range promise: "And, lo, I am with you alway, even unto the end of the world" (Matthew 28:20).

Here reference must once more be made to that event which constitutes the most important turning point by far in the history of Christ's church and is most meaningful for its glory: the outpouring of the Holy Spirit as related in the second chapter of The Acts of the Apostles.

Pentecost spells evangelism.   At Pentecost the Holy Spirit came upon the disciples and they received power to be Christ's witnesses in Jerusalem and all Judea and Samaria and unto the uttermost part of the earth (Acts 1:8).   Cloven tongues as of fire sat on the heads of the disciples, and "they were all filled with the Holy Ghost and began to speak with other tongues as the Spirit gave them utterance" (Acts 2:3, 4).   There were present both Jews and proselytes "out of every nation under heaven." Each of them heard the gospel "in his own language" (Acts 2:5-11).   Literally thousands of them were converted and received by baptism into the Christian church (Acts 2:41).

Pentecost has often been said to be the birthday of the Christian church.   While that statement is incorrect because already the believers of the old dispensation were members of the body of Christ, yet Pentecost certainly marks the founding of the church in its New Testament aspect.   It constitutes the transition from a national church to a universal.   That of necessity affected the outward form of the church.   The church had been bound up closely with the Israelitish nation; now it acquired an organization all its own.

Putting together the truths that Pentecost marks the founding of the church in its New Testament form and that Pentecost spells evangelism, we come unavoidably to the conclusion that on that day the Holy Spirit empowered the organized church for the accomplishment of its God-given task of world-wide evangelism.

No less significant is the account, in Acts 13, of the calling and sending forth of Paul and Barnabas as missionaries to the gentile world. It was the Holy Spirit who called them, but He called them through "the church that was at Antioch" (vs. 1). "The Holy Ghost said, Separate me Barnabas and Saul for the task whereunto I have called them" (vs. 2). Likewise, they were "sent forth by the Holy Ghost" (vs. 4), but again He sent them forth through the instrumentality of the church, for it is said: "When they had fasted and prayed and laid their hands on them, they sent them away" (vs. 3).

The words of Peter: "But ye are a chosen generation, a royal priesthood, a holy nation, a peculiar people; that ye should show forth the praises of him who hath called you out of darkness into his marvelous light" (I Peter 2:9), may well be described as an exhortation to evangelism. It is evident that the apostle regarded those to whom he addressed this exhortation not as so many individuals, but as a compact group, a "generation," a "priesthood," a "nation," a "people"; not as so many separate stones, but as "a spiritual house" (vs. 5). Beyond doubt he had in mind the church. The church must show forth the praises of God, its Saviour.

To the Scriptural evidence that has been adduced much could be added, but enough has been presented to prove conclusively that the church is the God-ordained agency for evangelism. God has assigned the task of evangelism specifically to the organized church. While evangelism may not be, and is not, the one and only reason why God has established the organized church on earth, evangelism certainly is a most significant reason for its existence. Whoever else may properly engage in evangelism, the organized church is the supreme Scriptural agency for evangelism.

SUBORDINATE AGENTS

That every Christian is in sacred duty bound to witness for Christ and, in so doing, to bring the gospel to his fellow men permits of no doubt. Besides being taught explicitly in many passages of Holy Writ, this duty is implicit in the universal prophethood of believers. It is just as clear that the individual Christian has a perfect right to engage in such activity without in every instance first securing the consent of the organized church. He does not need the approval of the officers of the church of which he is a member for the distribution of tracts or for telling Bible stories to the children of his unchurched neighbors. And yet it may not be forgotten that in this sort of work he is subordinate to the organized church. If, for instance, he should spread tracts containing consequential doctrinal error, the session of his church might well correct him. In fact, in case he should refuse to give heed, it would become the session's duty to discipline him.

Our age is one of depreciation of the organized church. That accounts for it that more and more voluntary associations are coming into being which aim to take over the functions of the organized church, in particular the function of evangelism. Numerous mission societies and boards exist, independent of church control. For an outstanding example, although the world-renowned evangelist Graham seeks the co-operation of churches in his campaigns and advises his "converts" to unite with churches, he does not operate, strictly speaking, under ecclesiastical auspices and control. The question arises to what extent that must be considered an evil. In recent years this problem has commanded the attention of some very able theologians. Although not one of them claims to have said the last word on the subject, the following observations appear to be in order.

If the individual Christian may, and even must, engage in evangelism, it is difficult to see why a number of individuals may not band together for such work. Practically all churches grant that this is permissible within certain limits. Obviously it does not lie within the province of a voluntary association of Christians to ordain evangelists, but an association of this kind certainly may engage, for but one example, in the translation, publication and distribution of Bibles. It should be remembered, however, that the members of such an association remain subject to the discipline of the churches to which they belong. Therefore, if, for example, the association should put out mistranslations of the Bible, the churches concerned might well hold such individuals co-responsible for that evil.

It is not unusual today for boards independent of ecclesiastical control to take over practically the whole missionary task of the church. Often they go so far as to send out ordained men as missionaries and in some instances they actually do the ordaining. In a word, evangelism by a voluntary association is substituted for evangelism by the organized church. Under normal conditions that surely must be regarded as a departure from Scriptural practice. However, whether conditions within a church may not become so abnormal as to justify even that practice is another matter. In comparatively recent times there have been at least two instances in which churchmen with a great zeal for strictly Biblical missions deemed it their duty to take so radical a step because of the prevalence of modernism in ecclesiastically controlled missions. That occurred in the Established Church of Holland before the reformation of 1886 and in the Presbyterian Church in the U. S. A. prior to the reformation of 1936. The former of these instances had the approval of so famous a churchman as Abraham Kuyper. Many readers will know that the latter reference is to the founding of the Independent Board for Presbyterian Foreign Missions by J. Gresham Machen and his associates. However, it is important to note that in both these cases the orthodox leaders concerned, before resorting to such extreme measures, did their utmost to reform ecclesiastical missions, and that the soundest among them desisted from such measures as soon as a new orthodox ecclesiastical organization had been brought into being. Thus they declared that their action was justifiable only as an exception, and they honored the Scriptural principle that the organized church is the supreme agency for evangelism.

Evangelism by the organized church is a *must*. Evangelism by a voluntary association is, within certain limits, a *may*. It hardly needs to be argued that what must be done should be given precedence over what may be done. If that rule is violated, there is grave danger that the latter will crowd out the former.

Numerous other reasons can be adduced why evangelistic activity should ordinarily be supervised and directed by the organized church. Following are a few. Thus the efforts put forth by individual believers and voluntary associations of Christians will be integrated with the work of the church, and the danger of overlapping and confusion will be lessened. Thus every believer by virtue of his being a church member will automatically have at least some part in evangelism, and it will not be left to a few who have a special liking for it. Thus by and large the likelihood that evangelism will be marred by doctrinal error will be reduced, for, no matter how great the inroads of unbelief upon the church both in the past and at present — in some cases so great as to transform erstwhile true churches into false ones — it remains true that the Spirit of truth has been given to the church and that this Spirit will continue to the very end of time to lead the church into the truth. And, last but by no means least, thus the subjects of evangelism will upon their conversion be led most directly into church membership.

A GLORIOUS PREROGATIVE

The evangelization of the world is a prerogative of the church. And that prerogative is a most glorious one. A brief statement of the ends of evangelism will bring this out.

Through evangelism precious souls are translated from darkness to light and from the power of Satan into the kingdom of God's dear Son. That is glorious indeed, but it is not the ultimate end of evangelism; rather it is a means to a higher end. Through the salvation of souls evangelism contributes to the growth and completion of the church, which is the body of Christ. That, too, excels in glory, but again it is but an approximate end of evangelism and a means to a still more comprehensive end. Through the expansion of Christ's church evangelism advances the recognition of Christ's kingship over every domain of human life — science and art, education and recreation, labor and industry, economics and politics included. That again is exceedingly glorious, but once more, instead of representing the final end of evangelism, it promotes its highest end. And that is the glory of God.

By entrusting to His church the task of evangelism God has bestowed upon it the high honor of being His chosen vessel for the accomplishment of all those glorious ends, and in particular of that end for which He has created the universe, upholds all things, does all that He does, has elected an innumerable multitude out of the lost race of men, has redeemed them and keeps them by His power unto "an inheritance incorruptible and undefiled and that fadeth not away" (I Peter 1:4) — His own glory.

Most certainly, all that the church does, and can do, when it brings the gospel to lost men is to plant and to water. For results it is completely dependent on God, who alone can give the increase. But even thus the church is God's co-laborer. Under God, to be sure, yet also together with God, it labors for the highest of all ends, the glory of the Most High.

Chapter 38

EDUCATIONAL EVANGELISM

It is rather generally supposed that the church, when bringing the gospel to those without the fold, must first move them to faith in Christ by an appeal to their wills and emotions, and, having succeeded in doing that and thereupon having received them into membership of the church, must subsequently instruct them. Those who hold that view may well be reminded that the most eloquent gospel appeal will not produce saving faith except the Holy Spirit apply it efficaciously to human hearts. And they must also be told that teaching constitutes a most important element of the message which the church is required to bring to the unsaved. In a word, the church's evangelism must not merely be followed up by instruction, but must itself be instructive. God demands of His church *educational* evangelism.

AN EXPRESS SCRIPTURAL DEMAND

The concluding verses of the gospel according to Matthew are known as the great commission. Although this is by no means the only missionary command of the Lord Jesus recorded in the New Testament, yet "the great commission" is not at all a misnomer for this passage, for it is clearly the most comprehensive of them all. In the Authorized or King James Version it reads: "All power is given unto me in heaven and in earth. Go ye therefore, and teach all nations, baptizing them in the name of the Father, and of the Son, and of the Holy Ghost: teaching them to observe all things whatsoever I have commanded you: and, lo, I am with you alway, even unto the end of the world."

A noteworthy feature of the great commission is that it bids the apostles and the church of all ages to *teach*. In fact, *teaching* is spoken of as their chief missionary task. They are to *go* in order to *teach*. *Going* is but a means to the end of *teaching*. And they are to *baptize* those who accept their *teaching*. But they must *teach*, whether or not men give heed. And, significantly, they are told not once, but twice, to *teach*. First Christ says: *"Teach* all nations"; in the next breath He adds: *"Teaching* them to observe all things whatsoever I have commanded you." To be sure, different Greek words are used in these two instances. The first means *to make learners, pupils, disciples;* the second means *to instruct*. But the word *teach* is a possible translation of both.

There are those who say that Jesus here enjoins His followers first to make men His disciples and as such to baptize them, and *afterwards* to teach men to observe His commands. However, if He had meant that, He would have expressed Himself differently. Likely He would have said: *"And* teach them to observe all things whatsoever I have commanded you." As it is, the ethical teaching here spoken of is not co-ordinate with, but subordinate to, making disciples of men. And that can only mean that Jesus thought of this ethical teaching as preparing men for discipleship. In his commentary on Matthew, F. W. Grosheide points out that the main verb in the great commission is the imperative *make disciples* and that Jesus here teaches that the nations are to be made disciples through baptizing and teaching.

As might be expected, the apostles and their helpers obeyed the great commission. Consequently the very first thing they did in their missionary labors was invariably to teach men the gospel. To name a few of many instances, Peter's Pentecostal sermon was not only strongly exhortative, but first of all highly instructive. By far the greater part of it, so far as recorded, was pure instruction (Acts 2:14-40). Before Philip the evangelist baptized the Ethiopian eunuch, he taught him about Jesus, with

Isaiah 53 as his text (Acts 8:26-40). According to Acts 16:31 Paul and Silas told the Philippian jailer: "Believe on the Lord Jesus Christ, and thou shalt be saved, and thy house," and according to verse 33 the apostle baptized him and his family. But between these two verses the statement is wedged in: "And they spake unto him the word of the Lord, and to all that were in his house" (Acts 16:32).

The fact that in the aforenamed instances converts were not instructed over an extended period hardly justifies a generalization as to how long or short a time prospective converts must be instructed prior to their baptism. Likely those assembled for the feast of Pentecost had considerable knowledge of the true religion, and we simply do not know how much knowledge the eunuch and the jailer may have possessed before Christ was preached to them. But we do know that in his encounter with the eunuch the evangelist Philip was led in a most remarkable way by the Holy Spirit and that Paul and his fellow apostles were supernaturally qualified to discern the hearts of men (John 20:22, 23). That gift and such guidance were peculiar to the church of the apostolic age.

How clear that Scripture expressly lays down as the first duty of the Christian church with reference to the unsaved that it teach them the Word of God!

A MOST REASONABLE DEMAND

While indubitably every demand made by God is a reasonable one, the reasonableness of a Scriptural demand is not in every instance self-evident. However, the reasonableness of the demand under discussion is perfectly apparent. What those who are outside the fold must do is to believe on the Lord Jesus Christ. Now knowledge is a prerequisite of saving faith, faith without knowledge being inconceivable. And knowledge is imparted by teaching. For that simple and conclusive reason the church must *teach* the unsaved.

Somehow the strange notion has entered certain religious circles that knowledge is an impediment rather than an aid to discipleship. It is held widely that faith and knowledge are antithetical one to the other. There are those who think that the less knowledge one has, the easier it will be for him to believe. Thus a premium is put on ignorance. A certain preacher is said to have boasted of having been to Calvary and not to seminary. It seemed not to have occurred to him that there is no good reason why a prospective minister should not go to both places, nor that by and large the minister who has been to seminary as well as to Calvary is likely to be an abler servant of the Lord than he who has been to Calvary only. Such outstanding leaders in the church as Moses, Paul, Augustine and Calvin, to name but a few, were all of them highly educated men. Throughout his book *What Is Faith* J. Gresham Machen drives home the point that, other things being equal, the more knowledge one has of Scripture, the simpler and stronger one's faith is going to be.

Those who disparage religious knowledge usually conceive of faith as a leap in the dark. They like a certain illustration. It concerns a house with a windowless basement. The entrance to this basement was a trap door. One day the father of the family was working in the basement, and the trap door stood open. Around it his little daughter was playing. He could see her in the light, but she could not see him in the dark. He called to her: "Jump through the open door, and daddy will catch you." Instantly she obeyed and in the next moment was caught in her father's strong embrace. That story is meant to illustrate the proposition that faith is a leap in the dark, but in reality it beautifully illustrates the exact opposite. Literally the little girl made a leap in the dark, but in a most real sense she did nothing of the kind. She recognized her father's voice. She knew that her father loved her. She was positive that her father was reliable. She knew a great deal about her father, and it was precisely because of this knowledge that she trusted him. The truth is that she made a leap in the light. So is saving faith a leap in the light, for it is rooted in knowledge of the Lord Jesus Christ.

Not only does faith presuppose knowledge, knowledge is also an essential element of saving faith. According to the Heidelberg Catechism, true faith is first of all, although by no means exclusively, "a sure knowledge whereby I hold for truth all that God has revealed to us in His Word" (Lord's Day VII, Question 21).

In *The Christ of the Indian Road* and other of his books Stanley Jones insists that missionaries must preach Christ, not Christianity. Under Christianity he subsumes much Christian doctrine. It is not unusual for evangelists to disparage the creeds. But the plain fact is that there is no such thing as preaching Christ without preaching the creeds of historic Christianity. He who would preach Christ must of necessity define the Christ whom he preaches. Is his Christ the God-given Christ of the Bible or the man-made Christ of modernism? Is his Christ God of God and therefore Himself very God, or is He divine only in the sense that a spark of divinity resided in Him as it is said to reside in all men, albeit it burned a bit more brightly in Him? Is He the resurrected and ever-living God-man at the right hand of God in the highest heaven, whence He will come to judge the quick and the dead, or is He the greatest religious teacher the world has ever known, whose bones are resting in a Judean sepulchre while His soul, like that of Confucius and Buddha and John Brown, goes marching on? These are questions of doctrine. The preaching of him who gives the wrong answers to them is incomparably worse than vain. The preaching of him who fails to answer them is sounding brass or a clanging cymbal.

And pray, what is the earthly use of asking a man whether he is saved unless he understands from what he needs to be saved and by whom alone he can be saved? And what boots it to ask a man whether he believes in Christ so long as he does not know who Christ is nor what it means to believe in Him? And what right has anyone to commit himself body and soul for time and eternity to Jesus unless he knows that Jesus is God? Thus to commit oneself to a mere man is idolatry. And how can one believe in Christ unto forgiveness of sins and life eternal without knowing that His death on the cross was not merely the death of a martyr, but a substitutionary sacrifice for the expiation of sin and the satisfaction of divine justice?

Surely, the simplest and plainest logic requires that the church *teach* the Word of God to those without the fold. Nothing could be more reasonable than this demand of Holy Writ.

A Particularly Timely Demand

From Wesley and Whitefield in the eighteenth century to Billy Sunday and the Gipsy Smiths of recent times, in much evangelistic preaching a strongly volitional and highly emotional appeal was wont to be made, with comparatively little emphasis on teaching. Although that was not as it should have been, it was not altogether as reprehensible as is the same type of evangelistic preaching today. Two centuries ago, and even as little as fifty years ago, the evangelist had a right to assume at least a modicum of religious knowledge on the part of his audiences in such countries as England and America. By and large his hearers were not totally ignorant of the gospel. But today the process of dechristianization has progressed to the point that even in so-called Christian lands the general public has little more knowledge of the way of salvation than do the heathen. It follows that the need for *educational* evangelism is especially great today. Billy Graham must be credited with apparently sensing something of that need. Although he hardly rates as a profound theologian, in fact does not claim to be one, he puts forth a concerted effort to inform his audiences what "the Bible says."

Beyond dispute, the ignorance of the American public, church members included, concerning Holy Scripture is nothing short of appalling. Whether or not it actually happened that a Sunday-school teacher told her pupils that Dan and Beersheba in Bible history were the names of a man and his wife, "just like Sodom and Gomorrah," it is true that a recent poll brought to light the sad fact that few persons can name the four Gospels. And undeniably, a majority of church members have not the remotest idea what it means to be saved by grace and take it completely for granted that the one and only way to be saved is by doing "one's best." If such ignorance prevails within the fold, what must be the plight of those without?

For another reason, too, the Scriptural demand that the church *teach* the unsaved is particularly timely. However ignorant men may be of the Christian religion, it cannot be denied that secular education, although lacking in thoroughness, is much more widespread than it was only a few decades ago. Therefore the general level of intelligence has risen. And that is true not only in these United States, but in other lands as well. It applies even to a number of pagan countries. In consequence many have lost much of whatever respect they may have had for predominantly emotional preaching. They rather demand that the evangelist show them the reasonableness of the Christian religion. In other words, they insist that the preacher of Christianity, if he would command their respect, instruct them. And who can deny them the right to that insistence? It must be granted especially by him who holds that much in Christian teaching transcends human reason, for it is eminently reasonable to assume that the self-revelation of the infinite God transcends the comprehension of finite man.

Few factors have contributed so much to the present flabbiness of most churches as their failure to instruct prospective members and their willingness to enroll as members such as are almost totally ignorant of the Word of God. What the church needs is a solid program of educational evangelism and a firm determination to receive into membership only those who make a creditable confession of the basic truths of Christianity. That would not only stem the tide of decadence which is now rolling over the church, it would also greatly enhance the glory of the Christian church.

Chapter 39

ANTITHETICAL TO THE WORLD

The term *world* does not always have the same meaning. It can properly be used in a considerable variety of senses. In distinction from the Christian church it is "the ungodly multitude, the mass of men alienated from God and therefore hostile to the cause of Christ." The term *antithesis* denotes "a strong contrast, the direct contrary."

It hardly needs to be argued that, the stronger the contrast of the church and the world, the greater is the glory of the church. White never seems quite so white as when it is seen against a black background. So the holiness and beauty of the church of Christ stand out most strikingly when contrasted with the filthiness and depravity of the world.

An Actual Antithesis

The charge is often laid at the door of the church that it closely resembles the world. All too frequently it does. Always there is some worldliness in the church, ofttimes much. Then the church must needs be rebuked for the sin of being conformed to the world and be reminded of the antithesis as a duty.

However, the antithesis may not be thought of merely as a duty which at times is observed, albeit imperfectly, by the church and at other times is largely neglected by it. The antithesis is also an actual fact. So long as the church has existed the antithesis has been a reality, and so long as the church will exist in this wicked world the antithesis will continue as a reality. The world will never be permitted to absorb the church, and the church, though always marred by worldliness, will never become identified with the world. To be the opposite of the world is not only necessary for the well-being of the church but is essential to its very being. If the church should cease being antithetical to the world, it would no longer be the church. That can happen, and every once in a while does happen, to a portion of the church, but it will never happen to the Christian church as such.

The reason is that God Himself has fashioned the church as the opposite of the world and that, according to His own promise, He will preserve His church. God, who made the church radically different from the world, will most certainly keep it so.

As was previously observed, the history of the church goes back all the way to the garden of Eden. No sooner had man sinned than God promised him a Saviour. Presumably Adam and Eve believed that promise. If so, they became the first members of the body of Christ. Significantly, at the very moment when God founded the church He also brought the antithesis into being. Said He to the tempter: "I will put enmity between thee and the woman, and between thy seed and her seed; it shall bruise thy head, and thou shalt bruise his heel" (Genesis 3:15). The seed of the tempter is the world; the seed of the woman is the church. It must be noted that God did not command them to be at enmity with each other and then leave it to them to obey or disobey as they might please. No, God Himself put enmity between them, and there it was. By a divine fiat the antithesis was established. And its continuation throughout the centuries is guaranteed by the unalterable will of God.

The apostle Paul told the believers at Ephesus: "Ye were sometimes darkness, but now are ye light in the Lord" (Ephesians 5:8). When they were of the world they were darkness; now that they have become members of Christ's church, they are light. One is the direct contrary of the other. Again it must be noted that the apostle did not command the Ephesians to stop being darkness and to become light in the Lord. That would have

made no sense for the simple and conclusive reason that
by the grace of God they had already as a matter of fact
been transformed from darkness into light. To be sure,
believers do not always manifest in their lives that they
are light in the Lord. Therefore the exhortation is in
order: "Walk as children of light." But that command
does not detract so much as an iota from the fact of their
being children of light. The truth of the matter is that
the command is predicated on that fact.

The conclusion is irrefutable that the antithesis of the
church and the world is actual. Now that has a direct
bearing on the glory of the church. Its being the opposite
of the world is not merely something to be desired without
necessarily being realized. Nor is its being the opposite
of the world a duty that may or may not be performed.
The antithesis is reality, actuality. The church is as a
matter of indisputable fact the opposite of the unholy
world. And that is a way of saying that it is supremely
holy.

An Absolute Antithesis

The persons who constitute the world are "dead in trespasses and sins" (Ephesians 2:1), whereas those who constitute the church, having been born again, are spiritually
alive. Because of that fact the contrast of the church and
the world is obviously not relative but absolute. For men
are either dead or alive; they cannot be both. Life and
death are mutually exclusive.

This is not to claim that the Christian is sinless. On
the contrary, the very best Christian is far from the goal
of perfection. The apostle Paul, great saint that he was,
readily granted that he had not apprehended the prize of
the high calling of God in Christ Jesus (Philippians 3:13,
14). And James, the brother of the Lord, said: "In many
things we offend all" (James 3:2). There is point to the
story of the minister who met a fellow minister on the
street, inquired of him where he was going, and, when
told that he was hurrying on to perfection, replied: "If

that is the case, I won't detain you, for I realize that you have a long way to go." Nevertheless, the new life which God the Holy Spirit has implanted in the Christian's soul dominates him. He is "dead unto sin" and "alive unto God" (Romans 6:11). And when he commits sin he does that which he would not and even hates. Therefore he dares to assert: "It is no more I that do it, but sin that dwelleth in me" (Romans 7:15, 17). In short, his sinning differs radically from that of the unregenerate.

Nor is this to say that the man of the world is less than human. In Shakespeare's *Merchant of Venice* Shylock contends that Jews are people, too. He argues: "Hath not a Jew eyes? hath not a Jew hands, organs, dimensions, senses, affections, passions? fed with the same food, hurt with the same weapons, subject to the same diseases, healed by the same means, warmed and cooled by the same winter and summer, as a Christian is? If you prick us, do we not bleed? If you tickle us, do we not laugh?" Certainly in that sense unbelievers, too, are people. In fact they are human in a more exalted sense. In them are remnants of the image of God in which man was originally created. They still possess rationality and morality. However, even the morality of natural, unregenerate man is, to quote the Canons of Dort, only "some knowledge of the difference between good and evil" and "some regard for virtue and good outward behavior" which "he is incapable of using aright even in things natural and civil" and "in various ways renders wholly polluted and hinders in unrighteousness" (Heads of Doctrine III and IV, Article 4). In the Christian, on the other hand, the image of God has in principle been restored to its pristine glory of true knowledge of God, true righteousness and true holiness. And that means that the difference between the image of God in the Christian and that image in the non-Christian is not merely quantitative, so that the former has more of it than the latter, but the difference is qualitative.

It has sometimes been contended that the gifts of the

common grace of God render the antithesis of the believer and the unbeliever, and consequently of the church and the world, less than absolute. It can hardly be denied that both are recipients of certain manifestations of divine benevolence. "He maketh his sun to rise on the evil and on the good, and sendeth rain on the just and on the unjust" (Matthew 5:45). Scripture even tells us that, certainly not by virtue of their innate goodness, which is non-existent, but by virtue of the common grace of God, unregenerate men can do good of a kind. Said Jesus: "If ye do good to them which do good to you, what thank have ye? for sinners also do even the same" (Luke 6:33).

However, it may be questioned seriously whether God is motivated — if one may speak of God as being motivated — by the same benevolence when He grants certain blessings to the unjust as when He grants the identical blessings to the just. He is indeed good, even loving, to the unjust, but only the just does He love as His children, adopted for Christ's sake. No doubt, He ever beholds them in Christ, also when bestowing upon them the blessings of nature. It must also be remembered that only the regenerate can do spiritual good; that is, good prompted by love for God, and that in all the good that the unregenerate do there is not manifest so much as a speck of that love. It must likewise be borne in mind that the use which the regenerate make of the gifts of common grace and the use of them by the unregenerate differ radically. In principle the Christian does his eating and drinking, as well as all other things, to the glory of God, whereas the man of the world does precisely nothing to God's glory. And never may the truth be forgotten that saving grace, which only Christians possess, differs so completely in kind from common grace that all the blessings of common grace that God has ever poured out upon mankind, together with those that remain to be poured out to the end of time, do not add up to so much as one grain of saving grace.

True, the complete separation of believers and unbe-

lievers will not take place until the consummation of that
process which we call history. Therefore they can, and
for the present should, co-operate in several worthy activities, albeit they are differently motivated in so doing.
It is also true that the God of sovereign grace will to the
day of judgment keep substituting hearts of flesh for
hearts of stone and thus translating men from the kingdom of Satan to that of His dear Son. But the fact remains that even now the antithesis of the regenerate,
who are spiritually alive, and the unregenerate, who are
spiritually dead, is absolute, not merely, as is sometimes
said, in principle, but in its very essence.

The absolute character of the antithesis of the church
and the world is undeniable. It is not true, as is often
supposed, that the church and the world run on the same
track for some distance and then diverge. They are divergent from beginning to end. And that, too, bears on
the glory of the church. So different is the church from
the world that the two are incomparable. That makes the
glory of the church transcendent.

An Active Antithesis

An antithesis may be absolute without being active.
Who will deny that black and white are opposites? White
is seen when sunlight is reflected without absorption of
any of the visible rays of the spectrum. Black is the
absence of all spectral color. But they may exist alongside each other and be purely passive. It is not unusual
nowadays to trim an otherwise white house with black.
The effect is striking because of the complete contrast of
white and black, but the two exist side by side in perfect
peace. Neither troubles the other in the least.

But now let us suppose that the house just referred to
has caught fire and that water is poured on the fire. There
you have another antithesis, but it is extremely active.
Fire and water work at cross-purposes. The one would
destroy the house, the other would save it. They would

even destroy each other. The water strives to put out the
fire, and the fire aims to transform the water into vapor.

The antithesis of the church and the world is not passive
but decidedly active.

That the world is actively opposed to the church is
abundantly clear from history. No sooner had God put
enmity between the seed of the tempter and that of the
woman than that enmity flared up. Cain killed Abel because his brother's works were good and his own evil
(I John 3:12). In cruel hatred the pagan Egyptians persecuted God's people. When Israel had occupied Palestine, the neighboring heathen nations were almost incessantly at war with it. The hatred of the world for the
seed of the woman came to its fullest and most violent
expression when it crucified the Son of man. But let no
one think that this hatred burned itself out on that occasion. The followers of Christ have ever since experienced
the truth of His words: "The servant is not greater than
his lord: if they have persecuted me, they will also persecute you" (John 15:20); and "If ye were of the world,
the world would love his own: but because ye are not of
the world, but I have chosen you out of the world, therefore the world hateth you" (John 15:19).

The church, too, must actively oppose the world, and in
the measure in which it truly is the church, it does that.
To be sure, the people of God do not hate the men of the
world as these hate them. Christ's disciples love all men,
even their enemies. Therefore they labor zealously and
pray fervently for the salvation of all who are alienated
from God and hostile to the cause of Christ. At the very
time of their martyrdom at the hands of the world they
plead: "Lord, lay not this sin to their charge" (Acts 7:
60). But that is not the whole picture. It has another
aspect. By His death Christ both saved the world and
vanquished it. And the church of Christ witnesses boldly
against the sins of the world, with might and main op-
poses the works of darkness perpetrated by the world,

and, unbelievable though it may sound, even hates the wicked.

Here is a paradox indeed. That the Christian must at all times love all men is true beyond the shadow of a doubt, but it is not the entire truth. This writer likes to describe the antithesis thus: while the ungodly hate the godly, the godly love the ungodly. That description is both true and pointed, but it is not exhaustive. The statement, often made, that the Christian hates the sins of the ungodly but loves their persons is altogether true, but as a solution of the paradox it suffers from oversimplification. This paradox, like every Scriptural paradox, must be allowed to stand in all its inspired boldness.

God, who loves all men, Esau included, declared: "Esau have I hated" (Romans 9:13). God's children, too, both love and hate the ungodly. They love them as their fellow men, their neighbors. They hate them in the very specific capacity of *haters of God*. Therefore the Psalmist exclaimed: "Do not I hate them, O Lord, that hate thee, and am I not grieved with those that rise up against thee? I hate them with perfect hatred" (Psalm 139:21, 22). According to several able expositors, among them F. L. Godet, Jesus had that hate in mind when He said: "If any man come to me, and hate not his father and mother, and wife and children and brethren and sisters, yea, and his own life also, he cannot be my disciple" (Luke 14:26). Without any doubt, the apostle Paul gave emphatic expression to that hate when he wrote to the churches of Galatia: "If any man preach any other gospel unto you than that ye have received, let him be accursed" (Galatians 1:9). So do the spirits of just men made perfect as they cry with a loud voice from under the altar in heaven: "How long, O Lord, holy and true, dost thou not judge and avenge our blood on them that dwell on the earth?" (Revelation 6:9, 10) And so will the inhabitants of heaven in the song of triumph: "Alleluia; salvation and glory and honor and power unto the Lord our God: for true and righteous are his judgments: for he hath judged the great whore which did corrupt the earth with her fornication and hath avenged the blood of his servants at her hand" (Revelation 19:1-3).

The Christian loves God. For that reason he loves his fellow men, none excepted; for the same reason he cannot but hate God's enemies. So says Scripture.

As the actuality and the absoluteness of the antithesis of the church and the world reveal the glory of the church, so does the active character of the antithesis. If the church loved God less, the world would persecute it less violently and it would oppose the world less vigorously. The activity of the antithesis results directly and inevitably from the church's love for God and thus reflects the church's resplendent glory.

Chapter 40

A BLESSING TO THE WORLD

That the church of Jesus Christ is an inestimable blessing to humanity, including those who are hostile to God and to the cause of Christ, is beyond question.

To enumerate all the blessings that accrue to the world from the presence of the church in its midst would, no doubt, prove impossible. They are countless. However, a great many of them may be subsumed under two sayings of the Lord Jesus. Said He to His disciples: "Ye are the salt of the earth" and "Ye are the light of the world" (Matthew 5:13, 14).

The Salt of the Earth

A certain preacher announced as his text: "Ye are the salt of the earth." Having done that, he said in effect: "When salt gets into an open wound, it bites; so we Christians must go through life biting." It hardly needs to be said that he was engaging in eisegesis rather than exegesis. To be sure, the truth of God, which Christians must proclaim, often hurts; but Scripture tells us that we are to love all men and, if it be possible, as much as lies in us, to live peaceably with all men (Romans 12:18).

In what sense, then, are believers the salt of the earth? The answer lies at hand. From time immemorial salt has been used the world over to season food and to prevent putrefaction. In those respects the people of God resemble salt. If it were not for them, the holy God would long ago have spewed this insipid world out of His mouth and in fiery indignation have consigned this putrid world to destruction.

An Old Testament story illustrates that truth strikingly.

The Lord had come to annihilate Sodom because of the extreme wickedness of its populace. However, Abraham, with whom God had recently established His covenant of grace, offered an intercessory prayer for the doomed city. In so doing he was acting as a preservative. By way of answer God promised to spare the city if fifty righteous men should be found in its midst. In response to His friend's importunate pleading God reduced that number, first to forty-five, then to forty, then to thirty, then to twenty, and finally to ten. Said He: "I will not destroy the city for ten's sake." If there had been but ten righteous persons in Sodom, the whole city would have been spared because of them. The ten would have served as a seasoning and a preservative (Genesis 18:16-33).

Of the many ways in which the church operates as the salt of the earth, a few follow.

The very presence of the church in the world constitutes a blessing to the world. As the holy God looks down upon the ungodly race of men, His wrath is stirred. It might be expected that He would manifest Himself to humanity as an all-consuming fire. But here and there, nearly everywhere, among the wicked He beholds such as through faith in His only begotten Son have become His children. He regards them in infinite love. Scripture tells us that for their sake the days of tribulation to come will be shortened (Matthew 24:22). Likewise for their sake the time of divine forbearance is being prolonged and the day of the ultimate wreaking of divine vengeance is postponed.

A nation which once was Christian may continue for a time to partake of the fruits of Christianity. These United States are a case in point. Our American liberties are in some measure products of the Christianity of the founding fathers. Because we are fast forsaking their God, we are in process of losing the freedoms which they bequeathed to us. And yet, in comparison with many other nations we are still "the land of the free."

In many other ways the ungodly are benefited by their

believing fellows. For instance, the moral tone of a community containing many Christians and several Christian churches is almost always much higher than is that of a purely pagan community.

That God has not yet destroyed crooked and perverse humanity is a matter of what theologians call the common grace of God. And one reason why God is longsuffering to the world is that the church operates as salt within it. The inference is warranted that the presence of God's people in the world is one — not necessarily the only — reason for the bestowal of the other blessings of common grace. The natural blessings of rain and sunshine (Matthew 5:45), the restraint of sin in the reprobate, in consequence of which more or less orderly human society remains possible (Genesis 6:3, 20:6), the endowment of unregenerate persons with talents in the fields of science and art (Genesis 4:20-22), and also the so-called civic good which the unsaved perform (Luke 6:33), are all of them crumbs that fall from the table of God's believing children. Says Robert S. Candlish in his famous work *The Atonement*: "The entire history of the human race, from the apostasy to the final judgment, is a dispensation of forbearance in respect to the reprobate, in which many blessings, physical and moral, affecting their characters and destinies forever, accrue to the heathen, and many more to the educated and refined citizens of Christian communities" (pp. 358f.).

Most important by far, by dispensing the Word of God the church operates in the world as preserving and seasoning salt. As men believe and obey that Word, God regards them no more in consuming wrath but in saving love. Those who were "by nature the children of wrath" (Ephesians 2:3) are made "accepted in the beloved" (Ephesians 1:6).

THE LIGHT OF THE WORLD

In no instance does Christ bestow greater honor upon His church than when He calls it "the light of the world."

In doing so He closely identifies the church with Himself, for He is in very deed the light of the world. Time and again He is so described in Holy Writ. When aged Simeon took the babe Jesus in his arms, he spoke of Him as a light to lighten the gentiles, and the glory of God's people Israel (Luke 2:29-32). Matthew referred to the beginning of Jesus' Galilean ministry as the fulfillment of Isaiah's prophecy: "The land of Zabulon and the land of Nephthalim, by the way of the sea, beyond Jordan, Galilee of the gentiles: the people that sat in darkness saw great light; and to them which sat in the region and shadow of death light is sprung up" (Matthew 4:15, 16). Our Lord testified of Himself: "I am the light of the world: he that followeth me shall not walk in darkness, but shall have the light of life" (John 8:12).

Thus it becomes evident at once how the church operates as the light of the world. It has no light of its own; whatever light it has is derived from Christ. As the moon reflects the light of the sun, so the church reflects the light of Him who is "the Sun of righteousness" (Malachi 4:2). By proclaiming Christ to the world the church of Christ becomes the light of the world.

"Behold, darkness shall cover the earth, and gross darkness the people." So spoke the prophet Isaiah (60:2). How accurate a description of every period of human history since the fall, and how applicable in particular to this day and age! The Christian nations are rapidly reverting to the darkness of paganism. A dense pall of unbelief has settled down upon the very church of Christ. Seemingly insuperable barriers are in many instances keeping the light of the gospel from reaching heathen lands. The grim prince of darkness appears to have been loosed from the bottomless pit and to be hurling his demoniac hordes relentlessly against Christendom. The sun of western civilization, largely the product of Christianity, seems about to set. The statesmen of the world are groping frantically for light, but the darkness keeps growing more intense. "Watchman, what of the night? Watchman, what of the night?" (Isaiah 21:11). Is there not a single ray of hope ? No, not one, except for Him who is the light of the world.

When the evangelist said of the personal and living Word: "That was the true light which lighteth every man that cometh into the world" (John 1:9), he likely referred to what has been called the common light of nature. Calvin comments: "We know that men have this peculiar excellence which raises them above other animals, that they are endued with reason and intelligence, and that they carry the distinction between right and wrong engraven on their conscience. There is no man, therefore, whom some perception of the eternal *light* does not reach." But he hastens to add that the common light of nature is "far inferior to faith; for never will any man, by all the acuteness and sagacity of his own mind penetrate into the kingdom of heaven," and "the light of reason which God implanted in men has been so obscured by sin that amidst the thick darkness and shocking ignorance and gulf of errors there are hardly a few shining sparks that are not utterly extinguished."

In a much more exalted sense is Christ the light of the world. Time was when our first parents walked in the full light of the divine countenance. But they perpetrated a black deed. Then was humanity steeped in the darkness of sin and death. However, the Son of God by His death and resurrection has vanquished sin and death and brought life and immortality to light (II Timothy 1:10). By faith in Him may men have the light of life, even of life eternal.

It is the high honor of the Christian church to consist of children of light who let their light shine by preaching Christ as Saviour and Lord to individuals and nations, and thus presenting Him who alone is able to translate sinners from darkness into light and to dispel the black clouds which envelop the peoples of earth as a shroud.

The members of Christ's church must do this by word and deed. The Christian life is no substitute for the Word of God, but the preaching of the Word must be complemented by Christian living. The Word of God is the one and only means by which sinners are brought to faith. "Faith cometh by hearing, and hearing by the word of God" (Romans 10:17). But true it is that Christ's disciples have no right to expect their preaching to be effective if they do not let their light shine before men in such a way that men may see their good works (Matthew 5:16), and if they are not themselves epistles of Christ, known and read of all men (II Corinthians 3:2, 3). Here too, man may not put asunder what God has joined together. Therefore Paul admonished the Philippians: "That ye may be blameless and harmless, the sons of God, without rebuke, in the midst of a crooked and perverse nation, among whom ye shine as lights in the world; holding forth the word of life" (Philippians 2:15, 16).

The apostle John saw "the holy city, new Jerusalem, coming down from God out of heaven, prepared as a bride adorned for her husband." It was the church of the future, but also the church of the present foreshadowing that which is to come. "The city had no need of the sun, neither of the moon, to shine in it; for the glory of God did lighten it, and the Lamb is the light thereof. And the nations of them which are saved shall walk in the light of it; and the kings of the earth do bring their glory and honor into it. And the gates of it shall not be shut at all by day, for there shall be no night there" (Revelation 21:2, 23-25).

Chapter 41

SEPARATED FROM THE WORLD

The Greek word used throughout the New Testament to designate the Christian church means *that which is called out*. Although the same word sometimes occurs in a looser sense, it is clear that that from which the church is called out is the world. Thus the very name which the Holy Spirit has given to the church denotes separation from the world.

That the separation of the church from the world is not, and need not be, complete in every respect is self-evident. While not *of* the world, the church is by divine appointment *in* the world. Jesus prayed for the members of His church: "I pray not that thou shouldest take them out of the world, but that thou shouldest keep them from the evil" (John 17:15). And the apostle Paul wrote to the church in the worldly city of Corinth: "I wrote unto you in an epistle not to company with fornicators; yet not altogether with the fornicators of this world, or with the covetous, or extortioners, or with idolaters; for then must ye needs go out of the world" (I Corinthians 5:9, 10).

The question arises in what sense and to what extent the church must needs be separated from the world. In seeking to answer that question it is of the greatest importance to distinguish between forbidden separation and required separation.

FORBIDDEN SEPARATION

Throughout the history of the Christian church there have been those in its midst who in their flight from the world went beyond the demands of Holy Writ. Usually they made the impression of exceptional piety, but in real-

The Glorious Body of Christ

ity they were guilty of impiety. To presume to be wiser than God and holier than the law of God is not sanctity but sanctimony, and sanctimony is a vice.

The Pharisee who refuses to touch a publican with a ten-foot pole and, on returning from the market place, where he has unavoidably mingled with all kinds of people, would not think of sitting down to eat without first having washed away the filth of the world (Mark 7:4), the hermit who withdraws to a dingy hut in the backwoods, the stylite who makes his habitat on the top of a slender pillar in some desert, the monk and the nun who take the vows of celibacy and poverty and consign themselves to the isolation of a monastery or convent, and he who thinks it sinful for a Christian to join any organization in which unbelievers hold membership or to participate in any amusement in which worldly folk indulge — all these have fallen into essentially the same error. They put undue emphasis on the spatial aspects of the Christian's separation from the world. And that is neither an innocent pastime nor a comparatively harmless foible. History teaches that it leads almost inevitably to heinous sin.

He who today forbids what God allows will almost certainly tomorrow allow what God forbids. The reason is obvious. Because of his emphasis on the commandments of men he is in imminent peril of neglecting the law of God. To come directly to the point at issue, he who makes the antithesis of the church and the world chiefly spatial is practically certain to forget that it is essentially spiritual. In other words, he who strives with all his might to escape from his worldly surroundings easily forgets that he is carrying the world about with him in his own heart. In consequence world flight frequently results in worldliness of the worst kind. It is not at all surprising that the Pharisees of Jesus' day resembled whited sepulchres and that our Lord thundered at them: "Woe unto you, scribes and Pharisees, hypocrites! for ye make clean the outside of the cup and of the platter, but within they are full of extortion and excess" (Matthew 23:25-27).

Nor is it strange that more than one monastery and convent has degenerated into a brothel.

He who would go beyond the precepts of Scripture in the matter of separation from the world is peculiarly liable to the abominable sin of spiritual pride. Almost unavoidably he will take an I-am-holier-than-thou attitude toward his fellow men. Did not the Pharisee of the parable thank God that he was not as other men: extortioners, unjust, adulterers, or as that despicable publican who at that very moment was standing afar off (Luke 18:11)? And because his supposed piety exceeds the demands of God's holy law the same person becomes exceedingly boastful. He glories: "I fast twice in the week, I give tithes of all that I possess" (Luke 18:12). In view of this teaching of the Lord Jesus the poet Tennyson may be said to have been on good ground when he put the following words, which reek with spiritual pride, into the mouth of Simeon the Stylite:

> Bethink Thee, Lord, while Thou and all the saints
> Enjoy themselves in heaven, and men on earth
> House in the shade of comfortable roofs,
> Sit with their wives by fires, eat wholesome food,
> And wear warm clothes, and even beasts have stalls —
> I 'tween the rise and downfall of the light
> Bow down one thousand and two hundred times
> To Christ, the Virgin Mother, and the saints;
> Or in the night, after a little sleep,
> I wake; the chill stars sparkle; I am wet
> With drenching dews, or stiff with crackling frost.
> I wear an undress'd goatskin on my back;
> A grazing iron collar grinds my neck;
> And in my weak, lean arms I lift the cross,
> And strive and wrestle with Thee till I die:
> O mercy, mercy! wash away my sin!

Still another sin in which too much emphasis on spatial separation from the world is almost sure to issue is that

of leading a negative rather than a positive life and therefore neglecting one's duty in the world. It is not sufficient
for the Christian to abstain from evil; he must be "zealous
of good works" (Titus 2:14). The members of Christ's
church are the salt of the earth and the light of the world.
As salt they act as a preservative in the world and impart
flavor to it. But salt can act thus only if it is in close
contact with that which is to be preserved and seasoned.
And obviously the followers of Christ cannot function as
the light of the world if they keep their light hidden
under a bushel or a bed. Therefore the oft-repeated saying that the church's strength lies in its isolation from
the world must, to say the least, be taken with several
grains of salt. In certain instances it may be true, but
as a generalization it is unwarranted. The church's
strength lies in its being radically different from the
world. The world is darkness, the church is light. But
light must shine into darkness in order to drive it away.

REQUIRED SEPARATION

The truth that the antithesis of the church and the
world is spiritual, not spatial, in its essence, may not
close the eyes of the members of Christ's church to the
fact that the spiritual antithesis has some very necessary
spatial implications. Following are a few examples.

Because children are exceedingly impressionable, it is
a matter of the greatest import that the children of the
covenant be kept ordinarily from evil associates and be
given the opportunity to grow up in wholesome surroundings. Their parents and the church must co-operate in
creating such surroundings and in preventing Christian
youth, as far as is possible, from being subjected to worldly influences. That is one of many good arguments for
providing Christian day schools for the children of
believers.

Marriage has both spiritual and spatial aspects. Because of the spiritual antithesis of the believer and the

unbeliever Scripture in no uncertain terms forbids their being joined in matrimony. No sooner did the sons of God take them wives of the daughters of men (Genesis 6:2) than the human race was headed for the deluge. God expressly forbade His people Israel to intermarry with the heathen Canaanites (Deuteronomy 7:3). King Solomon got off to an excellent start when he asked God for wisdom rather than riches and honor, but his pagan wives soon led him into idolatry. And the apostle Paul taught that a Christian widow is at liberty to marry whom she will; only in the Lord (I Corinthians 7:39). The phrase "only in the Lord" clearly restricts "whom she will." She is limited to that group which is the Lord's peculiar people. She may marry only within the circle of Christ's church.

Not only children are affected by their surroundings; so are adults. The influence of environment may be more potent in the case of a child than in that of an adult, but also in the latter instance it is far from negligible. Therefore an adult Christian has no right to expose himself needlessly to temptation. Admittedly, he cannot avoid all temptation. In the line of duty he is bound to encounter more than a little. It is also true that he grows stronger as he faces temptation and by the grace of God overcomes it. But to seek out temptation is sin. Did not our Lord teach us to pray: "Bring us not into temptation but deliver us from the evil one" (Matthew 6:13, ASV)? And the Psalmist sang: "Blessed is the man that walketh not in the counsel of the ungodly, nor standeth in the way of sinners, nor sitteth in the seat of the scornful" (Psalm 1:1).

There is in the New Testament a passage which demands in the strongest possible language the church's separation from the world. It reads: "Be ye not unequally yoked together with unbelievers: for what fellowship hath righteousness with unrighteousness? and what communion hath light with darkness? and what concord hath Christ with Belial? or what part hath he that believeth with an infidel? and what agreement hath the temple of God with idols? For ye are the temple of the living God: as God hath said, I will dwell in them and walk in them; and I will be their God, and they shall be my people. Wherefore come out from among them and be ye separate, saith the Lord, and touch not the unclean thing; and I will receive you, and will be a Father unto you, and ye shall be my sons and daughters, saith the Lord Almighty" (II Corinthians 6:14-18).

What is the exact meaning of this passage? Does it forbid all association of believers with unbelievers? Obviously not, for that would go contrary to the plain teaching of Scripture elsewhere. Does it forbid mixed marriages? If so, it does that only by implication, for neither this passage nor its immediate context makes mention of marriage. Does it forbid Christians ever to be members of the same organization with non-Christians? Again, that cannot be the case, for Abraham, the father of believers, made a league for mutual defense with Aner, Eshcol and Mamre, heathen chieftains in the land of Canaan, and Scripture gives not so much as an inkling of disapproval of that arrangement (Genesis 14:13). No, the teaching of this passage is quite another, and it is most specific. In the church at Corinth there were those who had not broken entirely with their former heathen religion and worship. The apostle enjoins them in uncompromising language to make the break complete.

The Christian may not worship with the adherents of other religions. In the early centuries of the Christian era the Roman emperors did not object to the worship of Christ by Christians if only they would also worship Caesar. Those who died a martyr's death for refusing to do that were obeying II Corinthians 6:14-18. Before its defeat in the second world war the Japanese government did not rule out the Christian religion as such but demanded of its Christian subjects, as indeed of all others, that they pay divine homage to the emperor at the Shinto shrines. Those Christians who suffered inhuman tortures for their refusal to obey were observing the same Scriptural command of separation.

The members of the Christian church may have no spiritual fellowship, for instance, with Buddhists, Confucianists, Shintoists, Mohammedans, Judaists, or, for that matter, with modernists. For, as J. Gresham Machen has shown conclusively in his *Christianity and Liberalism*, modernism, too, is a false religion. Not merely does it corrupt Christianity; by denying the most cardinal Christian truths it has forfeited every just claim to Christianity.

Of all the religions of the world Christianity alone is true; all others are false. To be sure, elements of truth are found in them, but at heart they are false; and even those elements of truth men "by their wickedness suppress" (Romans 1:18, RSV). Christianity is an exclusive religion, and the Christian church partakes of the exclusiveness of Christianity itself.

Chapter 42

CONQUEROR OF THE WORLD

In comparison with the glory of the world the glory of the church seems utterly despicable. The overwhelming majority of men constitute the world; the church consists of a small minority. The world is rich in material possessions; the church is poor. The world is powerful; the church is weak. The world boasts of its wisdom; the church declares the foolish gospel. How true it is that God has chosen not many wise men after the flesh, not many mighty, not many noble, but rather the foolish, weak, base and despised things of the world, yes, and things which are not (I Corinthians 1:26-29). To all outward appearances the church has ever been at the mercy of the world.

Amazing as it may seem, the insignificant church is out to conquer the imposing world. Not only is it striving to do this; it is succeeding. And, surpassing strange to say, not only is victory in sight for the church; it is a present reality.

THE DUTY OF CONQUEST

Far too often in the conflict of the ages the church, instead of taking the offensive against the world, has been content with a defensive role. Worse than that, frequently the church has deemed world flight rather than world conquest to be its duty. That attitude has the semblance of piety but actually represents a most heinous sin of omission.

An illustration may help to clarify the difference between world flight and world conquest. According to Greek mythology a certain island was inhabited by Sirens, creatures half woman and half bird. Their song was so irresistibly alluring that mariners who came within hearing distance invariably made their way to the island. But no sooner did they set foot on shore than the Sirens would tear them in pieces. Odysseus' ship was nearing the danger zone. Realizing the peril besetting him and his companions, he stopped their ears with wax that they might not be turned from their rowing, while he had himself bound firmly to the mast so that he might hear the song of the Sirens without danger. That resembled world flight. Orpheus and his Argonauts were also nearing the island of the Sirens, and he, too, was aware of imminent peril. But the safety measure which he employed was quite another. He himself produced music of such superior charm that no one gave the slightest attention to the Sirens. That resembled world conquest.

Let not the church think that it has performed its duty when it stops its ears to the temptations of the world or makes it physically impossible for its members to yield to those temptations. What the church must do is to drown out the voice of the tempter by proclaiming aloud the Word of God. And, to go far beyond our illustration, it must declare that Word not merely to its own members but to the world as well. It must indeed strive with might and main to keep its members out of the clutches of the world, but it must also exert itself to the utmost to bring the men and women of the world through the instrumentality of the gospel into the fold of Christ.

Judging by much of present-day evangelistic preaching one would think that the sum total of the church's efforts toward world conquest consists in seeking to persuade the unsaved to receive Christ as Saviour. That is indeed a most important aspect of world conquest, but it is by no means the whole of it. The church must proclaim Christ also as Lord and demand of men everywhere that they bend the knee in homage before Him and walk in obedience to His law. Did not the resurrected Christ say to His apostles and in them to the church of succeeding ages:

"All power is given unto me in heaven and in earth," and then give the charge to make disciples of all nations, "teaching them to observe all things whatsoever I have commanded you" (Matthew 28:18-20)?

Scripture teaches the mediatorial kingship of Christ. It is not merely a kingship over believers but a kingship of a far more comprehensive kind. Because the suffering Servant of Jehovah poured out His soul unto death, God divided Him a portion with the great, and He divided the spoil with the strong (Isaiah 53:12). And when God raised His Son from the dead and set Him at His own right hand in the heavenlies, He placed Him "far above all principality and power and might and dominion and every name that is named . . . and put all things under his feet, and gave him to be the head over all things to the church" (Ephesians 1:20-22).

That kingship of its Head the church must proclaim. It must require of men everywhere that they acknowledge Him as Head of all things, as King over every domain of their lives. It must insist on Christian marriage, Christian education, Christian science, Christian industry, Christian labor, Christian relationships between labor and industry, Christian culture, Christian recreation, Christian politics, Christian internationalism; in short, on a Christian society as well as a Christian church. Moving like a mighty army, the church of God must sing resoundingly:

> Onward, then, ye people,
> Join our happy throng;
> Blend with ours your voices
> In the triumph-song:
> Glory, laud and honor
> Unto Christ the King!
> This through endless ages
> Men and angels sing.

As to the results which the preaching of the gospel will bring, the ablest students of the Word of God are not unanimous. Some are of the opinion that this labor of the church will usher in a millennium, a golden age, characterized by well-nigh universal recognition of Christ as Lord. Others see no such beautiful prospect prior to Christ's return to establish a new heaven and a new earth. But beyond all doubt the church is God's chosen vessel to proclaim to the world Christ as Saviour and King, and it is God's co-laborer toward the conquest of the world for Him who is "the prince of the kings of the earth" (Revelation 1:5).

THE REALITY OF VICTORY

That the church will in the end overcome the world is a foregone conclusion, for it will share in the ultimate and complete triumph of Christ, its Head. But Scripture also teaches that the church's victory over the world is a present reality. That amazing aspect of the glory of the Christian church demands elaboration.

It cannot be denied that the members of Christ's church are frequently tempted by the sins of the world and all too often yield to that temptation. Yet they are assured of eventual victory over sin, for He who began a good work in them is certain to perform it until the day of Jesus Christ (Philippians 1:6). But that is by no means the whole truth. It is also true that in the midst of their conflict with sin they already have the victory over sin. However imperfect they may be in themselves, in Christ they are perfect. And by virtue of the grace of regeneration, which Christ has merited for them and the Holy Spirit has applied to them, they themselves are perfect in principle. Therefore the apostle Paul insisted that believers are as a matter of fact buried with Christ into death and that their old man is even now crucified with Him (Romans 6:4, 6). And immediately after his bitter self-accusation: "I am carnal, sold under sin . . . For what I would, that do I not; but what I hate, that do I," he asserted: "Now then it is no more I that do it, but sin that dwelleth in me" (Romans 7:14, 15, 17).

An astounding teaching of the apostle Paul is that Christians are the owners of all things. He wrote to the believers at Corinth: "Whether Paul, or Apollos, or Cephas, or the world, or life, or death, or things present, or things to come: all are yours" (I Corinthians 3:22). What may he have meant? Without an attempt at an exhaustive exegesis of this passage, one assertion may here be made. History tells us that worldly men have often excelled in the fields of science and art. Cain's descendants were the first to make musical instruments and to engage in metallurgy as well as husbandry (Genesis 4:20-22). It is a matter of common knowledge that the ancient Greeks were expert in art and literature, the ancient Romans in law. The members of Christ's church may justly claim such valuable products of the common grace of God as their very own. While they are warned not to use the world "to the full" (I Corinthians 7:31, ASV) because its fashion passes away, the fact remains that the world belongs to the children of light in a sense in which it does not belong to the children of darkness. It is theirs to use to the glory of Christ, whose they are, and of God, whose Christ is (I Corinthians 3:23). And so it is hardly surprising that "the glory and honor of the nations" will be brought into new Jerusalem (Revelation 21:26).

The apostle John declared: "This is the victory that overcometh the world, even our faith" (I John 5:4). The eleventh chapter of Hebrews presents a long list of men and women who by their faith overcame the world. Mention is made, for example, of Moses, who looked down disdainfully on the pleasures, riches and honors of the world and chose, instead, the reproach of Christ (vss. 24-26). We are told of those "who through faith subdued kingdoms, wrought righteousness, obtained promises, stopped the mouths of lions, quenched the violence of fire, escaped the edge of the sword, out of weakness were made strong, waxed valiant in fight, turned to flight the armies of aliens" (vss. 33, 34). Obviously these overcame the world. But, unbelievable though it may seem, also those overcame the world who were tortured, not accepting deliverance, had trial of cruel mockings and scourgings, of bonds and imprisonment, were stoned, sawn asunder, tempted and slain with the sword, wandered about, clothed in sheepskins and goatskins, in deserts, mountains, dens and caves of the earth (vss. 35-37). Well may it be asked whether these were not overcome by the world. But the answer is contained in the phrase "of whom the world was not worthy" (vs. 38). So far superior to the world were they that the world did not deserve to contain them. Their very rejection by the world was proof of their triumph over the world. In all these things they were more than conquerors (Romans 8:37). Small wonder that many a Christian martyr sang a paean of victory when the flames were about to consume him or the earth yawned to swallow him up. And how true it is that the blood of the martyrs became the seed of the church!

When the shadow of death was closing in on the Lord Jesus, He said: "Now is the judgment of this world: now shall the prince of this world be cast out" (John 12:31); and on the day before His crucifixion He declared: "I have overcome the world" (John 16:33). What, pray, may He have meant? Were not the world and its prince at the very point of scoring a complete triumph over Him, and was He not about to go down before them in crushing defeat? Seemingly so, but in reality not at all. When Christ died on Calvary's tree, the serpent did indeed bruise the heel of the woman's seed, but the woman's seed crushed the head of the serpent (Genesis 3:15). When Satan tempted Jesus in the wilderness, he promised Him all the kingdoms of the world if only He would fall down and worship him (Matthew 4:9). Had Jesus yielded, He would have been vanquished. But instead of yielding He chose to become obedient unto death, even the death of the cross. "*Wherefore* God also hath highly exalted him and given him a name which is above every name, that at the name of Jesus every knee should bow, of things in heaven and things in earth and things under the earth, and that

every tongue should confess that Jesus Christ is Lord, to
the glory of God the Father" (Philippians 2:8-11). Seated at the right hand of God, He now reigns supreme over
the world. Neither the world nor its prince can so much
as move without His royal permission, and He sovereignly overrules all their doings unto the consummation of His
glorious kingdom.

Not only must the church proclaim this mediatorial
kingship of Christ and demand its recognition by all men;
the church also participates in His rule. John "saw
thrones, and they sat upon them, and judgment was given
unto them"; and the souls which had overcome "lived
and reigned with Christ a thousand years" (Revelation
20:4). It is altogether likely that this vision describes
the present reign of the triumphant and glorified church
over the world. But also the militant church on earth
shares in Christ's reign. It is "a royal priesthood," a
royalty of priests and a priesthood of kings (I Peter 2:9).
In the words of several able commentators, it is "a priesthood possessing a royal character, inasmuch as it not
only offers up sacrifices but exercises sway over the world."
And, writing to the seven churches in Asia Minor, John
told their members that Jesus Christ, Himself the prince
of the kings of the earth, had made them "kings and priests
unto God and his Father" (Revelation 1:5, 6). That is
glory indeed.

Would that the church were fully aware of that aspect
of its glory! Then it would no longer cower before the
world. Nor would it continue to imitate the world. It
would exult in its triumph over the world. It would shout
for joy: "Thanks be unto God, which always causeth us
to triumph in Christ!" (II Corinthians 2:14)

Chapter 43

THE INCLUSIVENESS OF THE CHURCH

Those who were received into the Christian church on the day of Pentecost were required first to repent and believe. The Ethiopian eunuch and the Philippian jailer were not baptized until they had made confession of faith in Christ. In short, the apostolic church insisted upon faith in the Lord Jesus Christ as a prerequisite of membership. And the true church of succeeding ages has always done likewise.

That makes the Christian church an exclusive organization, and this is an important aspect of its glory. However, the church is also characterized by a glorious inclusiveness. There is room in the church *only* for true believers. That spells exclusiveness. There is room in the church for *all* true believers. That spells inclusiveness.

Following are a few aspects of the church's inclusiveness.

ALL RACES OF MEN

One of the most pressing problems of our day is the race problem. A factor that has made it particularly urgent is the current widespread revolt of other races against white supremacy. Race prejudice, more than any other one thing, makes the relationship of the various races to one another a problem. Each race seems to be prejudiced in its own favor and against all others. Let no one think that such prejudice is peculiar to the white race. Certain tribes of American Indians tell the following story of the creation of man. God formed the first man of clay and baked him in an oven. It so happened that the oven was not hot enough, and so the man that came out was very pale. Thus originated the white race.

God fashioned another man and put him into the oven. This time the oven was too hot, and consequently the man that came out was burned. That accounts for the black race. God made one more try. This time the oven was at just the right temperature, and the finished product was nicely browned. That was the Indian.

Nowadays one often hears a very simple solution of the race problem proffered. The only difference among the races is said to concern the matter of pigment in the blood and therefore to be quite negligible. But that is a clear case of oversimplification. The differences among the races go deeper than that. They concern not only the color of the skin and a few other superficial features, but also such matters as ingrained traditions and even traits of character. There is truth in the contention that each nation has its own "soul." If that holds of nations, it certainly does of races. To deny the differences among the races is to destroy the race problem, not to solve it.

The ultimate solution of the race problem is found in Christianity. No matter how great the differences among the races may be, in Christ they are one, and believers of all races are members of His body. When Scripture says that, where the old man has been put off and the new man put on, "there is neither Greek nor Jew, circumcision nor uncircumcision, Barbarian, Scythian, bond nor free; but Christ is all and in all" (Colossians 3:11), the plain meaning is that in Christ all the separating diversities have ceased. To be sure, racial differences continue among Christians and there is no need of minimizing them, but these differences no longer separate them. Not only the redeemed in glory, also the members of the militant church on earth may sing in beautiful harmony to the glory of the Lamb: "Thou wast slain and hast redeemed us to God by thy blood out of every kindred and tongue and people and nation" (Revelation 5:9).

The story is told of three men of different races — a Hindu, a Negro and a Chinese — traveling on a boat in the Orient. They were complete strangers to one another and completely ignorant of one another's language, until one of them named the name of Jesus. Immediately the others responded by repeating that blessed name. They had found each other as members of one family, the household of faith; as members of one body, the church of Christ.

This age is known as the age of Christian missions. For more than a century now the Christian church has devoted itself as never before in its history to the world-wide proclamation of the gospel. There is universal agreement among Christians that the church must welcome into its midst believers of any and every race. And yet, strange to say, there are still white Christians who would restrict colored believers to a branch of the church other than that to which they themselves belong. Some would have separate denominations for those of another race, many would have separate congregations for them. That is not a Christian position. Every congregation is a manifestation of the body of Christ. In theological language, every "particular" church is a "complete" church. Therefore there should be room for men of all races, not only in the church universal, but also in every constitutive portion of the universal church. Occasionally a Negro is installed as the minister of a white congregation. The writer knows of a congregation in which there is just one colored man, and his white fellow members have honored him with the office of elder. The conservative Christian Reformed Church now counts among its ministers one Negro and two Chinese. Such instances should occasion no surprise whatsoever. They are evidences of the glorious inclusiveness of the Christian church.

ALL STRATA OF SOCIETY

In many countries the rich are said to constitute the upper class of society, those with moderate means are rated as the middle class, while the poor are relegated to the lower class. That is undemocratic. It is also extremely unfair. And yet it can hardly be maintained that all men actually live and move on the same social level. Various factors contribute to the fact that there are different strata of society. It belongs to the glory of the Christian church that it embraces every stratum and does not favor one above another.

James, the Lord's brother, was zealous to wipe out the distinction between rich and poor in the churches to which he addressed his epistle. Therefore he wrote: "Let the brother of low degree rejoice in that he is exalted, but the rich in that he is made low" (James 1:9, 10). Again he said: "My brethren, have not the faith of our Lord Jesus Christ, the Lord of glory, with respect of persons. For if there come unto your assembly a man with a gold ring, in goodly apparel, and there come in also a poor man in vile raiment; and ye have respect to him that weareth the gay clothing and say unto him, Sit thou here in a good place; and say to the poor, Stand thou there, or sit here under my footstool: are ye not then partial in yourselves and are become judges of evil thoughts?" (James 2:1-4) To the present day some churches rent out pews at different prices. The inevitable consequence is that the better pews are occupied by the rich, the less desirable ones by the less well-to-do. That ought not to be. A certain small town has two churches of the same denomination. One is attended by the aristocrats of the community, the other by the common folk. But an aristocratic church is a contradiction in terms. In a great many churches the rich are customarily chosen for positions of honor and dignity, while the poor are not even considered. That, too, is contrary to the genius of Christianity.

Our age is characterized by strife between employers and employees. Some employers would, if they could, withhold a living wage from their employees, and not a few employees take advantage of their employers by such devices as the stealing of time. Sad to say, today the American scene is often marred by bitter warfare between these two classes. But in the church of Christ the distinction between them is erased. Both are reminded by the Word of God that Christ is their master. Servants are told: "Ye serve the Lord Christ," and masters are informed: "Ye also have a Master in heaven" (Colossians 3:24; 4:1). That places them on a par with each other. There is no good reason why the bank president and the bank janitor should not serve as elders of the same church, provided, of course, both possess the Scriptural qualifications for that office. And if the former does not qualify while the latter does, it is altogether proper that the janitor should, together with his fellow elders, "have the rule" (Hebrews 13:17) over the president.

Again, the highly educated and the comparatively uneducated are equally eligible for membership in the Christian church, if only they are believers. The church doors stand as wide open to the illiterate ditch-digger as to the university professor. This is not to say that the latter may not be more valuable to the cause of Christ than the former. That could easily be. God was pleased to use learned Paul more abundantly than his less learned fellow apostles. Yet Paul was not actuated by false modesty when he described himself as "the least of the apostles" (I Corinthians 15:9).

> One place there is — beneath the burial sod —
> Where all mankind are equalized by death;
> Another place there is — the fane of God —
> Where all are equal who draw living breath.

ALL TYPES OF CHRISTIANS

The twelve apostles constituted the nucleus of the New Testament church. With the obvious exception of Judas Iscariot, they were Christians. But let no one think that all of the eleven were cut after one pattern. Contrariwise, there was a striking variety of temperament and personality among them. For a few examples, think of Peter, John and Thomas.

Peter was characterized by a well-nigh uncontrollable impetuosity. When the Master walked on the waves of the Galilean sea, Peter could not refrain from attempting to do likewise (Matthew 14:28). When Jesus announced His approaching death, Peter objected: "Be it far from thee, Lord; this shall not be unto thee" (Matthew 16:22). On the very threshold of heaven, the mount of the transfiguration, where silence was becoming to mortal, Peter could not refrain his tongue from speaking (Mark 9:5, 6). And when the Lord predicted that all of His disciples would deny Him, Peter vowed violently: "Though I should die with thee, I will not deny thee" (Matthew 26:35). But let no one think of Peter's impetuosity solely as a fault. The Spirit of God could render it a virtue. It took impetuous Peter to confess Jesus to be "the Christ, the Son of the living God" (Matthew 16:16) and to preach the impassioned Pentecostal sermon of the second chapter of Acts.

How much less forward was John! He was the meditative type of Christian, a mystic in the good sense of that term. He excelled in depth of spiritual insight and in the sweetest of Christian graces — love. For that reason he came to be known as "the disciple whom Jesus loved." At the last supper he leaned on the Saviour's bosom (John 13:23). He alone of the eleven seems to have followed his Lord all the way to Calvary, and from the cross Jesus commended His mother Mary to John's loving care (John 19:26). Let no one think that his love lapsed when, together with his brother James, he mistakenly suggested that the Lord command fire to come down from heaven and consume the Samaritans who would not receive Him (Luke 9:51-54). Rather, that was proof of passionate love for his Lord. Small wonder that John made love the theme of his epistles.

How different again was Thomas! That he was warmly devoted to the Saviour is evident. When Jesus decided to return to Judea, where the Jews had recently threatened to stone Him, Thomas said to his companions: "Let us also go, that we may die with him" (John 11:16). But it can hardly be denied that he had a way of looking on the dark side of things and almost stubbornly refused to do otherwise. In his words just quoted he jumped to the conclusion that going to Judea would entail certain death for every one of the twelve. When Jesus, referring to His early departure, spoke of going to prepare a place for His disciples and added that they knew where He was going and also knew the way, Thomas, evidently irked, remarked: "Lord, we know not whither thou goest; and how can we know the way?" (John 14:1-5). And when Thomas was told by the other disciples that the risen Lord had appeared to them, he obstinately averred: "Except I shall see in his hands the print of the nails and put my finger into the print of the nails and thrust my hand into his side, I will not believe" (John 20:25).

Surely, Peter, John and Thomas were individuals, and as individuals they differed strikingly. Each of them was a character. And likely the same thing could be said of each of the other disciples. Evidently it took many kinds of believers to make up the nucleus of the New Testament church.

Martha and Mary of Bethany were sisters. Both were believers. Jesus loved both of them (John 11:5). But how their characters differed! During one of the Master's visits at their home Martha was cumbered about much serving. No doubt, she was on her feet all day long. Hardly was one meal finished, and the dishes washed, when she began to prepare the next repast. But all the time Mary sat at Jesus' feet, listening to His words. When Martha complained that her sister was letting her do all the work, Jesus said: "Martha, Martha, thou art careful and troubled about many things, but one thing is needful, and Mary hath chosen that good part which shall not be taken away from her" (Luke 10:38-42). With these words Jesus admonished Martha, but He did it mildly. Without condemning her work, He told her to

put first things first.   As a matter of fact, much of the
serving which she did was necessary too.

In the twelfth chapter of his first epistle to the Corinthians Paul describes the church at length as the body
of Christ.   Two matters are stressed: the unity of the
body and the diversity of its members.   Says the apostle:
"If the whole body were an eye, where were the hearing?
If the whole were hearing, where were the smelling?   But
now hath God set the members every one of them in the
body, as it hath pleased him.   And if they were all one
member, where were the body?   But now are they many
members, yet but one body.   And the eye cannot say unto
the hand, I have no need of thee; nor again the head to
the feet, I have no need of you.   Nay, much more those
members of the body which seem to be more feeble are
necessary" (I Corinthians 12:17-22).

There is room in the Christian church only for true
believers.   But it takes all kinds of true believers to make
a church.   To name but a few, there is need of quiet
members and talkative members, meditative members and
bustling members, conservative members and progressive
members, timid members and courageous members, mem-
bers with five talents and members with one talent, san-
guine members and phlegmatic members, constructive
critics and enthusiastic promoters, leaders and helpers.
And each must learn to esteem others better than himself
(Philippians 2:3).

As the beauty of the human body is brought out by the
variety of its parts, so the glory of the body of Christ
appears in the diversity of its members.

Chapter 44

THE EXCLUSIVENESS OF THE CHURCH

Through faith in the Lord Jesus Christ sinners become members of His mystical body, the invisible church. As the visible church is not another church alongside the invisible, but merely the manifestation of the invisible church, it follows of necessity that there is room in the visible church only for believers — together, of course, with their children. That is clear as broad daylight.

But just how must the church go about the exclusion of unbelievers from its membership? On that question there is no unanimity. As was previously suggested, by and large three views are held, one of which is extremely strict, another extremely lax, while the third is moderate, reasonable and — what is most important by far — Scriptural.

There are those who claim the ability to a very high degree of determining who are born again and who are not. Therefore, when some one seeks communicant membership in the church, they think they can tell with certainty approaching infallibility whether he is a real Christian or a nominal one, a true believer or a hypocrite. That view is highly presumptuous. It reeks with spiritual pride. Those who hold it forget that only God omniscient knows the hearts of men.

There are those — and they are exceedingly numerous today — who say that the church must willingly receive into its membership all who *say* they are believers. The church, it is said, should make no attempt whatever to pass judgment on their sincerity or the correctness of their appraisal of themselves. It is not difficult to see that those who take that position throw the church doors wide open to deniers of the faith. Almost any modernist will insist that he is a Christian. The opinion is widely held that observance of "the golden rule" is a sufficient test of Christianity. Many who blatantly deny the deity of Christ declare boldly that they believe in Him.

There is a view of this matter which is plainly Scriptural. On the one hand, only God is omniscient. The church is not omniscient and therefore is fallible in judging who are believers and who are not. On the other hand, it is the solemn duty of the church to keep unbelievers out of its membership just as far as that is humanly possible. Time and again the Word of God admonishes the church to bar from its midst any who give evidence of not being believers.

It follows that the church is solemnly obligated to apply certain tests to those who seek membership. Three indispensable tests may be named.

ARE THE PREREQUISITES OF SAVING FAITH PRESENT?

Anti-intellectualism abounds in the Christian church today. Emotional experience and the will to be and do good are stressed at the expense of doctrine. Faith is thought to be a gamble.

But that is precisely what saving faith is not. It presupposes knowledge. To be sure, saving faith is more than mere knowledge of what the Bible teaches about the Saviour. It is nothing less than trust in Him for eternal life. But one cannot trust Him thus without first knowing what the Bible teaches concerning Him and assenting to that teaching. It is precisely because of the teaching of Scripture concerning Jesus Christ that the believer commits himself to Him for salvation.

The Ethiopian eunuch needed to be instructed from the Word of God before he could believe (Acts 8:29-38). Paul and Silas said to the Philippian jailer: "Believe on the Lord Jesus Christ, and thou shalt be saved, and thy house." That very night he and all his were baptized. But it is recorded that before they were baptized the apostle and his companion "spake unto him the word of the Lord, and to all that were in his house" (Acts 16:31-33). The command to teach is most prominent in our Lord's great missionary commission (Matthew 28:18-20). As a matter of course the thing a missionary does as he seeks to win men for Christ is to teach them the way of salvation. "Faith cometh by hearing and hearing by the Word of God" (Romans 10:17).

While assuredly not every church member needs to know all the niceties of systematic theology, it is not difficult to name specific truths knowledge of which and assent to which are prerequisite to saving faith. For example, he who is ignorant of the deity of Christ cannot possibly believe in Him unto life eternal. He who regards Jesus as a mere human being does not even have the right to commit himself to Him for salvation. If he does, he is giving divine honor to a man, for only God can save. And that is tantamount to saying that he is guilty of idolatry. And how can he who has no conception of the Biblical interpretation of Christ's death trust in Christ crucified for salvation? The substitutionary atonement constitutes the very heart of the Scriptural doctrine of salvation. He who is ignorant of it cannot believe that Christ suffered and died on the accursed tree in his stead.

It follows that, when someone wishes to make profession of faith, the church may not take his word for it that he is a believer, but the church is in duty bound to investigate whether he possesses the doctrinal knowledge which is prerequisite to saving faith. If it appears that he does not, the church must insist on his receiving further instruction as a condition of his reception into communicant membership.

Another prerequisite of saving faith is conviction of sin. Ordinarily one does not consult a physician unless one feels ill. Certainly no one will flee to the great physician of souls, Jesus Christ, who does not realize that he is spiritually sick. Only he who is oppressed by the guilt

and the pollution of sin will run to Calvary with the
prayer:

> Rock of ages, cleft for me,
> Let me hide myself in Thee;
> Let the water and the blood,
> From Thy wounded side which flowed,
> Be of sin the double cure:
> Save from guilt and make me pure.

The Larger Westminster Catechism is quite right in
defining "justifying faith" as "a saving grace, wrought
in the heart of a sinner by the Spirit and Word of God,
whereby he, *being convinced of his sin and misery, and of
the disability in himself and all other creatures to recover
him out of his lost condition* . . . receiveth and resteth upon
Christ and His righteousness . . ." (Question 72).

And so, when someone wishes to unite with the church
because he feels that he is in himself good enough for
membership, he must be rejected, for the question is not
how good he is but how guilty and foul and helpless he is
in his own estimation. He who considers himself worthy
of membership in the church of Christ is by that very
token utterly unworthy. There is room in the Christian
church only for such as, realizing that they are deserving
of hell, despair of saving themselves and therefore aban-
don themselves to Jesus Christ.

Is the Essence of Saving Faith Present?

Many who are cocksure of being believers apparently
have no idea what saving faith really is. Therefore it is
essential that the church inquire whether the essence of
saving faith is found in candidates for membership.

As was already said, one cannot believe in Christ unto
eternal life without knowing in the main what the Bible
teaches concerning Him and assenting to that teaching.
But now it must be stated that such knowledge and such
assent alone do not constitute saving faith. The very

essence of saving faith is a consequent committing of oneself to Christ for salvation.

Saving faith is not merely faith in certain *propositions* concerning Jesus Christ; it is trust in His very *person*. The Bible teaches that Jesus was conceived by the Holy Ghost and born of the virgin Mary, that during a public ministry of approximately three years He spoke many words of divine wisdom and wrought many miracles, that He died for sinners on Calvary's cross, that on the third day He was raised from the dead for their justification and after forty days ascended into heaven, where He intercedes for His own. These are a few of a great many Scriptural propositions concerning the Saviour. Let no one think that he can reject those propositions and believe in the person of Christ. That is a manifest impossibility. But it is not inconceivable that one might accept those propositions with his intellect and yet not believe with his heart in Christ's person. Theologians call that sort of faith speculative. Dead orthodoxism is another name for it. The abandonment of oneself for salvation to the person of the Christ of Scripture — that is the very essence of saving faith.

Preachers often tell their audiences that to believe in Christ means to be fully assured that He died for one's sins on the cross. That statement does not excel in precision. It identifies the essence of saving faith with the assurance of saving faith. And that is a mistake. To be sure, the essence and the assurance of faith are inseparable. A measure of the latter is inherent in the former. Every believer has some assurance. But by no means every believer has full assurance all the time.

The church demands too much when it insists that only those are eligible for communicant membership who never question their Christianity but can at every moment say: "I know that my Redeemer liveth" (Job 19:25). But it requires too little when it is willing to receive into membership any who have not cast themselves upon, and aban-

doned themselves to, Jesus Christ for salvation from sin
and death.

The Westminster Shorter Catechism gives as clear and
precise a definition of saving faith as is found anywhere.
It says: "Faith in Jesus Christ is a saving grace, whereby we receive and rest upon Him alone for salvation, as
He is offered to us in the gospel" (Question 86). A most
significant word in that definition is *alone*. The true believer does not trust for salvation in any creature, whether
on earth or in heaven, but solely in Jesus Christ. He
trusts neither in angels nor in saints. And he trusts
neither in his own works nor in his own character. He
sings:

> Just as I am, without one plea,
> But that Thy blood was shed for me
> And that Thou bidd'st me come to Thee,
> O Lamb of God, I come! I come!

That is an expression of the very essence of saving faith.
In questioning applicants for membership, the church must
make as sure that it is present as is humanly possible.

ARE THE FRUITS OF SAVING FAITH PRESENT?

"By their fruits ye shall know them," said the Lord
Jesus. And He added: "Not every one that saith unto me,
Lord, Lord, shall enter into the kingdom of heaven; but
he that doeth the will of my Father which is in heaven"
(Matthew 7:20, 21). Scripture throughout teaches emphatically that men are saved, not by works, but by grace
through faith; but nowhere does Scripture tell us that
men are saved by a faith that does not work. On the
contrary, it is extremely insistent that saving faith is a
faith that works. Paul taught that no less emphatically
than did James. Shall the church fail to apply that test?

The notion is abroad in the Christian church that one
can receive Jesus as Saviour without acknowledging Him
as Lord; that one can have his sins forgiven without for-

saking his sins; that, to use theological terminology, one can have the benefit of justification without the grace of sanctification. That notion is completely false and exceedingly pernicious. Not for a moment may the church give quarter to it. The church must unqualifiedly refuse to recognize as members such as seem to revel in Jesus as Saviour but neglect to keep His commandments. They show themselves to be hypocrites. Without holiness no man will see the Lord (Hebrews 12:14). Without holiness no man should be recognized as a member of Christ's church.

This is not to say that only such as have attained the goal of moral perfection may be received into the church. The very best Christian still offends in many things. But it does mean that only such may be welcomed into the church as can answer affirmatively the question: "Do you declare that you love the Lord, and that it is your heartfelt desire to serve Him according to His Word, to forsake the world, to mortify your old nature, and to lead a godly life?" (Form of the Christian Reformed Church for the Public Profession of Faith). There is room in the Christian church only for perfectionists, not in the sense that they lay claim to perfection, but in the sense that they strive with might and main for perfection and are dissatisfied with anything short of perfection.

Sometimes one hears the fear expressed that, if the requirements for church membership are made so stringent, few, if any, will dare to unite with the church. The Bible gives a most pointed reply to that objection.

The fifth chapter of The Acts of the Apostles relates the tragic story of Ananias and Sapphira. They were church members and professed Christians, but their lives belied their profession. They pretended to be more pious than they were. In so doing they lied to the Holy Spirit. By way of punishment both of them fell dead. Small wonder that we are told: "Great fear came upon all the church and upon as many as heard these things . . . And of the rest durst no man join himself to them; but the people magnified them" (vss. 11, 13). Then comes a great surprise. In the very next verse Luke says: "And believers were the more added to the Lord, multitudes both of men and women" (vs. 14).

Here was an exclusive church. According to human calculation its prospects for growth were nil. But through the divine working its prospects proved excellent. It grew as never before.

The growth of His church is God's concern. He will bless the church that is as exclusive as He requires in His Word. He will add to its membership. And only additions made by God are additions at all. Man-made additions are always subtractions from the glory of the church.

Chapter 45

THE KEYS OF THE KINGDOM

The Westminster Confession of Faith states that to the officers of the church "the keys of the kingdom of heaven are committed, by virtue whereof they have power respectively to retain and remit sins, to shut that kingdom against the impenitent, both by the word and censures; and to open it unto penitent sinners, by the ministry of the gospel, and by absolution from censures, as occasion shall require" (Chapter XXX, Section II). And the Heidelberg Catechism's answer to the question, "What are the keys of the kingdom of heaven?" reads: "The preaching of the holy gospel, and church discipline, or excommunication out of the Christian Church. By these two the kingdom of heaven is opened to believers and shut against unbelievers" (Lord's Day XXXI, Question 83).

Assuredly, to be entrusted with the keys of the kingdom of heaven is an exceedingly great distinction for the church. It should prove eminently worth while to seek to discover what the Word of God has to say on that matter.

CHRIST AND THE KEYS

Obviously, the expression *the keys of the kingdom of heaven* must not be taken literally but figuratively. Christ said to Pilate: "My kingdom is not of this world" (John 18:36). His kingdom is spiritual. This does not mean that it is less real than are the kingdoms of this world. As a matter of fact, it is incomparably more real, for it alone is destined to endure throughout eternity. But it does follow that the keys of the kingdom are not to be thought of as made of metal or any other material, but are also themselves spiritual. They represent the author-

ity to admit sinners into the kingdom or to exclude them
from it.

In Scripture the terms *church* and *kingdom* are not
always interchangeable. For example, while the church
is a communion of persons, the kingdom is sometimes
said to consist of spiritual blessings. It is "not meat and
drink, but righteousness and peace and joy in the Holy
Ghost" (Romans 14:17). Often, too, the kingdom is
regarded as more extensive than the church. When, for
instance, God is said to have given Christ to be the head
over all things to the church (Ephesians 1:22), the plain
import is that His reign extends not only over the church
but also over the family, the state, society, in fact, over
the whole of the universe. However, in the expression
the keys of the kingdom the kingdom is synonymous with
the church. The only place in Scripture where this precise expression occurs is Matthew 16:19. In the foregoing verse Jesus said: "Upon this rock I will build my
church." Evidently He was thinking of the church as a
house. When in the next breath He says: "And I will
give unto thee the keys of the kingdom of heaven," He can
have in mind only the keys of the selfsame house. So
here the church is the kingdom of heaven, and the kingdom of heaven is the church. In view of the Scriptural
teaching that the church consists of the saved (Acts 2:
47), those who are on the way to heaven together with
those who have gone to heaven, this identification is not
surprising. Therefore the keys of the kingdom represent
the authority to receive men into the church or to exclude
them from it, and likewise the authority to admit men
into heaven or to exclude them from it.

That being the meaning of *the keys of the kingdom of
heaven,* it is clear that in the absolute sense they belong
to Christ, the Head of the church and the King of the
kingdom, and to Him alone. He only can forgive sins.
"He only could unlock the gate of heaven and let us in."
Again, He alone has the right to sentence men to everlasting damnation. To the Son, and to Him alone, has

the Father "given authority to execute judgment" (John 5:27). It is He "that openeth, and no man shutteth; and shutteth, and no man openeth" (Revelation 3:7).

Once upon a time a man sick of the palsy was brought to Jesus for healing. But, instead of at once commanding him to rise up and walk, the Lord first said to him: "Son, thy sins be forgiven thee." Certain of the scribes who were present were appalled. Said they in their hearts: "Why doth this man thus speak blasphemies? Who can forgive sins but God only?" (Mark 2:3-7). Their premise was that Jesus was a mere man. It was a false premise, but on it their conclusion was irrefutable. For a man to presume to forgive sins is blasphemy indeed. To forgive sins is a divine prerogative. Precisely and solely because of His deity did Jesus have the right to say: "Thy sins be forgiven thee."

One day the King will come in His glory and all the holy angels with Him. Before Him, as He sits on the throne of His glory, all nations will be gathered. And He will separate them as a shepherd divides his sheep from the goats. To the sheep He will say: "Come, ye blessed of my Father, inherit the kingdom prepared for you from the foundation of the world." The goats He will address thus: "Depart from me, ye cursed, into everlasting fire, prepared for the devil and his angels" Matthew 25:31-46). With the sword that goes out of His mouth will He divide humanity in two for the endless ages of eternity. Surely, thus to exercise the keys of the kingdom is the sole prerogative of the King.

THE APOSTLES AND THE KEYS

Christ holds the keys of the kingdom by His own right. That can be said of Him alone. But He has seen fit to entrust the keys to His apostles. Certain New Testament passages here demand special attention.

When Peter had confessed Jesus to be the Christ, the Son of the living God, the Lord said to him: "I will give

unto thee the keys of the kingdom of heaven: and whatsoever thou shalt bind on earth shall be bound in heaven;
and whatsoever thou shalt loose on earth shall be loosed
in heaven" (Matthew 16:19).

Largely upon this passage the church of Rome has constructed its doctrine of the papacy. To Peter as an individual, Christ is said to have entrusted the keys of the
kingdom. That made him the first pope. And his authority has since passed to his successors. Of the many
arguments that may be arrayed against that interpretation, one of the most conclusive is afforded by a parallel
passage. Subsequently Jesus said to the twelve: "Whatsoever *ye* shall bind on earth shall be bound in heaven;
and whatsoever *ye* shall loose on earth shall be loosed in
heaven" (Matthew 18:18). Here precisely the same authority that was given to Peter is bestowed upon all the
apostles. How clear that in the former passage Jesus
must have regarded Peter as a representative of the
twelve! Not to one of them, but to all of them, Christ
gave the keys of the kingdom.

Some expositors are of the opinion that the binding of
which Jesus speaks in these passages has reference to
the retention of sins and that the loosing refers to the
forgiveness of sins. But that view is hardly tenable.
Much more likely Jesus meant: "Whatsoever ye shall forbid on earth as disqualifying for entrance into the kingdom will be forbidden in heaven; and whatsoever ye
shall allow on earth as not disqualifying for entrance into
the kingdom will be allowed in heaven." In a word, the
Lord authorized the apostles to lay down conditions for
entrance into the kingdom of heaven.

That the conditions laid down subsequently by the
apostles do not differ from the conditions laid down by
Christ Himself in the days of His flesh goes altogether
without saying. They may be summed up as faith in
Christ as Saviour together with preceding repentance
from sin and consequent obedience to Christ as Lord. Yet
it may not be supposed that special revelation ceased at

Christ's return to heaven. The ascended Christ Himself sent down the Holy Spirit to guide the apostles into all truth (John 16:13). In consequence the writings of the apostles shed fuller light than was previously given on the precise nature of repentance unto salvation, the precise meaning of faith in Christ, and the precise requirements for a life to His glory. And, not to be forgotten, these writings were divinely inspired and therefore infallible.

Although the Matthew passages just discussed do not speak of the forgiveness and retention of sins, elsewhere Christ did give His apostles authority with reference to that very matter. In one of His appearances He said to them: "Whose soever sins ye remit, they are remitted unto them; and whose soever sins ye retain, they are retained" (John 20:23).

At first blush there is something truly amazing about that statement. For its proper understanding some important distinctions are essential. Christ did not assign to the apostles authority actually to forgive or retain sins. As was already shown, that authority belongs to God alone. Christ authorized His apostles merely to *declare* the forgiveness or retention of sins. But He authorized them to declare those matters *infallibly*. If that seems well-nigh unbelievable, it must be remembered that just before making this statement the Lord breathed on the apostles and said: "Receive ye the Holy Ghost" (vs. 22). Beyond all doubt we are face to face here with what a very able expositor has described as "a specific charismatic endowment" and "the peculiar authority of the apostolical office." Only the apostles were endowed by the Holy Spirit with the ability to declare infallibly the forgiveness or the retention of an individual's sins.

Likely the story of Ananias and Sapphira affords an instance of the exercise of that peculiar apostolic authority. Under the very special influence of the Holy Spirit, Peter saw through their deceit. Supernaturally enabled to look into their hearts, he accused them of being filled with Satan and of lying to the Holy Spirit. Immediately they were punished with death. Beyond all reasonable doubt their sins were retained (Acts 5:1-10).

THE CHURCH AND THE KEYS

The divine Head of the church exercises the keys of the kingdom in the most absolute fashion. His apostles, upon whom the church was built, were authorized by Him to exercise the keys in a subordinate way, but nonetheless infallibly. That leaves the question in what sense the keys have been committed to the church of subsequent times.

God forbid that the church should presume to exercise the keys of the kingdom as does the King. For, Rome to the contrary notwithstanding, the church is not divine. It was indeed divinely originated; God brought it into being. It has a divine Head, even the Lord Jesus Christ. And it is supernatural in its essence; those born of the Spirit constitute its membership. But it is not divine and never will be. The church on earth consists of sinful saints, and even the perfected members of the church triumphant in glory continue as finite creatures of the infinite Creator.

Rome also errs when it teaches that the church, like the apostles, is authorized to lay down infallibly conditions for entrance into the kingdom and to declare infallibly in specific instances the forgiveness or the retention of sins. Underlying that teaching are the false assumptions that the apostolic office is continuous, that the church is infallible, and that special revelation is not complete in the Bible.

Must we then conclude that the Westminster Confession of Faith and the Heidelberg Catechism are in error when they ascribe the keys of the kingdom to the church of all ages? By no means. In a very real sense the church employs the keys when it preaches the Word of God and when it exercises judicial discipline according to the commands of Christ and the teaching of His apostles.

Both in its preaching and in its discipline the church must distinguish between believers and unbelievers. Although it cannot determine infallibly who are believers and who are not, yet in its dealings with men the question of supreme importance for the church is whether or not they are believers. In Scriptural preaching and in Scriptural discipline the church opens the doors of the church and the gate of heaven for believers, and it closes those doors and that gate for unbelievers.

For the proper use of the keys of the kingdom it is absolutely essential that the church neither subtract from nor add to the Scriptural requirement for salvation — faith in Jesus Christ. The church may only declare, not augment, the conditions laid down by Christ and the apostles for entrance into the kingdom, but those conditions it must declare fully.

When, for example, an individual is highly respected by his neighbors and himself, but gives no evidence of being under conviction of sin; has the highest regard for Jesus of Nazareth as an exemplary and perhaps perfect man, but does not believe that He is the Son of God and therefore Himself very God; admires Christ's indomitable courage in dying for His convictions, but has no understanding of the vicariousness of His death; says he believes in the man of Galilee, but expects to go to heaven because he is doing "his best"; or expresses a willingness to be saved by Jesus, but is manifestly unwilling to deny himself, take up his cross, and follow Christ — the church has no right to regard him as a believer and it must so inform him. The church is in duty bound to close its doors to him and to tell him that he has no part in the kingdom of God.

On the other hand, when a person is guilty of murder or adultery but, kneeling at the bleeding feet of Christ crucified, cries out: "Wash me, Saviour, or I die"; does not know, as regards the order of the divine decrees, whether to be a supralapsarian or an infralapsarian, nor,

as regards the origin of the individual soul, whether to
call himself a creationist or a traducianist, but makes
Peter's confession his own: "Thou are the Christ, the
Son of the living God"; is unable to refute the govern-
mental theory of the atonement because he has never
heard of it, but is certain that the good Shepherd gave His
life for the sheep (John 10:11) and that "Christ died for
the ungodly" (Romans 5:6); is not always ready to affirm
that he is going to heaven when he dies, but has abandoned
himself as a helpless and hell-deserving sinner to the crucified One; must complain every hour of the day that, instead of doing the good that he would do, he does the
evil that he would not do (Romans 7:19), yet in utter
dependence on the grace of God keeps working out his own
salvation with fear and trembling (Philippians 2:12,
13) and pressing toward the goal of perfection (Philippians 3:14) — such a one the church must deem to be a
true believer. It is its sacred duty and blessed privilege
to receive him with open arms into its membership and
to unlock for him the gate of heaven.

For it is the church of Him who welcomed into paradise
a thief when that criminal in his dying moments judged
himself deserving of the accursed death of crucifixion,
confessed his faith in Christ in the words, "Lord, remember me when thou comest into thy kingdom," and by that
very prayer not merely lifted a cup of cold water to the
Saviour's burning lips but held a cup of heavenly comfort
to His anguished soul (Luke 23:41-43).

Of such is the kingdom of heaven.

Chapter 46

SALUTARY DISCIPLINE

The marks of the true church are three in number: the sound preaching of the Word of God, the proper administration of the sacraments and the faithful exercise of discipline. By those standards the present plight of almost all churches is sad indeed. Some have forfeited every claim to being true churches, and the validity of the claim of a great many others has become questionable.

As for discipline, many churches neglect it because they fear it will reduce their membership and thus detract from their glory. But the truth of the matter is that the church which fails to exercise discipline is sure to lose both its self-respect and the respect of those without. Strange though it may seem, the world today despises the church precisely because the church is so worldly, and the members of the church by and large take no pride in their membership because it carries with it no distinction. On the other hand, the faithful exercise of discipline is sure to enhance the church's glory.

In other words, the proper exercise of ecclesiastical discipline is decidedly salutary. It will contribute greatly to the church's health. The following aspects of church discipline help to bring out its salutariness.

ITS SCRIPTURAL WARRANT

Frequently a church fails, under the guise of piety, to exercise discipline. It is said, for instance, that God will take care of His church and that He is abundantly able to do so without human help. Or it is said that the disciplining of erring church members is conducive to their destruction rather than their salvation because it is almost sure to drive them out of the church. But the Word of

God plainly requires church discipline. Those who disparage it presume to be wiser than God. And that is a vice, not a virtue.

Of the passages of Scripture that undeniably prescribe ecclesiastical discipline the following may be cited. Jesus taught that if one church member sins against another, the offended party, after having tried in various ways but in vain, to bring the offender to repentance, is to report the matter to the church, and if the offender neglects to hear the church, he is to be regarded as "a heathen man and a publican" (Matthew 18:15-17). That can only mean that he is no longer to be regarded a member of the body of Christ. The apostle Paul commanded the church at Corinth to "put away" from its midst a member who was living in the sin of incest (I Corinthians 5:13). And the same apostle instructed the evangelist Titus: "A man that is a heretic, after the first and second admonition reject" (Titus 3:10).

The thirteenth chapter of the Gospel according to Matthew contains the parable of the tares. A man sowed good seed in his field. An enemy of his sowed tares in the same field. When both wheat and tares had appeared, the servants of the owner of the field suggested to him that he permit them to pluck out the tares. But he forbade them do this lest they should root up the wheat with the tares. Instead, he bade them let the two grow together until harvest, at which time the wheat would be gathered into the barn and the tares would be burned. Thus, taught Jesus, the children of the kingdom and the children of the world will be separated in the end of the world (vss. 24-30; 36-43). From this parable it has sometimes been inferred that church discipline is a matter for the final judgment and that its present exercise is contrary to the teaching of Jesus. What is the answer to that argument?

On the one hand, it must be insisted that there are no contradictions in the Word of God and that therefore an interpretation of this parable which goes contrary to the unmistakable teaching of Scripture elsewhere cannot be allowed. On the other hand, those who conclude from the statement, "The field is the world" (vs. 38), that this parable has no bearing whatever on *church* discipline but merely teaches that the righteous and the wicked will until the end of time exist alongside each other in the *world* are guilty of serious oversimplification. The field is indeed the world. Into that field the good seed is sown, and thus the church comes into existence. But Satan sows tares among the wheat and thus introduces the children of the wicked one into the church. That is the presentation of the parable. Practically all the ablest expositors of Scripture are agreed that this parable does present a picture of the imperfect visible church.

In *The Teaching of Jesus Concerning the Kingdom of God and the Church* Geerhardus Vos offers a most reasonable explanation of this parable. The disciples entertained the notion, so prevalent among the Jews of that day, that the very first work of the Messiah on His arrival would be the absolute separation of the good and the evil. Jesus here corrects that notion by telling them that the complete separation will not occur until the end of time, and that in the meantime the kingdom, which is the church, must partake of the limitations and imperfections to which a sinful environment exposes it (pp. 165-168). Thus understood, the parable of the tares is a strong warning against excesses in church discipline, notably against the view that men are able to determine infallibly who are born again and who are not and, in reliance on their supposed infallibility, must establish a perfectly pure church. But by no manner of means does this parable forbid, or even discourage, ecclesiastical discipline.

ITS SPIRITUAL CHARACTER

The authority of the church differs widely in character from the authority of the state. That is indicated by the Scriptural symbols of the two. The sword is the Scriptural symbol of civil authority. Of the civil magistrate it is said: "He beareth not the sword in vain: for he is the minister of God, a revenger to execute wrath upon him that doeth evil" (Romans 13:4). But keys are the Scriptural symbol of ecclesiastical authority. Said Jesus to Peter as representative of the twelve apostles, upon whom the church is built: "I will give unto thee the keys of the kingdom of heaven: and whatsoever thou shalt bind on earth shall be bound in heaven; and whatsoever thou shalt loose on earth shall be loosed in heaven" (Matthew 16:19). Obviously, keys are wont to be used in a wholly different way from a sword. A sword suggests force; keys do not. And that means that, in distinction from civil authority, ecclesiastical authority is spiritual.

For that reason church discipline must always be exercised in a spirit of deep humility. Never may the members of the church assume an I-am-holier-than-thou attitude. Rather should each member be mindful that he is not a whit better than the offender and that but for the grace of God he would be the offender. Said the apostle Paul: "Brethren, if a man be overtaken in a fault, ye which are spiritual restore such an one in the spirit of meekness; considering thyself, lest thou also be tempted" (Galatians 6:1).

The methods of church discipline differ from those employed by the state. The latter often uses force in dealing with criminals, but the church, in dealing with offenders, may never resort to force. It must be content with such spiritual measures as persuasion and admonition.

The state punishes evil-doers. Strictly speaking, the church never punishes its erring members. So long as at all possible it keeps regarding erring ones as Christians. And did not Christ crucified bear the punishment due to His own for their sins? Therefore it is far better to say that the church *censures* its offending members than to say that the church *punishes* them. And its censures are never physical but always spiritual. Never may the church impose fines on its erring members, consign them to prison, or boycott them in business. All it should do is admonish or rebuke them, in certain instances deprive them of such privileges of membership as, for example, the use of the sacraments, and in last instance exclude them from membership. But even excommunication must remain a purely spiritual transaction.

While a member is in process of being disciplined the church may never cease praying for him. Not only should the officers of the church intercede for him; the membership should be reminded of this duty. Excommunication must be an occasion for mourning. And when the church has been compelled to regard an offender as "a heathen man and a publican," it will not yet despise him but keep remembering him before the throne of grace and beseeching him to be reconciled to God. If he repents, he should be welcomed back into the fold with joy and thanksgiving.

In summary, ecclesiastical discipline should ever be exercised in the spirit of Christian love.

Its Exalted Aim

The aim of church discipline must ever be the salvation of the offender, never his destruction. Sometimes there is need of this reminder. It seems that in practically every church there is at least one member who is adept at stirring up trouble. At times the temptation becomes very real to employ discipline as a device to get rid of such an individual. But never may the church yield to that temptation. Discipline may unavoidably issue in expulsion from the church, but its aim must be the correction of the offender, not his elimination.

That is plainly taught in the Matthew 18 passage to which reference was already made (vss. 15-17). Jesus does not say: "If thy brother shall trespass against thee, forthwith bring charges against him before the church." Quite to the contrary, He says: "Go and tell him his fault between thee and him alone: if he shall hear thee, thou hast gained thy brother." Nor does He proceed: "But if he will not hear thee, report the matter without further delay to the church in order that it may take summary

action against him." No, He says: "Then take with thee
one or two more, that in the mouth of two or three witnesses every word may be established." Only as a last
resort are Christians to report one another's offenses to
the church. They may not leave a stone unturned to gain
the offender before referring his case to the church. And
when that has become necessary, the first duty of the
church still is to seek to reclaim the erring brother.

The salvation of the offender is indeed a high aim of
church discipline, but there is a higher aim. The spiritual welfare of the individual member is a means to
the end of the promotion of the purity and edification of
the church as a whole. Who will deny that the well-
being of any one member is conducive to the well-being
of the whole body? If an eye is diseased, the whole body
will be benefited by the healing of that eye. And who
will deny that the well-being of the body as a whole is
more important than the well-being of any one member?
It is far better that a gangrenous foot be amputated than
that the whole body be destroyed by disease. One significant reason for the decadence of certain churches has
been their failure to resort in time to the surgery of
discipline.

The highest aim of ecclesiastical discipline remains to
be named. It is the glory of the Head of the church,
even Jesus Christ. As the welfare of the individual
member is a means to the end of the welfare of the church
as a body, so the welfare of that body is a means to the
glorification of its Head. And that is a way of saying
that the church which neglects discipline is not only
destroying its own glory but also shows a serious disregard of the glory of Christ. The faithful exercise of discipline is in very deed a mark of the true church. The
church which is not deeply concerned about the honor
of Christ simply is no church of His. On the other
hand, passionate love for Christ and a consequent consuming zeal for His glory will impel the true church to
be faithful in discipline.

ITS WHOLESOME OPERATION

Following are a few of many possible suggestions as to the wholesome operation of ecclesiastical discipline.

Those churches which still exercise some discipline today are ordinarily much less concerned about the beliefs of their members than about their behavior. That is a grave mistake. According to Scripture the church should show an equal concern for both. The same apostle who commanded the church at Corinth to put away a member who was guilty of incest instructed Titus to reject a heretic after the first and second admonition and boldly declared: "Though we, or an angel from heaven, preach any other gospel unto you than that which we have preached unto you, let him be accursed" (Galatians 1:8). Nothing could be more logical. One's beliefs determine one's behavior. That may not always be immediately evident, but in the long run it is inevitable. Besides, error itself is sin. To adulterate the truth is as immoral as to commit adultery in the literal sense of that term.

The Roman Catholic Church makes a sharp distinction between venial and mortal sins. Many Protestants, too, presume to be able to tell which sins are great and which are small. And so the notion has become prevalent that the church properly resorts to discipline if one of its members holds up a bank or commits premeditated murder, but not if he occasionally, or even frequently, tells a lie. Those who make such distinctions are treading on dangerous ground. Every sin is heinous and, while there are more heinous and less heinous sins, God's judgment of that matter may differ widely from ours. God is not influenced, as we are, by traditions and popular prejudices. The eighth commandment forbids stealing and the ninth forbids the bearing of false witness. What right has anyone to take the ninth less seriously than the eighth? It follows that in the exercise of discipline the church must take into account not only the seriousness of the offense committed but also, and especially, the attitude of the offender toward his sin. If the murderer gives evidence of heartfelt repentance, he can be dealt with gently. If the slanderer gives no evidence of sorrow but hardens his heart, excommunication may be in order.

In Reformed and Presbyterian churches it is often supposed that discipline is a task of the elders only and that the other members have no responsibility in this matter. That is a serious error. The members of the church are primarily responsible for disciplining those who err. If my brother insults me, I have no right to report his sin to the session until I have done my utmost to get him to apologize. If I see my brother in an intoxicated condition, I have no business telling others until I have done everything possible to bring him to repentance and all my efforts have proved futile. In fact, I sin against the law of love if I expose him sooner. Again, if I am convinced that my brother is guilty of doctrinal error, I must do all in my power to convince him of the truth before bringing him to trial.

In conclusion, two great principles may be named, the observance of which will contribute much to the wholesome operation of church discipline. One is that discipline must concern itself with both the purity and the peace of the church. Nothing disturbs the peace of the church as much as impurity. Peace at the expense of purity is utterly unworthy of its name. And while insistence on purity may temporarily disturb the peace, in the end it is sure to prove highly conducive to peace. The other principle is that discipline must be exercised with both justice and mercy. Mercy without justice is sheer sentimentalism. Justice without mercy is unworthy of a church which has the command: "Be ye merciful as your Father also is merciful" (Luke 6:36), and every member of which needs daily to repeat the prayer of the publican: "God, be merciful to me a sinner" (Luke 18:13).

Chapter 47

THE SOVEREIGNTY OF THE CHURCH

Sovereignty is correctly defined as "the possession or exercise of supreme authority; dominion; sway." A most important word in that definition is *supreme*. The English word *sovereign* is derived from the Latin *supremus,* which means *highest* or *supreme.* In the light of this derivation the less usual spelling *soveren* is correct. The spelling *sovereign* seems to have come into use because *soverenty* usually involves *reigning.*

God alone is sovereign in the absolute sense, for His authority is truly supreme. He holds unlimited sway over the whole of the universe. "He doeth according to his will in the army of heaven and among the inhabitants of the earth; and no one can stay his hand or say unto him, What doest thou?" (Daniel 4:35)

However, the term *sovereignty* has also come to be used in a relative sense. The sovereign God has seen fit to lend authority to some of His creatures over others. In consequence, while no creature has an iota of sovereignty in relation to the Creator, certain creatures do possess a measure of sovereignty in relation to other creatures.

Therefore it is proper to ascribe sovereignty, for example, to the state; and that is commonly done. Much less frequently are men wont to ascribe sovereignty to the Christian church, and yet to do that is not a whit less proper. Its sovereignty is a significant aspect of its glory.

A RESTRICTED SOVEREIGNTY

Let us suppose that a certain village has three churches, that each of those churches has a high spire, and that all three of those spires are of exactly the same height. No matter how high they may be, not one of them is the highest. Manifestly there can never be more than one highest. It follows that there is but one who is truly sovereign. That one is God. No matter how great the power and authority of, shall we say, the state or the church may be, God alone is sovereign.

Therefore the church has no sovereignty whatever with reference to God. God is sovereign over the church, and that is the entire truth. The church is wholly subject unto God. Its one duty is to obey the law of God, and it has no right to make laws of its own that contradict or even augment the law of God. It may neither allow what God forbids nor forbid what God allows.

As the church is subject to God, so it is subject to its Head and King, Jesus Christ. He reigns over it as its absolute monarch. His word is law for the church, and the church has no right to amend His law whether by alteration, addition, or subtraction. It is entirely correct to say that the church has no legislative power, for Christ has given it a perfect law. When it makes certain rules and regulations in the interest of good order, as it often must, these are never to be equated with the law of Christ.

How clear that the church's sovereignty is severely restricted! With reference to God and Christ it is simply non-existent.

God has, however, given a measure of authority to the church with reference to men, and that authority may somewhat loosely be denominated sovereignty. The question whether this sovereignty is restricted or unrestricted has been the subject of much contention throughout the church's history. While Protestantism insists that it is restricted, the Church of Rome teaches that it is unrestricted. The authority which Rome claims for itself is truly totalitarian. But that claim cannot be substantiated.

When God made man in His image, He endowed him with certain inherent rights. By man's fall into sin that image was severely marred and even largely lost, but not annihilated. In consequence, every human being remains in possession of certain inalienable rights. And in the case of the regenerate, in whom the image of God has been restored, those rights are accentuated. Freedom of speech and freedom of worship are but two of them. To be sure, in the exercise of those rights each man must respect the rights of his fellow men and, above all else, the law of God, but nobody may seek to deprive him of those rights. Rome has often done precisely that. There was a time when it forbade not only the reading, but the possessing, of a Bible; and frequently it has inflicted the penalty of death on those who dared to criticize the teachings and practices of the church. Beyond all doubt, the church's sovereignty with reference to the individual is restricted.

So is the sovereignty of the church with reference to the family restricted. God established the human family in the garden of Eden. He created woman and gave her to Adam that she might be his wife. He commanded them: "Be fruitful and multiply and replenish the earth" (Genesis 1:28). Significantly, God, not the church, brought the family into being, and it antedates the founding of the church. It follows undeniably that the family, like the individual, has certain rights on which the church may not encroach. It is not the church's business to stipulate the precise percentage of the family budget that is to be given to the church, nor to prescribe a menu for the family dinner, nor yet to dictate to a bereaved family where it is to bury its dead.

More instances of restrictions on the church's sovereignty might be named, but in this context the relation of the church to the state deserves special attention.

For centuries two opposite views of the relation of church and state have vied with each other. The western church, under the leadership of the bishop of Rome, has long taken the position that the church must exercise authority over the state. Pope Pius IX declared that the pope as head of the church "possesses the right, which he properly uses under favorable circumstances, to pass

judgment even in civil affairs on the acts of princes and
of nations." Contrariwise, the eastern church early took
the position that the church is but a phase of the state
and that it is the state's duty to appoint the officers of the
church, to define its laws, and to support it. Constantine
the Great, who was the first Roman emperor to give official recognition to the Christian church and in 330 A.D.
moved his capital eastward to the city which he named
Constantinople for himself, was regarded not only as head
of the empire but also as head of the church. In later
times the Russian czars claimed the same double honor.
It is not strange that the churches of the Protestant
Reformation, by way of opposition to Rome, adhered in
the main to a more or less similar view. Since one of its
ablest advocates in the Reformation era was a Swiss
physician and theologian by the name of Erastus, it came
to be known as Erastianism.

Today a large part of Protestantism, American Protestantism in particular, is convinced that the Bible teaches
what is commonly — and rather loosely — called the separation of church and state. On this score some Anabaptists of the Reformation period and that famous American Baptist, Roger Williams, must be credited with having
been ahead of their contemporaries. What is meant by
the separation of church and state is that the church may
not seek to govern a commonwealth nor interfere with the
purely political affairs of the state, and that the state
may not seek to govern the church nor interfere with its
spiritual affairs. In short, both the church and the state
are sovereign, each in its own sphere; and each must
recognize the other's sovereignty. That is implied in the
saying of the Lord Jesus: "Render unto Caesar the things
that are Caesar's, and unto God the things that are God's"
(Matthew 22:21), on which Calvin has commented that
the Lord here "lays down a clear distinction between
spiritual and civil government." The same truth is implicit in the fact that at Pentecost the church, which had
been largely — although not entirely — national, became

universal. A universal church must needs transcend the bounds of nationalism. And is it not obvious that neither did the state create the church nor did the church create the state, but God originated both and endowed each with its own specific authority?

The conclusion is inescapable that, while the sovereignty of the state with reference to the church is restricted, the sovereignty of the church with reference to the state is also restricted. The church is sovereign only in its own sphere. Its authority is not totalitarian.

A POSITIVE SOVEREIGNTY

Let no one infer from the foregoing that the sovereignty of the church amounts to little or nothing. The truth is that it is very real, most actual and decidedly positive.

Time and again in its history the church has found it necessary to assert its sovereignty over against usurpation by the state.

It is an interesting fact that already under the theocracy of the Old Testament, when church and state were much more closely joined than has been the case since Pentecost, the church on various occasions exercised its sovereignty vigorously in opposition to the encroaching state. King Saul was ready to go to battle against the Philistines. It seems to have been customary for the Israelites before joining battle to bring a sacrifice to God. That was a function of the priests, to be performed in this instance by Samuel. When Samuel was late in coming, Saul became impatient and himself offered the sacrifice. Presently Samuel arrived and informed Saul that because of this sin the kingdom would be taken from him (I Samuel 13:9-14). King Uzziah once upon a time insisted on burning incense on the altar of incense in the temple. This again was a prerogative of the priests. When the king ignored the vigorous protest of the priests, God smote him with leprosy, and his son reigned in his stead (II Chronicles 26:16-20). In both those instances a repre-

sentative of the state was severely punished for encroaching upon the sovereignty of the church.

The New Testament records some striking instances
of the same sort of thing. To name but one, when the
Sanhedrin, the supreme court of the Jews, forbade the
apostles to preach in the name of Jesus, Peter declared
boldly: "We ought to obey God rather than men" (Acts
5:29) ; and so they did.

When the Diet of Worms demanded that Luther recant
his supposedly heretical teachings, he sovereignly uttered
the memorable words: "Here I stand; I cannot do otherwise; God help me; Amen." John Knox sovereignly de-
fied both the tears and the wrath of Queen Mary, and over
his grave Melville spoke: "Here lies one who never feared
the face of man." Said Lord Macaulay of the Puritan:
"He bowed himself in the dust before his Maker, but he
set his foot on the neck of his king."

Ours is an age of state totalitarianism. All over the
world statism is in the ascendancy. In the second world
war three totalitarian states, Germany, Italy and Japan,
suffered a crushing defeat, but Russia, another totalitarian
state, has since risen to incomparably greater heights of
power and influence than ever before. And in the so-called
democracies, the United States of America included, there
is a strong trend toward statism. In consequence, in many
lands the church finds itself utterly at the mercy of a
state whose mercy often proves cruelty, while in others
the notion is rapidly gaining ground that the church exists
and operates by the state's permission. Now, if ever, is
the time for the church to assert its sovereignty over
against encroachments by the state. The church is in
sacred duty bound to rise up in majesty and proclaim to
the world that it enjoys freedom of worship, not by the
grace of the state, but as a God-given right and that it
preaches the Word of God, not by the grace of human
governments, but solely at the command of the sovereign
God and its sovereign King, seated at God's right hand.

In another respect, too, the sovereignty of the church

is positive indeed. It must sovereignly lay down the law of God to the individual, the family, society and the state.

No individual has the right to say that his private life is his own to lead and is none of the church's business. That would be far too sweeping an assertion. The law of God concerns every aspect of human life, and the church has been charged with the proclamation of that law in all its Scriptural fullness. It must condemn every sin in the life of the individual. To be sure, there are a number of practices which the law of God neither commands nor forbids. They are commonly called *adiaphora* or *indifferent things*. But even such matters are not beyond God's law. An accurate definition of an *adiaphoron* is a *practice which the law of God allows but does not require*. That means that the so-called indifferent things have divine sanction. In themselves they are neither immoral nor amoral, but good, although not required. But only then is their performance truly good when they are performed in faith and out of love. While the church must be scrupulously careful not to forbid what God allows, it must also tell men what is the proper use according to the Word of God of that which God allows.

Never may the family tell the church defiantly to refrain from meddling with any of its affairs. That would be exceedingly rash. With reference to the family, too, the church must sovereignly proclaim the whole law of God. When a husband and his wife are contemplating divorce, they may not bid the church leave them alone. It must acquaint them with the teaching of Scripture on divorce and demand of them that they live accordingly. That church is remiss in the performance of its duty which does not proclaim the teaching of the Word of God on "mixed marriages" and "planned parenthood." And whether parents give their children a truly Christian training is not merely their concern, but the church's as well. For on that subject, too, God has spoken, and He has done so emphatically.

For many decades the social gospel has been popular

with liberals. In their righteous indignation with the
social gospel of modernism many fundamentalists have
illogically jumped to the conclusion that the gospel must
be presented only on a strictly individual basis. In consequence, conservative churches generally have neglected
the social aspects of the gospel. But that is a way of
saying that those churches have failed to assert their
sovereignty in relation to society. For but one example,
society is sorely troubled today by juvenile delinquency.
All too often the church is satisfied with the role of a mildly interested, if not altogether disinterested, onlooker. It
must inculcate in its own children the fear of the Lord.
But that is not enough. It must declare from the house-
tops that Christian education and training for the youth
of the land are the indispensable requisite for godly behavior.

It must be admitted to the church's shame that it has
often cowered before the state. It was not ever thus.
When David had stolen Bathsheba from her husband
Uriah and had then got rid of him by what amounted to
murder, the prophet Nathan told him off in utter fearless-
ness. And when King Ahab had robbed and killed Na-
both, the prophet Elijah unflinchingly pronounced upon
him and his house the judgments of God. A noble company of God's servants has followed in the train of those
prophets, but that company has never been as large as it
should have been. Today it is small indeed. The church
of God should lift up its voice with strength against lying
and theft and bribery and vice, which are so frightfully
rampant in high places. It must proclaim aloud that
"righteousness exalteth a nation, but sin is a reproach
to any people" (Proverbs 14:34). It is much more than
time for the church to call to repentance and, in case
of failure to repent, to discipline to the point of excommunication those rulers of the world who are at once
members of Christ's church and putrid politicians. And
those power-hungry potentates who neither fear God nor
regard man but take counsel together against the Lord

and His Anointed, saying: "Let us break their bands asunder and cast away their cords from us," must be told by the church that He that sits in the heavens will laugh, that the Lord will have them in derision, and that, if they fail to kiss the Son, He will break them with a rod of iron and dash them in pieces like a potter's vessel (Psalm 2).

Let the church speak sovereignly for the sovereign God and "the blessed and only Potentate, the King of kings and Lord of lords" (I Timothy 6:15).

Chapter 48

GOD'S ELECT

The church consists of God's elect. To be sure, not all who are listed as members of the visible church were chosen by God unto eternal life. There are those within the church who are but nominal Christians and will never be believers. They are not of the number of the elect. But all true members of the church of Christ belong to the elect.

Perhaps no other teaching of the Word of God is as unpopular as that of election. Even some Bible-believing and Bible-loving Christians come close to detesting it. That is difficult to account for. Not only is election taught unmistakably in Scripture, but this doctrine sets forth most emphatically and most beautifully the infinite and eternal love of God for His own.

Thus the fact that the church consists of God's elect imparts great glory to it.

SPECIFIED BY GOD THE FATHER

Let us suppose that a congregation is going to erect a church, a house of worship. The first step toward the realization of that project is the engagement of an architect, who will draw up a plan for the proposed building and will specify what material is to go into it. As the architect of His church, God the Father planned it from eternity and specified precisely what persons would constitute it. He chose them out of the whole human race to that end.

Of the Old Testament church God spoke as "Jacob, my servant" and "Israel, mine elect" (Isaiah 45:4). In the opening sentence of his letter to the church at Ephesus

Paul exulted: "Blessed be the God and Father of our Lord Jesus Christ, who hath blessed us with all spiritual blessings in heavenly places in Christ; according as he hath chosen us in him before the foundation of the world, that we should be holy and without blame before him in love; having predestinated us unto the adoption of children by Jesus Christ to himself, according to the good pleasure of his will" (Ephesians 1:3-5). And Peter addressed those to whom he wrote his first epistle as "elect, according to the foreknowledge of God the Father" (I Peter 1:2).

There are those who tell us that God has elected all men to be members of the body of Christ. Nothing could be more absurd. The very word *election* means choosing out of a larger number, and choosing all of a certain number simply is not choosing at all. Three men, let us say, are running for the governorship of a given state. A certain voter, unable to make up his mind which of them is the best man for that position, casts a ballot for all three. How clear that he has thrown his vote away! It is no less clear that, if all other voters did likewise, there would be no election. It follows that, if God elected all men to be members of His church, He elected no one. That conclusion is inescapable.

Interestingly enough, some who hold that God elected all men do actually come to that very conclusion. They say that the only reason why anybody becomes a member of Christ's church is that of his own volition he chooses to join the church. In other words, one becomes a member of the church, not of God's choice, but of one's own choice. Thus election is of man, not of God. But a more flagrant contradiction of Scripture is hardly imaginable.

Karl Barth teaches that all men are elected by and in Christ to life eternal. Having taken that position, which is clearly at odds with Scripture, he faces a serious dilemma. Either he must, in concord with universalism, conclude that in the end all men will be saved, or he must, after the manner of Arminianism, make salvation de-

pendent in last instance on the will of man. However,
he refuses to seat himself on either horn of that dilemma.
Thus his doctrine of election becomes puzzling in the
extreme.

The all-important question arises why God from eternity specified certain persons in distinction from others
as members of His church. Two contradictory answers
have been given. Arminianism teaches that God chose
certain individuals because He foreknew that they would
believe in Christ. Reformed theology insists that the sole
reason for God's choice was the divine sovereign love.
That is to say, from eternity God viewed the objects of
His choice in Christ, His Chosen One. According to
Arminianism the ground for God's choice lay in man;
according to Calvinism it lay in God. In still other words,
Arminianism holds that faith is the ground of election,
while the Reformed faith holds that faith is a fruit of
election and also its proof.

Not only does Scripture substantiate the Reformed
teaching by affirming explicitly that God predestinated
the members of His church "according to the good pleasure of his will" (Ephesians 1:5) and by concluding from
God's statement to Moses: "I will have mercy on whom
I will have mercy, and I will have compassion on whom
I will have compassion" that "it is not of him that willeth,
nor of him that runneth, but of God that sheweth mercy"
(Romans 9:15, 16); but the very passages of Scripture
which the Arminian is wont to adduce in support of his
view actually teach the Reformed view. Prominent
among them is Romans 8:29 — "Whom he did foreknow
he also did predestinate to be conformed to the image of
his Son." Says the Arminian: "How clear that election
is based upon foreknowledge!" So it is. But just what
is meant here by foreknowledge? That is the question.
Is it a mere prescience on the part of God that the person concerned would believe? Nothing whatever is said
about that. What the text says is that God foreknew
certain persons. Beyond the shadow of a doubt *knew* here

has that rich, pregnant meaning which it so often has in Scripture. It means nothing less than *loved*. And when we are told that God foreknew certain persons, this means that God loved those persons from eternity. Because He loved them from eternity He predestinated them to be conformed to the image of His Son.

What mortal can tell why God loved them? Divine love is not human love. Human love is finite; God's is infinite. This we know: the reason why God loved certain individuals from eternity lay not in those individuals but in God Himself. In a word, His love is sovereign. Election spells the infinite and sovereign love of God for the members of His church. He chose them in Christ, His Beloved (Ephesians 1:4).

PURCHASED BY GOD THE SON

Let us suppose again that a congregation is going to build a house of worship. The plans and specifications having been adopted, a next step is the purchase of the building material. That, too, God attended to in the building of His church. God the Son bought the elect, those whom the Father had specified as members of His church. Paul reminded the elders of the church at Ephesus of their duty to feed the church of God, "which," said he, "he hath purchased with his own blood" (Acts 20:28).

Some of the early church fathers were of the opinion that Christ paid to Satan the price with which He purchased the elect. But that is a gross misrepresentation. Christ's doing that would have constituted a recognition of the devil as at one time the rightful owner of elect sinners. It is self-evident that Satan has never been that. The facts of the case are rather as follows. When man sinned, God as Judge sentenced the human race to imprisonment. Satan was, as it were, keeper of the prison. Christ came to give His life as a ransom for certain prisoners. Most certainly He presented the ransom, not to the jailer, but to the Judge. The Judge accepted the ran-

som and ordered those prisoners released. Thus are sinners delivered from the power of darkness and translated
into the kingdom of God's dear Son (Colossians 1:13).

In our day another misrepresentation of that transaction
is prevalent. It is said that Christ bought not only the
elect, but all men, with His blood and that, having done
that, He left it to each individual's choice whether or not
to accept the saving benefit of His death. But that presentation fails utterly to do justice to the dying Saviour's
love for His own. To be sure, Christ's death is sufficient
for the salvation of all men. However, it must be asserted
emphatically that not one whom Christ has bought with
His blood will remain in the power of the devil. His love
makes certain that all whom He has bought will become
believers in Him and members of His church. He will
bring that to pass, not by external compulsion, but by
the gracious influence of His Holy Spirit. "The good
shepherd giveth his life for the sheep" (John 10:11).
And He will see to it that every last sheep for which He
gave His life is brought into the fold.

Scripture often speaks in superlative terms of the love
of God for His church. For example, God exclaims: "Can
a woman forget her sucking child that she should not have
compassion on the son of her womb? yea, they may forget,
yet will not I forget thee. Behold, I have graven thee on
the palms of my hands; thy walls are continually before
me" (Isaiah 49:15, 16). That language is both exceedingly strong and supremely tender. But the revelation of
God's love for His church reaches its acme in the purchase of that church by the Son of God with His own
blood. Looking up to the crucified Christ, every member
of His church whispers: "Who loved me and gave himself for me" (Galatians 2:20). In unison the church
reads: "God commendeth his love toward us in that, while
we were yet sinners, Christ died for us. Much more then,
being now justified by his blood, we shall be saved from
wrath through him. For if, when we were enemies, we
were reconciled to God by the death of his Son, much

more, being reconciled, we shall be saved by his life"
(Romans 5:8-10). And it sings:

> See, from His head, His hands, His feet,
> Sorrow and love flow mingled down:
> Did e'er such love and sorrow meet,
> Or thorns compose so rich a crown?

ASSEMBLED BY GOD THE HOLY SPIRIT

Once more let us suppose that a congregation is in
process of erecting a church. The plans and specifications have been approved and the building material has
been bought. Obviously, one thing remains to be done —
the material must be fitted together. That having been
done, the structure will be complete. That, too, God does
as He builds His church. The elect, those who were specified by God the Father from eternity and purchased by
God the Son when He died on Calvary's cross, are in the
course of history assembled as the Christian church by
God the Holy Spirit.

The Spirit accomplishes this by granting to the elect
the grace of regeneration. By nature they are dead in
trespasses and sins, but the Spirit of God makes them
alive (Ephesians 2:1). It is a foregone conclusion that
in consequence they will believe on the Lord Jesus Christ.
Some of the elect are foreordained to die in infancy. All
of these are certain to be regenerated before their departure from this life, and from the very moment of
regeneration they possess what theologians call the *habi-
tus*, the disposition, of saving faith. That makes them
members of the body of Christ. As for the elect who are
foreordained to reach the years of discretion, although
no human being can tell at what age it may please the
Holy Spirit to grant them the new birth, they, too, are
certain to be born again, and in their case regeneration
will issue in conscious reception of the Saviour as He is
offered in the gospel. That is a way of saying that sooner

or later by the grace of the Holy Spirit they are bound to
become living members of Christ's church.

The notion is widely held in Christian circles that all
human beings, the unregenerate included, are able of their
own free volition to accept Christ as Saviour and by so
doing to join His church. In fact, God is said to have left
that part of salvation to man. And the new birth is declared to be a consequence, not a prerequisite, of man's
act of faith. That is one of the most prevalent and, it
must be said, most serious errors of present-day fundamentalism. By ultimately making man his own saviour
this heresy does the greatest violence to that cardinal
doctrine of the Word of God — salvation by the grace of
God. Scripture teaches unmistakably that no one can
come to Christ in faith except the Father draw him (John
6:44) ; that, before faith becomes an act of man, it is a
gift of God (Philippians 1:29) ; and that "no man can
say that Jesus is the Lord but by the Holy Ghost" (I Corinthians 12:3). Scripture teaches just as clearly that it
is God who gathers His elect into the church. It was God
the Holy Spirit who, by the application of Peter's sermon
to their hearts, assembled three thousand men and women
into the church on the day of Pentecost. And it was "the
Lord" who subsequently "added to the church daily such
as should be saved" (Acts 2:47).

How glorious a manifestation of the divine love is the
assembling of God's elect into the church! If God had
chosen certain individuals to constitute the body of His
Son but had made the realization of that choice contingent on their consent, not one of them would be saved.
If, in addition to choosing them, God had purchased them
with His blood to be members of His church, but had made
the completion of that transaction dependent on their acceptance of its terms, all would be lost. So great is the
love of God for His own that He accomplishes their salvation to the utmost. Not only did He choose them from
the foundation of the world and purchase them on Calvary, but He makes that choice and that purchase effec-

tive by the operation of His Spirit within them. The Holy Spirit brings them from death to life, imparts to them saving faith and thus makes them members of Christ. From its first beginning to its ultimate end their salvation is of the sovereign grace and infinite love of God.

The church consists of those whom God loves so exceedingly.

SAVED FOR SERVICE

At this point attention must be called to an aspect of election which is sometimes neglected by those who confess that doctrine. Most certainly election is unto salvation, but Scripture teaches no less emphatically that it is unto service. In fact, salvation and service are inseparable. Salvation is unto service.

The members of Christ's church are God's "workmanship, created in Christ Jesus unto good works" (Ephesians 2:10): Because they were bought with a price, they are under the solemn obligation to glorify God in their bodies and their spirits, both of which are God's (I Corinthians 6:20). Christ gave Himself for them that He might redeem them from all iniquity and purify unto Himself a peculiar people, zealous for good works (Titus 2:14). And let it be said with all possible emphasis — God chose His church in sovereign love, the Son bought it with His precious blood, and the Holy Spirit came to dwell within it, *to the end that it might witness.* It is a chosen generation, a royal priesthood, a holy nation, a peculiar people; that it might show forth the praises of Him who called it out of darkness into His marvellous light (I Peter 2:9).

The church consists of those who love and serve the Triune God because He first loved them.

Chapter 49

GOD'S FRIENDS

The church consists of God's covenant people. This is a way of saying that it consists of God's friends. For the covenant of grace spells friendship between God and His own.

In essence the covenant of grace was established when, immediately after the fall of man, God said to the serpent: "I will put enmity between thee and the woman, and between thy seed and her seed; it shall bruise thy head, and thou shalt bruise his heel" (Genesis 3:15). Enmity with Satan implies friendship with God.

More explicitly God established His covenant with Abraham when He said: "I will establish my covenant between me and thee and thy seed after thee in their generations for an everlasting covenant, to be a God unto thee and to thy seed after thee" (Genesis 17:7). Thus Abraham became God's friend. Repeatedly Scripture calls him by that name. When many strong enemies came against King Jehoshaphat, he called upon God for help and pleaded: "Art not thou our God, who didst drive out the inhabitants of this land before thy people Israel and gavest it to the seed of Abraham thy friend for ever?" (II Chronicles 20:7) God Himself declared: "But thou, Israel, art my servant, Jacob whom I have chosen, the seed of Abraham my friend" (Isaiah 41:8). And James says: "The Scripture was fulfilled which saith, Abraham believed God, and it was imputed unto him for righteousness: and he was called the friend of God" (James 2:23).

The Psalmist equates the covenant of grace with friendship between God and His people in the words: "The friendship of Jehovah is with them that fear him; and he will show them his covenant" (Psalm 25:14, ASV).

Inasmuch as the believers of all ages are Abraham's seed (Galatians 3:7, 29), they are God's covenant people, God's friends.

SOVEREIGN FRIENDSHIP

Let no one think that our first parents, when they had fallen into sin, sought God. Quite to the contrary, they fled from His presence. But God in His sovereign grace sought them. Nor did God merely suggest to them that they become enemies of the prince of darkness and invite them to become friends of the Father of lights. He did incomparably more. He *put* enmity between the woman and the serpent and between the seed of the two and, by so doing, *established* friendship between Himself and His people. No sooner had God spoken than that enmity and that friendship were realities.

Likewise it must not be supposed that Abraham sought God's friendship. Contrariwise, God sovereignly offered him His friendship. Nor did God make this offer contingent on Abraham's acceptance. Without consulting Abraham He made him His friend. Said God: "I will establish my covenant between me and thee," and established it was.

What is true of Abraham holds also of his seed. God did not inform Abraham that the covenant which He was establishing with him would be continued with his seed in case his seed should care to have it continued. From its very inception God included in the covenant Abraham's seed as well as Abraham.

At this point election and the covenant of grace converge, and the latter complements the former. In election God was absolutely sovereign. "According to the good pleasure of his will" He foreordained individuals unto salvation (Ephesians 1:5). He loved Jacob and hated his twin-brother Esau (Romans 9:13). But that is not the whole truth. Without being bound in His choice by family relationships, He nevertheless chose to take them into account. By and large He elected unto eternal life cer-

tain persons together with their seed. And in doing that
He was again completely sovereign.

The sovereign character of the divine friendship comes
to forceful expression in the word employed in the Greek
New Testament to designate the covenant of grace. It is
not the word which is commonly used for a covenant or
agreement made by men with equal rights. On the contrary, it specifically denotes a disposition made by one
person in behalf of another. In some contexts it is properly translated *testament*. As one in his last will of his
own free choice bequeaths his possessions to another, so
God in the covenant of grace sovereignly bestows His
friendship upon the elect.

Never may it be forgotten that in the very nature of
things a covenant has two parties. The covenant of grace
is no exception. God alone established it, but in its operation God's people may not sit idly by. Friendship must
needs be mutual. The covenant of grace places God's
people under the obligations of faith and obedience. Therefore Scripture says: "Abraham believed God, and it was
imputed unto him for righteousness: and he was called
the friend of God" (James 2:23), and Jesus told His
disciples: "Ye are my friends if ye do whatsoever I command you" (John 15:14). And yet, let no one think that
this responsibility of God's people detracts aught from
the sovereignty of the divine friendship. Rather, it
stresses that sovereignty all the more. For it is of the
sovereign grace of God that His own comply with the demands of the covenant. Both faith and obedience are gifts
sovereignly imparted by the Holy Spirit to the elect. They
work out their own salvation because God once worked,
and ever keeps working, in them both to will and to do of
His good pleasure (Philippians 2:12, 13).

INTIMATE FRIENDSHIP

How the Creator can regard mere creatures as His
friends defies human understanding. How the holy God
can bestow His friendship on sinful men is utterly incom-

prehensible. Suffice it to say that here we witness a supreme manifestation of divine condescension. And the intimacy of that friendship renders the divine condescension all the more marvelous.

The derivation of the Hebrew word employed in the Old Testament to designate the covenant of grace is uncertain. Perhaps it was derived from a root meaning *to bind*. That God should willingly be bound to man is indeed condescension. It is also possible that the word under consideration was derived from a root meaning *to cut*. In making a covenant it was customary in the Orient to cut certain animals in two and to place the pieces at a short distance over against each other. Then the parties to the covenant would walk between the pieces, signifying that, if they broke the covenant, they would be willing to be cut in pieces as these animals had been. When God established His covenant with Abraham, He actually condescended to do that very thing. At God's command Abraham arranged the pieces of various animals, and, when the sun had set, "behold, a smoking furnace and a burning lamp that passed between those pieces. In the same day the Lord made a covenant with Abraham" (Genesis 15: 8-18). That, too, was extreme condescension. Again, it has been suggested by some scholars that the Hebrew word for covenant may mean *eating together*. When making a covenant, Orientals would often banquet with each other. Whether or not that is the meaning of the word, as a matter of fact the Lord condescended to visit Abraham in his tent and to eat the fare served by His friend (Genesis 18:1-8).

The intimacy of God's friendship with Abraham is revealed strikingly in a rhetorical question asked by the Lord on the latter occasion. On leaving Abraham's tent He and the angels attending Him walked toward the doomed city of Sodom. Abraham accompanied them. Said the Lord: "Shall I hide from Abraham the thing which I do?" (Genesis 18:17) Because Abraham was His friend God disclosed to him secrets that He would tell no other.

God deals likewise with all His covenant people. It makes little difference whether in Psalm 25:14 we follow the King James Version or the American Revised. The former speaks of "the secret of the Lord," the latter of "the friendship of Jehovah." Friendship comes to expression in the revealing of secrets. One tells a friend everything. To be sure, it may not be inferred that today God gives the members of His church special revelations in addition to Holy Writ. Special revelation is complete in the Bible. But God imparts to His friends, in distinction from others, the inward illumination of His Spirit for the proper understanding of divine revelation, so that it may be said to them: "Ye have an unction from the Holy One, and ye know all things" (I John 2:20).

The climactic revelation of the intimacy of God's friendship for His own is found in the incarnation of His Son and the outpouring of His Spirit. The Word that was in the beginning, that was not only with God but was very God, was made flesh and dwelt among us (John 1:1, 14). His own saw Him with their eyes and handled Him with their hands (I John 1:1). And when He was about to return to the Father He spoke to His friends: "I will pray the Father, and he shall give you another Comforter, that he may abide with you for ever; even the Spirit of truth, whom the world cannot receive because it seeth him not neither knoweth him: but ye know him, for he dwelleth with you and shall be in you" (John 14:16,17). God *with* His people; nay, God *in* them — that is at once unfathomable mystery and supreme intimacy.

DEVOTED FRIENDSHIP

Genuine friendship is more than a feeling of good will. Also, it is more than an expression of good will in words. It manifests itself in deeds of love, in acts of devotion.

The friendship of God toward His covenant people is so devoted as to defy appraisal. All we can do is to repeat a few Scriptural statements on that exalted theme. But the import of those statements no mortal can fully comprehend.

When God made His covenant with Abraham and his seed, He, marvelous to say, gave *Himself* to them (Genesis 17:7). Henceforth they were not merely His people, but He was their God. That is the all-embracing blessing of the covenant of grace. And of that blessing God repeatedly assured His church of both dispensations (Leviticus 26:12, Jeremiah 31:33, Hebrews 8:10).

The God who gave Himself to His people gave His only-begotten Son for them. And the Son of God willingly gave His life a ransom for the elect. "Greater love hath no man than this, that a man lay down his life for his friends" (John 15:13).

Bound up with the gift of God's Son is the gift of life everlasting. "The gift of God is eternal life through Jesus Christ our Lord" (Romans 6:23).

Again, the Spirit of truth and holiness, who operated already in the church of the old dispensation and was poured out upon the church of the new, is a gift of God to His people (Romans 5:5); and that Spirit imparts to the church "all spiritual blessings in heavenly places" (Ephesians 1:3).

If God spared not His own Son but delivered Him up for us all, "how shall he not also with him freely give us all things?" (Romans 8:32) Paul wrote to the Corinthians: "All things are yours: whether Paul, or Apollos, or Cephas, or the world, or life, or death, or things present, or things to come; all are yours. And ye are Christ's, and Christ is God's" (I Corinthians 3:21-23).

Friendship is always mutual. There may be unreciprocated affection or unrequited love, but never unreciprocated or unrequited friendship. It follows that the members of Christ's church are not only obligated to manifest friendship for God in their lives, but they are certain to do this. If any who are listed as church members fail to do this, they prove themselves not to be members of the body of Christ. And while the best members of that body

fall far short of that fullness of devotion which they owe
their heavenly Friend, every true member does serve Him
devotedly. He delights in the law of God after the inward
man (Romans 7:22). Albeit only in principle, he loves
the Lord his God with all his heart, soul, strength and
mind. In that love he walks (Ephesians 5:2). And his
devotion is all the stronger because he knows that it is
through the grace of God that he is what he is (I Corinthians 15:10).

EVERLASTING FRIENDSHIP

The friendship of God for His people is from everlasting
to everlasting. Because it is from eternity it will be unto
eternity.

No aspect of the covenant of grace looms larger in
Scripture than its everlastingness. When God established
His covenant with Abraham He at once described it as
"an everlasting covenant" (Genesis 17:7). Jehovah com-
forted His people: "The mountains shall depart and the
hills be removed; but my kindness shall not depart from
thee, neither shall the covenant of my peace be removed"
(Isaiah 54:10).

In consequence, God, who founded His church, has sus-
tained it in ages past and will sustain it to the end of time.
The gates of hell never have prevailed against it and never
will. Often the foe within the city of God is more dangerous and more destructive than the enemy without.
Who can deny that such is the case in many instances
today? Nothing is laying waste the church of Christ as
effectively as the unbelief of its leaders. But God will
keep His promise: "No weapon that is formed against
thee shall prosper, and every tongue that shall rise against
thee in judgment thou shalt condemn" (Isaiah 54:17).
The history of the church tells us that, when God's people
broke His covenant, He still remembered it and renewed
it and — wonder of grace — in renewing it, greatly en-
riched it. That is the meaning of the glorious promise

of the new covenant given by Jeremiah to God's people of the old dispensation and appropriated by the author of Hebrews for the church of the new: "Behold, the days come, saith the Lord, that I will make a new covenant with the house of Israel and with the house of Judah: not according to the covenant that I made with their fathers in the day that I took them by the hand to bring them out of the land of Egypt, which my covenant they brake, although I was an husband unto them, saith the Lord. But this shall be the covenant that I will make with the house of Israel: After those days, saith the Lord, I will put my law in their inward parts and write it in their hearts; and I will be their God, and they shall be my people" (Jeremiah 31:31-33, Hebrews 8:8-10). They will be His people, not merely to the end of time, but throughout the endless ages of eternity.

Not only to the church as a body, but to each of its living members, the everlastingness of the covenant offers unspeakable comfort. He goes through life singing:

> I've found a Friend, oh, such a Friend!
> He loved me ere I knew Him,
> And drew me with the cords of love,
> And thus He bound me to Him.
> And round my heart still closely twine
> Those ties which naught can sever,
> For I am His and He is mine
> Forever and forever.

When earthly friends and kindred forsake him, he knows that the Lord will take him up (Psalm 27:10). When indwelling sin perturbs him, his faith looks up to the Lamb of Calvary. When Satan assails him, he calmly affirms: "The prince of darkness grim, I tremble not for him." When the world leads him as a sheep to the slaughter, he glories: "Nay, in all these things I am more than conqueror through Him that loved me" (Romans

8:37).   And when at last he stands on the brink of the dread river of death, which he must needs pass over, his divine Friend takes him by the hand, and he whispers: "I will fear no evil, for thou art with me" (Psalm 23:4). Presently he has crossed.   Now he enters the house of the Lord, where he beholds his Friend face to face.   That is his dwelling forever.

Chapter 50

GOD'S ABODE

Scripture tells us repeatedly that the church is God's dwelling-place.

In the old dispensation God dwelt in the midst of His people Israel, first in the tabernacle and subsequently in the temple. The Old Testament speaks of Him as dwelling between the cherubim that stood with outspread wings over the mercy-seat, the covering of the ark of the covenant.

The new dispensation knows of no holy places comparable to those of the old. Therefore, to denominate the place of public worship "sanctuary" is, to say the least, of questionable propriety. At best it is an anachronism. Jesus told the woman of Samaria that the time was at hand when it would make no difference whether men worshiped God on Mount Zion, the holy place of the Jews, or on Mount Gerizim, the holy place of the Samaritans, so long as they worshiped Him in spirit and in truth (John 4:21-24). The Old Testament sanctuaries belonged to the period of shadows, which was concluded by Christ's death on the cross. Although we have the custom of dedicating a church building and properly call it God's house, God dwells among His people in just as real a sense when they gather for worship in a home or under the dome of heaven. The church in which God dwells is the communion of believers. That is His sanctuary.

How inestimable an honor it is for the church that "the blessed and only Potentate, the King of kings and Lord of lords, who only hath immortality, dwelling in the light which no man can approach unto, whom no man hath seen or can see" (I Timothy 6:15, 16), makes it His abode!

339

A HUMBLE ABODE

It might seem almost sacrilegious to say that the infinite God, whom "the heaven and heaven of heavens cannot contain" (I Kings 8:27), occupies a humble abode. Yet such is the teaching of His Word.

The church consists of created men. Between the Creator and His creatures yawns a gulf which cannot be measured. "Behold, the nations are as a drop of a bucket and are counted as the small dust of the balance . . . . All nations before him are as nothing, and they are counted to him less than nothing, and vanity" (Isaiah 40:15, 17). What condescension that the infinite Creator makes His abode among finite, nay infinitesimal, creatures!

The church consists of sinful human beings. But in the sight of God's resplendent holiness the very seraphs cover their faces with their wings and cry one to another: "Holy, holy, holy is the Lord of hosts: the whole earth is full of his glory." As His people behold Him in His temple, it behooves each of them to exclaim: "Woe is me, for I am undone, because I am a man of unclean lips, and I dwell in the midst of a people of unclean lips" (Isaiah 6:1-5). How incomprehensible that the Holy One of Israel should make His abode with an unclean people!

But not all created men belong to the church of God. Nor are all sinful human beings counted among its members. It consists of such as cry from the depths: "Have mercy upon me, O God, according to thy lovingkindness, according unto the multitude of thy tender mercies blot out my transgressions. Wash me throughly from mine iniquity and cleanse me from my sin. For I acknowledge my transgressions, and my sin is ever before me" (Psalm 51:1-3). Only with such does God dwell as stand afar off, dare not lift up so much as their eyes unto heaven, but smite upon their breast, and say: "God, be merciful to me a sinner" (Luke 18:13). "For thus saith the high and lofty One that inhabiteth eternity, whose name is Holy: I dwell in the high and holy place, with him also that is of a contrite and humble spirit, to revive the spirit of the humble and to revive the heart of the contrite ones" (Isaiah 57:15).

Truly, the church is an exceedingly humble abode for the Most High.

A HOLY ABODE

However humble God's abode may be and actually is, it is also holy. The holiness of God demands that. Therefore the Psalmist said: "Holiness becometh thy house, O Lord, for ever" (Psalm 93:5).

Holiness is one of the most outstanding attributes of the church of God. As was previously pointed out, it is holy in a twofold sense. Having been called by God out of the world and set aside for His service, it is objectively holy. In that sense it is holy regardless of the sin that is found in its midst. Only when a church becomes so steeped in sin that it ceases to be a church does it forfeit that objective holiness. But the church is also subjectively holy. Its true members have been regenerated by the Holy Spirit. By virtue of the new birth they are holy indeed. Sinful though they still are, in principle they are perfect. They are "saints," and the apostle Paul recognized as such even the members of the corrupt Corinthian church (I Corinthians 1:2, II Corinthians 1:1). The Holy Spirit dwells in each of them, and collectively they are His holy house.

Although the Holy Spirit dwelt also in the church of the old dispensation, at Pentecost He was poured out upon the church as never before. To be sure, the church can never be abstracted from the individuals that constitute it; yet it would be a serious error to suppose that at Pentecost the Spirit was imparted merely to certain persons. He was shed forth upon the disciples when "they were all with one accord in one place" (Acts 2:1). In short, the Spirit of holiness was given to the church as a body. And that makes the church supremely holy.

The fact that God dwells in the church presupposes its

342   *The Glorious Body of Christ*

holiness. That is clear, for the holy God would not dwell in any but a holy place. The fact that God dwells in the church renders the church holy. That, too, is self-evident. But never may it be forgotten that the fact of God's dwelling in the church also requires of the church that it be holy. Therefore Paul wrote to the church at Corinth: "Know ye not that ye are the temple of God, and that the Spirit of God dwelleth in you? If any man defile the temple of God, him shall God destroy: for the temple of God is holy, which temple ye are" (I Corinthians 3:16, 17). Again, admonishing the same church against participation in worship with unbelievers, he wrote: "For ye are the temple of the living God; as God hath said, I will dwell in them and walk in them; and I will be their God, and they shall be my people. Wherefore come out from among them and be ye separate, saith the Lord, and touch not the unclean thing" (II Corinthians 6:16, 17). There was much sin in the Corinthian church. Discord, immorality, and compromise with paganism were prevalent. By and large the church of this day is hardly less sinful. Both the truth of God and His law are trodden in the mire. The voice of God resounds: "As he which hath called you is holy, so be ye holy in all manner of conversation; because it is written, Be ye holy, for I am holy" (I Peter 1:15, 16).

A Blessed Abode

When God is said to dwell in His church, the reference is not merely to the divine omnipresence. The Psalmist addressed the omnipresent God when he said: "Whither shall I go from thy Spirit? or whither shall I flee from thy presence? If I ascend up into heaven, thou art there: if I make my bed in hell, behold, thou art there" (Psalm 139:7, 8). God is not only in heaven, but also in hell; not only in the church, but also in the tents of wickedness. However, He dwells in His church in a sense that is unique.

When Scripture localizes, so to speak, the presence of God, the reference is invariably to the manifestation of one or more specific attributes of God. For example, God dwells in heaven in the sense that His glory and majesty are displayed there in all their fullness. The question arises in which of His attributes God is peculiarly present in His church. No doubt, the answer is that He there reveals Himself in His great love for His own, as their Saviour and Benefactor. It was the Saviour who said: "Where two or three are gathered together in my name, there am I in the midst of them" (Matthew 18:20). One of the prophets assured the people of God: "He that toucheth you toucheth the apple of his eye" (Zechariah 2:8). Moved by His infinite love for the church, God dwells in its midst to bless it with "all spiritual blessings in heavenly places" (Ephesians 1:3), so that the members of the church on earth even now "sit together in heavenly places in Christ Jesus" (Ephesians 2:6).

The blessing which God bestows upon His abode is the Holy Spirit Himself together with His gifts. To the apostolic church the Spirit imparted special gifts, such as speaking with tongues and miraculous healing, which have ceased; but His most valuable gifts are permanent. Prominent among them are "love, joy, peace, longsuffering, gentleness, goodness, faith, meekness and temperance" (Galatians 5:22, 23). The greatest of them all is love. It is inseparable from faith and hope but is even greater than these (I Corinthians 13:13).

Love is a blessing which God bestows upon His church. And this blessing in turn begets a divine blessing. On the one hand, love dwells within the church because God has blessed it. On the other hand, God will bless the church if love dwells within it. Of that the sweet singer of Israel was aware when he sang: "Behold, how good and how pleasant it is for brethren to dwell together in unity! It is like the precious ointment upon the head, that ran down upon the beard, even Aaron's beard: that went down to the skirts of his garments; as the dew of Hermon, and as the dew that descended upon the mountains of Zion: for there the Lord commanded the blessing, even life for evermore" (Psalm 133).

How richly blessed is God's abode! It is thrice blessed, for in it dwells the Triune God.

A PERMANENT ABODE

God dwelt in the church of the old dispensation, and He dwells in the church of the new. The church is His permanent abode.

When the Lord Jesus was about to return to the Father, He gave His disciples the comforting assurance: "I will pray the Father, and he shall give you another Comforter, that he may abide with you for ever" (John 14:16). Only a few weeks later, on the day of Pentecost, the Comforter, the Spirit of truth, was poured out upon the church to abide with it and in it forever.

For that reason it is quite out of place for the church to pray for another Pentecost. Well may it plead for fuller manifestations of the presence and power of the Spirit in its midst, but never for a second bestowal of the Spirit comparable to that of Pentecost. The outpouring of the Spirit on that day was a once-for-all event, as unique as the incarnation of the Son of God. The Spirit was given to the church to abide with it forever. Never since has the Spirit departed from the church, nor will He depart at any time in the future.

That truth bears most directly on the glory of the Christian church. Again and again in the course of its history it has seemed forsaken of God. Time and again the complaint "The glory is departed from Israel" (I Samuel 4:21) has seemed warranted. To all outward appearances *Ichabod* might well have been written at various times over the doors of Christ's church. The era preceding the Protestant Reformation is a striking example. Our own day affords an instance that is hardly less striking. Unbelief is rampant in the church. A great many of its teachers and leaders have rejected the Word of God. They have become blind leaders of the blind. The church has grieved the Spirit of truth, and He seems to have left the church to the spirit of error. And yet He has not really done that. Possibly an overwhelming majority of church members either openly denies the truth or has lost interest in it; yet the Spirit's abiding presence in the church guarantees that there always will be "seven thousand in Israel, all the knees which have not bowed unto Baal and every mouth which hath not kissed him" (I Kings 19:18). Those seven thousand faithful ones constitute the true church of God, and they sing now, as they did in the sixteenth century:

> The prince of darkness grim,
> We tremble not for him;
> His rage we can endure,
> For lo! his doom is sure,
>   One little word shall fell him

> That word above all earthly powers,
>   No thanks to them, abideth;
> The Spirit and the gifts are ours
>   Through Him who with us sideth:
> Let goods and kindred go,
> This mortal life also;
> The body they may kill:
> God's truth abideth still,
>   His kingdom is for ever.

Not only throughout time will God abide in His church, but unto eternity. John saw a new heaven and a new earth: for the first earth and the first heaven were passed away; and there was no more sea. And he saw the holy city, new Jerusalem, coming down from God out of heaven, prepared as a bride adorned for her husband. And he heard a great voice out of heaven, saying: "Behold, the tabernacle of God is with men, and he will dwell with them, and they shall be his people, and God himself shall be with them and be their God" (Revelation 21:1-3).

Chapter 51

THE ESSENCE OF CORPORATE WORSHIP

The Lord Jesus commanded individual worship when He said: "When thou prayest, enter into thy closet, and when thou hast shut thy door, pray to thy Father which is in secret; and thy Father which seeth in secret shall reward thee openly" (Matthew 6:6). Joshua must have had in mind — perhaps not exclusively — family worship when he vowed: "As for me and my house, we will serve the Lord" (Joshua 24:15). Scripture abounds in references to church worship. For instance, it is said of Jesus: "As his custom was, he went into the synagogue on the Sabbath day" (Luke 4:16). The context informs us that He participated in worship there. And the author of Hebrews admonished his readers not to forsake the assembling of themselves together (Hebrews 10:25). This mode of worship has been described as public or common, but perhaps the best name for it is corporate worship, for that name designates it as worship by a body, even the body of Christ.

In its worship the glory of the Christian church is manifested resplendently. That will become clear from the consideration of the sublime essence of corporate worship.

WITH GOD

The tabernacle of the old dispensation was known as the tent of meeting. Was it called by that name because the people of God were wont to meet one another within its precincts? Possibly so, but there was a far more important reason. God Himself said: "There I will meet with the children of Israel, and the tabernacle shall be

346

sanctified by my glory" (Exodus 29:43). God and His people met in the sanctuary.

Referring, no doubt, to a gathering of His disciples for worship, the Son of God said: "Where two or three are gathered in my name, there am I in the midst of them" (Matthew 18:20).

In a very real sense God's people of the new dispensation draw even closer to God in worship than did His people of the old dispensation. In the tabernacle and the temple God dwelt in the holiest place of all. Only once a year, on the great day of atonement, one man, the high priest, was permitted to enter that place. Even he might not enter without sacrificial blood, which he had to sprinkle on the mercy-seat in order to make atonement for his own sins and those of the people. But when Christ died on Calvary's cross, the veil separating the holiest of all from the rest of the sanctuary was torn in two from the top to the bottom (Matthew 27:51). This signified that since the shedding of Christ's atoning blood all believers are privileged to come at any time into the immediate presence of the Holy One of Israel.

How lofty a conception of corporate worship Scripture presents! When God's people assemble for worship they enter into the place where God dwells. God meets them, and they meet God. They find themselves face to face with none other than God Himself. Their worship is an intimate transaction between them and their God.

If the church were fully conscious of that truth, what dignity and reverence would characterize its worship! Of levity and frivolity there would not be a trace. The worshipers would exclaim, as did Jacob at Bethel: "How dreadful is this place! This is none other than the house of God and this is the gate of heaven" (Genesis 28:17). Realizing that they are standing on holy ground, they would, as it were, remove their shoes from their feet, as did Moses when God spoke to him from the burning bush (Exodus 3:5). As John, when on Patmos he saw in the midst of the seven candlesticks one like unto the Son of man, clothed with a garment down to His feet and girt about the paps with a golden girdle; His head and His hair white like wool, as white as snow; His eyes as a flame of fire; His feet like unto fine brass as if they burned in a furnace; His voice as the sound of many waters; His right hand clasping seven stars; His mouth holding a sharp two-edged sword; His countenance shining as the sun in His strength — at this resplendent sight fell at His feet as dead (Revelation 1:13-17), so would every worshiper.

Since corporate worship is offered to God in a meeting of God and His people, it must consist of two sorts of transactions. In some, as the reading of Scripture, the preaching of the Word and the benediction, God addresses His people and they worship by reverently attending. In others, as prayer, song and the offering of gifts, they respond in holy fear to what God has spoken. In every part of their worship God's people either listen to God or reply to God.

What glory for the church that the great God condescends thus to commune with it and that it is privileged thus to commune with Him!

OF GOD

Worship originates with God, not with man.

The desire to worship the true God is wrought in the human heart by His Spirit. But for the renewing grace of God, men would turn their backs upon Him. They might worship idols, as many do, but not Him of whom it is written: "Thou art God alone" (Psalm 86:10). No man would ever seek after the living God if the living God did not first seek him.

Every act of worship, too, is evoked by God. God commands His children to worship Him, and they obey. They love Him because He has first loved them. They praise Him for all the benefits He has bestowed upon them. They adore Him both for what He is and for what He does. Each act of their worship is performed in response to His revelation. Each word they utter in His presence is spoken in reply to His Word. And may they never forget that what God says to them is of incomparably greater importance than anything they can say to Him.

Nor would God's people know how to render worship worthy of the great and holy God if He Himself had not instructed them. If He were a man, however illustrious, they might well discover through their own imagination what would please Him, for in that case they could put themselves in His place. But the truth is that He is God. Only through revelation can man know Him at all. And even thus it remains impossible for man to comprehend Him, for the finite cannot contain the infinite. Therefore it is sacrilege for man to worship God according to his own devices. Never may the creature assay to worship the Creator in any manner not prescribed by the Creator.

What has been said constitutes a most important principle governing the content of worship in general and of corporate worship in particular. Sad to say, not all churches subscribe to it. The church of Rome takes the position that everything is permissible in public worship which is not forbidden by the Word of God. That has led to a multitude of unscriptural and even anti-scriptural elements in its worship. Some Protestant churches, too, which have not purged out all Romish leaven, take the same position. The Reformed churches have upheld the principle that only that is permissible in the content of public worship which has the positive sanction of Holy Scripture. And that principle is Biblical. It is plainly implicit in the second commandment of the moral law (Exodus 20:4-6). While the first commandment forbids the worship of false gods, the second forbids worship of the true God in a wrong way. In the words of the Westminster Shorter Catechism, "The second commandment forbiddeth the worshiping of God by images, or in any other way not appointed in his Word" (Question 51). And the Lord Jesus said of the scribes and Pharisees of His day: "In vain do they worship me, teaching for doctrines the commandments of men" (Mark 7:7).

Lest the principle under discussion be misunderstood, it may be remarked that it does not apply to such mere circumstances of public worship as, for example, the place of meeting, and that it takes into account the fact that, while some teachings concerning worship are explicit in Scripture, others are implicit, as, for instance, the setting aside in the new dispensation of the first day of the week for corporate worship. It may also be observed that most Reformed churches hold that Scriptural sanction of the elements of common worship need not always come as a command, but may also come in the form of permission. For example, Scripture nowhere commands the church to commemorate the Saviour's birth on the twenty-fifth of December, or for that matter, on any other day; yet few will deny that the church is at liberty to do so. And those who insist on this liberty contend that such divine institutions as the passover and the holy supper are evidence that the commemoration of important events in the history of redemption is pleasing to God. Thus they claim positive Scriptural sanction for the celebration of the so-called Christian festivals.

The principle stands that there is room in the content of corporate worship only for that which God Himself has appointed. And that is an emphatic way of saying that in its very essence corporate worship is of God.

UNTO GOD

It can hardly be denied that in their worship services God's children sometimes have evil aims. Not infrequently their aim centers on themselves, not on God. That makes their aim evil. Perhaps they go to church to have their craving for theatricals or entertainment satisfied.

They want to see "a good show" and have "a good laugh" or, still better, "a good cry." For the minister the temptation is ever present to seek his own glory. All too often he looks forward to the plaudits of men rather than the divine approval. To put it popularly, he is out to "make a hit" for himself. Such worship is worship of self, not of God. It can only be an abomination in God's sight.

The danger is no less real that the aim of the worshiping church will be distorted. What should be secondary is made primary. What should be a means is regarded as the end. Christians go to church to enjoy the communion of saints. That certainly is good, but only so far as it goes, and it does not go nearly far enough. They should go to church to have communion with God. Worship services are conducted in the hope that sinners may be saved through the preaching of the Word. Most assuredly that is good, but it may never be forgotten that the salvation of men is a means to the glorification of God. Saints go to church that they may be built up in faith, hope and love. That, too, is excellent, but it again is only a means to the highest of all ends — the honor of God.

Corporate worship must be unto God. When properly performed, it is unto God. It is oriented to the glory of God rather than the blessedness of man, and it aims at man's blessedness only as a means to the end of God's glory.

All that the Christian does must be done to the glory of God. That holds even of his eating and drinking (I Corinthians 10:31). But in nothing does he glorify God as directly as in worship, and in nothing does the church glorify God as immediately as in its corporate worship. It stands in the very presence of God. It is overawed by the holiness and majesty of God. It prays: "Hallowed be thy name, thy kingdom come, thy will be done in earth as it is in heaven" (Matthew 6:9, 10). It chants in adoration:

Holy, Holy, Holy, Lord God Almighty!
Early in the morning our song shall rise to Thee;
Holy, Holy, Holy, Merciful and Mighty!
God in Three Persons, blessed Trinity!

Now, if ever, it has an eye single to the glory of God.

Nor is that all. Not only does the church glorify God
in its services of worship, but through those services its
members are stimulated to do all their living to God's
glory — to serve God not merely on the Lord's Day, but
all the days of the week; not merely in God's house, but
also in their homes; not merely on the day of rest, but
also in their daily work; not merely when partaking of
the holy supper, but also when eating their daily bread;
not merely when singing psalms and hymns and spiritual
songs, but also when listening to the symphonies of
Brahms; not merely when praying, but also when playing. Even while engaged in corporate worship, God's
children appropriate the quaint but meaningful petition
of George Herbert:

> Teach me, my God and King,
>   In all things Thee to see;
> And what I do in any thing
>   To do it as for Thee.

And, pondering the phrase, "for the glory of God," they
sing:

> This is the famous stone
>   That turneth all to gold;
> For that which God doth touch and own
>   Cannot for lesse be told.

Chapter 52

THE QUALITY OF CORPORATE WORSHIP

The worship which the Christian church offers to God is sublime in its essence. Inasmuch as its quality is of necessity determined by its essence, that worship is sublime also in its quality.

What follows is a brief description of a few of the exalted characteristics of corporate worship.

It Is Humble

On the occasion of corporate worship God meets with His people, and they find themselves in the presence of "the high and lofty One that inhabiteth eternity, whose name is Holy" (Isaiah 57:15). As creatures the deepest humility becomes them. And as sinners it behooves each of them to cry out: "Depart from me; for I am a sinful man, O Lord" (Luke 5:8).

The worshipers should know that they have no right to draw nigh to God but through the Mediator Jesus Christ. Did not He Himself declare majestically: "I am the way, the truth, and the life: no man cometh unto the Father but by me" (John 14:6)? He that assays to come to God in his own right can only find Him to be a consuming fire.

The worshipers should realize that apart from the qualifying grace of Christ they are utterly unable to worship God aright. Did not their Lord tell them that, as the branch cannot bear fruit except it abide in the vine, so they are completely dependent on Him for the bearing of fruit? "Apart from me," said He, "ye can do nothing" (John 15:4, 5, ASV). That applies also to worship.

The worshipers should be conscious of it that even with

the enabling grace of Christ they cannot render to God that worship of which He is worthy. Not only does their noblest worship fall far short of glorifying God as He ought to be glorified, it is also marred by sins of commission. So much sin cleaves to the best works of God's children that their very righteousnesses are as filthy rags (Isaiah 64:6). When that truth is related to corporate worship, it can only mean that such worship is ever in need of being purified and perfected by the sacrifice and the intercession of the great High Priest Jesus Christ.

It Is United

Whenever a congregation is worshiping, it does this, not as an aggregate of individuals, but as a body. Those present sing the same songs, pray the same prayers, attend to the same Word, contribute to the same offering, receive the same benediction. And they perform all those activities under the control of one Spirit. To be sure, there may be in attendance some who participate only in appearance, not in reality. But those aside, the church engages in public worship unitedly.

Nor is that all. The particular churches of a denomination usually have similar, if not identical, modes of worship. The content of worship, too, in any one of them ordinarily resembles closely that in every other. Therefore in a real sense the churches of a denomination worship together. Although the time for worship differs in various longitudes, nevertheless all the particular churches of a denomination, whether they be located in Connecticut, Colorado, or California, worship unitedly.

Even that is but one aspect of the matter. God's people are scattered throughout many denominations. And all truly Christian churches the world over worship the only true God with more or less fidelity to the demands for worship contained in His Word. That is a way of saying that the church universal worships unitedly. For instance, the church in America, Australia and Argentina, employing the words of the Apostles' Creed, makes confession of its common faith in unison.

The whole truth has not yet been told. The church of all ages worships unitedly. The church of the twentieth century joins the church of past centuries in praying the prayer that Jesus taught His disciples. And the church of the new dispensation joins the church of the old in singing the Psalms of Holy Writ.

To cap the climax, the worshiping church may be said to have come "unto mount Zion, and unto the city of the living God, the heavenly Jerusalem, to an innumerable company of angels . . . and the spirits of just men made perfect" (Hebrews 12:22, 23). It worships in the company of angels and the church triumphant.

IT IS SPIRITUAL

To the query of the Samaritan woman which was the proper place for public worship: Mount Zion, the holy place of the Jews, or Mount Gerizim, the holy place of the Samaritans, Jesus replied: "The hour is coming, and now is, when the true worshipers will worship the Father in spirit and truth, for such the Father seeks to worship him. God is spirit, and those who worship him must worship in spirit and truth" (John 4:23, 24, RSV).

The phrase *in spirit* does not refer primarily to the Holy Spirit, the third person of the Trinity, but to the spirit of the worshiper. Paul used a similar expression when he said: "God is my witness, whom I serve with my spirit" (Romans 1:9). Yet only he will truly worship God in his spirit whose spirit is controlled by the Holy Spirit.

The phrase *in truth* may possibly contrast New Testament worship with the ceremonialism of the old dispensation. More likely it means *in harmony with the truth that God is spirit.* In that case *in truth* is synonymous with *in spirit.*

In effect Jesus said: "Since God is spirit, worship of

Him must be spiritual, and only spiritual worship is true worship."

It cannot be that the Lord meant to condemn all *forms* in public worship. How the church in glory worships we cannot say in detail, but certain it is that so long as the church finds itself in this world of time and space it cannot get along without certain forms in worship. The Lord Jesus Himself prescribed such a form as the commemoration of His death in the holy supper. However, all *formalism* in the worship of God stands condemned. Going through the forms of worship in routine fashion is not worship at all. In the sight of God it is an abomination. Our Lord denounced it scathingly in the words of the prophet Isaiah: "This people draweth nigh unto me with their mouth, and honoureth me with their lips; but their heart is far from me" (Isaiah 29:13, Matthew 15:8).

Spiritual worship, on the contrary, glorifies God greatly, for it recognizes Him for what He truly is. Nothing that man can do glorifies God more directly and immediately. And such is the worship of the true church of Christ.

It Is Free

Closely related to the spiritual quality of corporate worship is its quality of freedom. The more spiritual it is, the more it will excel in spontaneity.

Like all true liberty, freedom in worship is freedom under law. However, it is of utmost importance to distinguish at this point between the law of God and the laws of men. The law of God is "the law of liberty" (James 1:25, 2:12). God gave it to man, not to restrict his liberty, but that he might enjoy liberty to the full. Disobedience to God's commandments is slavery, obedience to them is genuine liberty. Contrariwise, the laws of men, if they are not based upon the law of God, invariably tend to destroy liberty. Applied to corporate worship this means, on the one hand, that, in order to be free, it must be performed in strict accord with the prescriptions of God's Word, and, on the other hand, that it ceases to be free in the measure in which it is controlled by human regulations and traditions. Never may a church presume to add to the divine precepts for worship. Nor are the Roman Catholic and Greek Catholic churches the only ones that have thus destroyed freedom in worship. Many Protestant churches, too, may well be reminded that "God alone is lord of the conscience, and hath left it free from the doctrines and commandments of men which are in any thing contrary to his word, or beside it, in matters of faith or worship" (Westminster Confession of Faith, Chapter XX, Section II), and that it is their solemn duty as well as God-given privilege to "reject all human inventions, and all laws which men would introduce into the worship of God, thereby to bind and compel the conscience in any manner whatever" (Belgic Confession, Article XXXII).

If worship is to be free, it is no less necessary that the worshiper take the proper attitude to the law of God. He who keeps God's commandments under external compulsion and contrary to his own desires is not keeping them at all. Only that is true obedience which is prompted by love. Only he worships God freely who delights in His worship after the inward man. And only he finds that delight in the worship of God who is controlled by God's free Spirit.

That means that the Christian church is qualified to worship freely, for the Holy Spirit has been given to it. The Spirit operated already in the church of the old dispensation, but upon the church of the new He was poured out as never before. That accounts for it, on the one hand, that the New Testament contains far fewer detailed prescriptions for corporate worship than does the Old. But it also follows that upon the church of the new dispensation especially rests the obligation to worship God freely, spontaneously, lovingly. "Where the Spirit of the Lord is, there is liberty" (II Corinthians 3:17).

It Is Beautiful

Repeatedly Scripture enjoins God's people to worship Him "in the beauty of holiness" (e.g., Psalm 29:2, 96:9).

The Old Testament sanctuaries and their furnishings, made after the pattern which Jehovah had showed Moses (Numbers 8:4), were beautiful. So were the garments of the priests, especially those of the high priest. In the new dispensation, too, it is well that the place of worship and its appurtenances be beautiful. However, in public worship there is no room for art for art's sake, and ornamentation that distracts from the worship of God must be banned. What is beautiful elsewhere may be out of place, and therefore unbecoming, in the house of God. For instance, portraits of Washington and Lincoln are appropriate for a school, but not for a church. And one might well wish that he had the original, or even a copy, of Rembrandt's Night Watch in his living room, but that masterpiece would disgrace a place of worship. Never may a sense of aesthetic satisfaction derived from the stately rhythm of the choral with lofty organ accompaniment or from dim light filtering in through windows of stained glass be mistaken for the spirit of worship. Not all ornamentation and symbolism need be excluded, for God Himself commanded Moses to adorn the tabernacle with pomegranates and to fashion cherubim for the holiest place of all. Yet whatever tends to image worship and thus to transgression of the second commandment of the moral law must be excluded from the house of God. This means that there is no room for any creature as a representation of the Creator and hence, as an object of worship. The place of worship is beautiful if it excels in simple dignity and dignified simplicity.

However, in this dispensation the *place* of public worship is relatively unimportant. The church has worshiped acceptably in catacombs and log cabins. What is of supreme importance is that public worship *itself* be beautiful. And it is beautiful when it is in harmony with Holy Scripture.

Corporate worship is beautiful if its content is Scriptural and if, as to form, every part is performed "decently and in order" (I Corinthians 14:40) ; if it is characterized by reverence and holy fear on the one hand and by joyful spontaneity on the other; if it issues forth from regenerate hearts aflame with gratitude for all that God is and does for His people, particularly for the full and free salvation which He has provided in His Son; if in it God's children humbly, yet boldly, draw nigh to the throne of grace; if it is the holy communion of a holy priesthood with the thrice holy God. In short, beauty in worship is the reflection of holiness.

It Is Festive

Corporate worship should be a festive occasion. The Psalmist exhorted God's people: "Enter into his gates with thanksgiving, and into his courts with praise: be thankful unto him, and bless his name. For the Lord is good; his mercy is everlasting; and his truth endureth to all generations" (Psalm 100:4, 5).

To be sure, in every service of public worship confession of sins must needs be made. But from their sins God's children must look up to the Saviour. Introspection must result in contemplation of the Christ crucified. And every song begun on a note of self-abhorrence may well end in a burst of gratitude to God for His great salvation.

There is room for special services of confession and humiliation. In times of war and other calamities such services are highly proper. Yet even then the note of joy may not be absent. In fact, it must be prominent. The church may exult: "God is our refuge and strength, a very present help in trouble. Therefore will not we fear, though the earth be removed, and though the mountains be carried into the midst of the sea; though the

waters thereof roar and be troubled, though the mountains
shake with the swelling thereof.   There is a river the
streams whereof shall make glad the city of God, the holy
place of the tabernacles of the most High.   God is in the
midst of her; she shall not be moved: God shall help her,
and that right early.   The heathen raged, the kingdoms
were moved: he uttered his voice, the earth melted.   The
Lord of hosts is with us; the God of Jacob is our refuge"
(Psalm 46:1-7).

What greater joy have God's people than that afforded
by communion with God?   They sing: "As the hart panteth after the water brooks, so panteth my soul after thee,
O God.   My soul thirsteth for God, for the living God:
when shall I come and appear before God?   (Psalm 42:
1, 2).   God Himself is their highest joy.   Therefore they
pray: "O send out thy light and thy truth: let them lead
me; let them bring me unto thy holy hill and to thy tabernacles.   Then will I go unto the altar of God, unto God
my exceeding joy" (Psalm 43:3, 4).   Communion with
God is what makes heaven heaven.   In corporate worship
the church of God has a foretaste of heavenly bliss.   It
begins to understand what it is to glorify God as He
would be glorified and to enjoy Him to the full and
forever.

Chapter 53

THE BRIDE OF THE LAMB

Scripture frequently compares the relationship of God and His people to that of husband and wife, and it likens the relationship of Christ and His church to that of a bridegroom and his bride. It may well be questioned whether the Word of God bestows upon the church any honor greater than that.

How beautiful upon the mountains are the feet of him who brings to Zion the good tidings: "Thy Maker is thy husband; the Lord of hosts is his name" (Isaiah 54:5)! And the whole of Scripture hardly contains a more exquisite portrait than that of "the holy city, new Jerusalem, coming down from God out of heaven, prepared as a bride adorned for her husband" (Revelation 21:2).

This meditation on the church as the bride of the Lamb will dwell on her betrothal, her cleansing and her marriage.

Her Betrothal

The betrothal of Christ and His church took place in the quietude of eternity, before the world was. Not only was it included in God's eternal counsel, embracing all that would come to pass in the course of history; from everlasting it was reality.

Time and again Christ designated the members of His church as those whom the Father had given Him. In His high-priestly prayer, which one cannot ponder without sensing that one is standing on holy ground, even within the holiest place of all, He thus described them seven times. Said He: "Thou hast given him power over all flesh that he should give eternal life to as many as thou

hast given him . . . . I have manifested thy name unto the
men whom thou gavest me out of the world: thine they
were, and thou gavest them me . . . . I pray not for the
world, but for them which thou hast given me . . . . Holy
Father, keep through thine own name those whom thou
hast given me . . . .Those that thou gavest me I have
kept . . . . Father, I will that they also whom thou hast given
me be with me where I am, that they may behold my
glory" (John 17:2, 6, 9, 11, 12, 24). The Father gave
them to Him from eternity. He gave them to Him that
they might be His bride.

Christ paid a dowry for His bride. It consisted not of
gold or silver or costly stones, but of His own precious
blood. In the plan of Him who inhabits eternity and with
whom the beginning and the end are one, this, too, took
place from everlasting. Christ is "the Lamb slain from
the foundation of the world" (Revelation 13:8). In the
fullness of time He came into this world and on Calvary's
tree laid down His life for His bride. He loved her so
exceedingly that He "gave himself for her" (Ephesians
5:25).

> From heaven He came and sought her
> To be His holy bride;
> With His own blood He bought her,
> And for her life He died.

Ten days after His return to the Father He sent His
betrothed a most valuable gift. It was His Holy Spirit.
That Spirit is proof of His continued, though invisible,
presence with her, pledges His perfect fidelity to her,
and constantly reminds her of His many precious promises, notably of the promise that one day He will return
to take her to Himself as His spouse. And, prone as she
is to infidelity, the selfsame Spirit, abiding with her and
in her, keeps and prepares her for that day.

Because the betrothal of the Lamb and His bride is of
God, nothing can annul it. Sealed with the blood and the

Spirit of Christ, it cannot be broken. Conceived in eternal love, it must of necessity be unto eternity.

Amazing to say, not even the bride's unfaithfulness can make void her betrothal. Will a man love her who was his betrothed but has played the harlot? It is hardly conceivable. But the God of all grace assures His adulterous people: "I will betroth thee unto me forever; yea, I will betroth thee unto me in righteousness, and in judgment, and in lovingkindness, and in mercies. I will even betroth thee unto me in faithfulness, and thou shalt know the Lord" (Hosea 2:19, 20). That is a declaration of love eternal, infinite, unchangeable, incomprehensible.

He whose name is Faithful has never forsaken His church, and never will. In His great and eternal faithfulness He brings it to pass that in the darkest periods of its history there is never wanting "a remnant according to the election of grace" (Romans 11:5). When countless numbers in the church prove not to be of it and when numerous churches of Christ are transformed into abodes of Satan, that remnant continues as the true church. And when, toward the end of time, "all that dwell upon the earth," many of them on the roll of the church, shall worship "the beast," then by the grace of God they will be excepted whose names are written in the Lamb's book of life (Revelation 13:8).

HER CLEANSING

First and foremost of the virtues required in a bride is chastity. First and foremost of the virtues which Christ demands of His church is holiness.

Although she has been called out of a sinful world, the church will be marred by sin until, at the dawn of eternity, the marriage of the Lamb and His bride is consummated. Not until then will it be "a glorious church, not having spot or wrinkle or any such thing" (Ephesians 5:27). Therefore from the time of its founding in the garden of Eden until the day of its entrance into the paradise of God, where flows the pure river of the water of life and where grows the tree of life (Revelation 22: 1, 2), the church is in constant need of cleansing.

In the process of her cleansing Christ does not leave His bride to her own devices. In that case, not only would her purification never be perfected; contrariwise, her filthiness could only increase. But in His great love the Lamb has made provision for her cleansing. He gave Himself for the church "that he might sanctify and cleanse it with the washing of water by the word" (Ephesians 5:26).

That the expression "the washing of water" is an allusion to the purifying bath of the bride previous to marriage, permits of no doubt. Just as clearly there is a reference here to the sacrament of holy baptism. But significantly no cleansing power is ascribed to the sacrament apart from the Word of God. As the great Augustine said: "Take away the Word, and what is the water but water? Add the Word to the element, and it becomes a sacrament, itself as it were the visible Word." Was it not to the Word that the Lord Jesus Himself ascribed cleansing power when He prayed for His own: "Sanctify them through thy truth," and added: "Thy word is truth" (John 17:17)? However, Scripture teaches that the Word effects cleansing only when it is applied to human hearts by the Holy Spirit. "Sanctification" is "of the Spirit" (I Peter 1:2). Christ, then, cleanses His bride by the Holy Spirit, whom He merited for her by His atoning death, and the means employed in her cleansing is the Word of God.

At the very moment when God founded His church He put enmity between it and the world (Genesis 3:15). Throughout the centuries that enmity is conducive in no small measure to the purification of God's people. In all its history one of the greatest perils besetting the church is conformity to the world. The danger is ever present that the line of demarcation between the seed of the woman and the seed of the serpent will be erased. In every age the danger is imminent that Jerusalem, the bride of the Lamb, will become identified with Babylon, "the great whore" (Revelation 19:2). But by the working of His Spirit through the Word in the hearts of His own, as well as by the providential control of His enemies, Christ ever keeps alive the enmity between them.

This accounts for it that the Head of the church, omnipotent though He is, nevertheless permits the world to persecute His saints, often most bitterly, not infrequently unto death. His reason is that He would keep them from becoming allied with the world. He is purifying them as gold is wont to be purified by fire. He is cutting them, so to speak, as diamonds are wont to be cut that they may sparkle the more brilliantly. As He Himself, the sinless One, was made perfect through sufferings (Hebrews 2:10), so He sanctifies them through many tribulations. In a word, He permits the cruel whore to persecute His bride for the very reason that He loves His bride so exceedingly.

Knowing that, she raises from caves of the earth, from lions' dens, from prison cells, from scaffolds and from flaming piles the song of love: "Who shall separate us from the love of Christ? Shall tribulation, or distress, or persecution, or famine, or nakedness, or peril, or sword? As it is written, For thy sake we are killed all the day long; we are accounted as sheep for the slaughter. Nay, in all these things we are more than conquerors through him that loved us. For I am persuaded that neither death, nor life, nor angels, nor principalities, nor powers, nor things present, nor things to come, nor height, nor depth, nor any other creature, shall be able to separate us from the love of God, which is in Christ Jesus our Lord" (Romans 8:35-39).

HER MARRIAGE

The church is even now the bride of Christ, but their marriage remains to be consummated in the future. That will occur when a great voice, "as it were the voice of a great multitude, and as the voice of many waters, and as the voice of mighty thunderings," will proclaim: "Alleluia: for the Lord God omnipotent reigneth. Let us be glad and rejoice and give honor to him: for the marriage of the Lamb is come, and his wife hath made herself ready" (Revelation 19:6, 7).

That marriage will indeed be glory for the bride.

It will take place on the day of her complete victory over her arch-foe, the great whore which did corrupt the earth with her fornication. God will avenge the blood of His servants at her hand, and her smoke will rise up for ever and ever. Nevermore will the bride of Christ be troubled by the whore. Then the church triumphant will make the vault of heaven ring with Alleluias (Revelation 19:1-6).

The Bridegroom will greatly desire His bride for her beauty. A gorgeous bridal gown will adorn her. It will be granted to her to be "arrayed in fine linen, clean and white, which is the righteousness of saints" (Revelation 19:8). Her righteous deeds, manifesting her holy character, are a gift to her, God having placed them in readiness beforehand that she should walk in them (Ephesians 2:10). And they are white because she has washed them in the blood of the Lamb (Revelation 7:14). Then will the queen in gold of Ophir stand upon the King's right hand (Psalm 45:9). An angel spoke to John, the apostle: "Come hither, I will show thee the bride, the Lamb's wife." And he saw "the holy Jerusalem, descending out of heaven from God, having the glory of God: and her light was like unto a stone most precious, even like a jasper stone, clear as crystal" (Revelation 21:9-11). Its foundations were garnished with all manner of precious stones; its twelve gates were twelve pearls; and its street was pure gold, as it were transparent glass (Revelation 21:19-21).

God will wipe away all tears from the eyes of the inhabitants of that city, and there will be no more death, neither sorrow nor crying, neither will there be any more pain (Revelation 21:4). Broken bodies will have been restored and broken hearts healed.

> Then eyes with joy shall sparkle
> That brimmed with tears of late;
> Orphans no longer fatherless,
> Nor widows desolate.

All the consequences of sin will be dispelled because sin itself will have been destroyed. And because the bride's holiness has been perfected, the cup of her bliss will be full.

Better still, what will cause that cup to run over is communion with the Bridegroom. It will be good, even heaven, for the bride to be near unto her Beloved. She will follow Him whithersoever He goes (Revelation 14:4). Keeping her gaze fixed upon Him, she will be like Him, for she will see Him as He is (I John 3:2). She will dwell with Him in the secret of His tent. A great voice will declare: "The tabernacle of God is with men and he will dwell with them, and they shall be his people, and God himself will be with them and be their God" (Revelation 21:3).

Best of all, the Lamb's wife will find her greatest joy in serving her Beloved. As the woman was made for the man, not the man for the woman, so the church was made for Christ. In serving the Bridegroom the bride will accomplish her highest end and reach her highest joy. Lost in wonder, love and praise, she will cast her crown at His feet. In glorifying Him she will enjoy Him to the full. Therefore she will fall down before Him and sing: "Thou, O Lamb, wast slain and hast redeemed us to God by thy blood out of every kindred and tongue and people and nation" (Revelation 5:8, 9). Without ceasing she will adore Him in His temple, chanting the song of Moses and the Lamb.

And that perfect marriage will not be for a day, or a week, or a month, or a year, or a decade, or a century, or a millennium. It will last throughout the endless ages of eternity — world without end.

Outline

OUTLINE

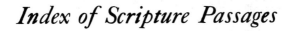

Index of Scripture Passages

INDEX OF SCRIPTURE PASSAGES